Introduction to Modern Philosophy

Custom Edition for Oakland Community College

Taken from:

Introduction to Modern Philosophy: Examining the Human Condition, Seventh Edition
by Alburey Castell, Donald M. Borchert, and Arthur Zucker

Introduction to Modern Philosophy: Examining the Human Condition, Sixth Edition
by Alburey Castell, Donald M. Borchert, and Arthur Zucker

Learning Solutions

New York Boston San Francisco
London Toronto Sydney Tokyo Singapore Madrid
Mexico City Munich Paris Cape Town Hong Kong Montreal

Cover Art: *Girl on Couch*, by Bettina Burch

Pedagogy taken from:

Introduction to Modern Philosophy: Examining the Human Condition, Seventh Edition
by Alburey Castell, Donald M. Borchert and Arthur Zucker
Copyright © 2001, 1994, 1988, 1983, 1976, 1963, 1943 by Pearson Education, Inc.
Published by Prentice Hall
Upper Saddle River, New Jersey 07458

Introduction to Modern Philosophy: Examining the Human Condition, Sixth Edition
by Alburey Castell, Donald M. Borchert and Arthur Zucker
Copyright © 1994, 1988, 1983, 1976, 1963, 1943 by Macmillan College Publishing Company, Inc.
Englewood Cliffs, New Jersey 07632

Pearson Learning Solutions, 501 Boylston Street, Suite 900, Boston, MA 02116
A Pearson Education Company
www.pearsoned.com

Printed in the United States of America

099900000270508838

LB/JR

ISBN 10: 0-558-31027-3
ISBN 13: 978-0-558-31027-1

Contents

CHAPTER **4**

What Shall I Say About Ultimate Reality?   116

CHAPTER **5**

Am I Free or Determined?   137

Glossary   156

What Is Philosophy?*

This book is an introduction to philosophy. It is written with the beginning student of philosophy in mind. We must, therefore, try to get clear from the outset what "philosophy" is.

People use the word "philosophy" in a number of contexts. Perhaps you have heard breweries advertise their philosophy of beer making, and innkeepers proclaim their philosophy of innkeeping, and coaches debate their philosophies of football or basketball. When people speak of "philosophy" in these settings they usually take the word to mean "a point of view," or "a personal outlook," or "a personal way or technique for doing something." And while these people use the term "philosophy" quite unhesitatingly, most of them would probably be somewhat reluctant to call themselves philosophers. Indeed, would we not find it rather strange if we heard one of them say, "As a philosopher, I think a hotel should be managed to ensure that every unit turns a profit"?

This hesitancy of people to call themselves "philosophers" at the same time that they find themselves expounding on their "philosophies" of this or that suggests that they sense that the philosophy of the philosopher is something other than a personal point of view or a certain technique for doing something.

What, then, does philosophy mean for the philosopher?

The term "philosophy" is derived from two Greek words: *philein* meaning "to love" and *sophia* meaning "wisdom." *Philosophy,* then, is "the love of wisdom," and a *philosopher* is a "lover of wisdom." According to an ancient tradition, the first person to call himself a "philosopher" was the sixth century B.C. Greek thinker, Pythagoras.

But what does it mean to call oneself a lover of wisdom? And what is this "wisdom" that the philosopher loves, seeks, and pursues? Clearly, what we are looking for is a definition of philosophy. An engaging and instructive way to formulate one is to observe a philosopher in action and then to single out those characteristics of the philosopher which seem to make that person a philosopher. Let us try such an approach, and let us consider as our model philosopher Socrates whose status as a philosopher is eminent and secure. The material we have selected to represent Socrates is basically the account of his trial recorded by one of his most celebrated students, Plato. As you read Plato's account of Socrates defending

* Taken from *Introduction to Modern Philosophy: Examining the Human Condition*, Seventh Edition by Alburey Castell, Donald M. Borchert, and Arthur Zucker.

himself before a citizen jury in Athens almost 2,500 years ago, try to figure out what it is about Socrates that has led people to regard him as a notable philosopher.

---

1   SOCRATES
The Examined Life

Socrates was born about 470 B.C.—shortly after the Persian invasions of Greece had been repulsed and just before a golden age of Athenian culture flourished under the leadership of Pericles. From 460 B.C. until his death in 430 B.C., Pericles was the political leader of an increasingly democratic and culturally creative Athens. The flowering of Athenian culture at this time was magnificently symbolized by Pericles' reconstruction of the Acropolis with its new majestic Parthenon—a temple dedicated to the goddess Athena whose colossal statue, carved in gold and ivory by Phidias and set within the Parthenon, reminded the Athenians that their success over the Persians and the glories of their expanding empire were gifts of the gods.

As democracy developed in Athens a key factor in a politician's success became the ability to influence the citizenry through eloquent speeches. Accordingly, when various itinerant scholars called the Sophists—who tried to popularize knowledge and who offered lessons in rhetoric—appeared in Athens during the fifth century B.C., they were sought out by young Athenians with political ambitions. These Sophists concentrated on the techniques of persuasion and refutation. They taught their clientele how to defend and oppose various conflicting opinions with the consequence that serious questions were raised whether or not there was any abiding truth to which all humans could assent. In such an intellectual climate it is not surprising that belief in the traditional gods came to be questioned. Nor is it surprising that the conservative and traditional sectors of Athenian society viewed the teachings of the Sophists with great alarm. Indeed when one of Pericles' friends among the Sophists was prosecuted for his alleged pernicious religious ideas, not even the intervention of Pericles himself could save the Sophist from condemnation.

As Athens entered its protracted struggle with Sparta, the Athenian democracy became the victim of incompetent leadership, treachery, and fickle public opinion, all of which contributed to the humiliating defeat of Athens in 404 B.C. No clearer evidence of the weakness of Athenian democracy can be found than the situation that prevailed in the courts. Citizen juries, which had been introduced by Solon in the sixth century as a court of appeal, were enlarged until they comprised some six thousand jurors. These jurors were subdivided into smaller juries, each of which contained five hundred and one jurors. To enable even the poorest of citizens to leave their work to participate in juries, the Athenians legislated payment for jury service. This truly noble idea, however, was corrupted when the state treasury became exhausted and juries found it convenient to lay heavy fines on accused citizens, irrespective of their guilt or innocence, in order to insure that the funds would be available for their salaries. In this environment, the additional decadent practice developed whereby wealthy citizens would be accused of fictitious crimes to entice them to settle out of court with their accusers rather than face the greed of a citizen jury. It was before such a jury that

Socrates was hauled in 399 B.C. to respond to charges that he was corrupting the youth of Athens with his teachings. And it is to Socrates' defense on that occasion that we wish to direct our attention to view a philosopher in action.

Bear in mind that Athenian society was far from stable. In the aftermath of Sparta's victory over Athens, the nobles were struggling with the democratic masses for control of the state; and the ideas of the Sophists were vying with the traditional beliefs for the intellectual commitment of the citizenry. It was not an enviable time to stand before a citizen's jury in Athens. Yet the seventy-year-old Socrates presents a courageous and noble defense.

Socrates begins with a plea that he be allowed to speak in his accustomed manner, the power of which resides not in the force of eloquence but in the force of truth.

> How you, O Athenians, have been affected by my accusers, I cannot tell; but I know that they almost made me forget who I was—so persuasively did they speak, and yet they have hardly uttered a word of truth. But of the many falsehoods told by them, there was one which quite amazed me—I mean when they said that you should be upon your guard and not allow yourselves to be deceived by the force of my eloquence. To say this, when they were certain to be detected as soon as I opened my lips and proved myself to be anything but a great speaker, did indeed appear to me most shameless—unless by the force of eloquence they mean the force of truth; for if such is their meaning, I admit that I am eloquent. But in how different a way from theirs! Well, as I was saying, they have scarcely spoken the truth at all; but from me you shall hear the whole truth; not, however, delivered after their manner in a set oration duly ornamented with words and phrases. No, by heaven! but I shall use the words and arguments which occur to me at the moment; for I am confident in the justice of my cause; at my time of life I ought not to be appearing before you, O men of Athens, in the character of a juvenile orator—let no one expect it of me. And I must beg of you to grant me a favor—if I defend myself in my accustomed manner and you hear me using the words which I have been in the habit of using in the agora, at the tables of the money-changers, or anywhere else, I would ask you not to be surprised, and not to interrupt me on this account. For I am more than seventy years of age, and appearing now for the first time in a court of law, I am quite a stranger to the language of the place; and therefore I would have you regard me as if I were really a stranger, whom you would excuse if he spoke in his native tongue and after the fashion of his country—Am I making an unfair request of you? Never mind the manner, which may or may not be good; but think only of the truth of my words, and give heed to that; let the speaker speak truly and the judge decide justly.

Socrates proceeds to identify the charges leveled against him. It is alleged that he is a student of the physical world, with the implication that such studies are incompatible with traditional religious belief. After all, if you demythologize heavenly bodies by saying the sun is rock and the moon is earth, have you not discarded the notion that the sun and the moon are divine beings? Furthermore, it is alleged that Socrates has traditional values all mixed up when he debates with people. That is to say, what most people would regard as "good," he considered to be "evil," and vice versa. And furthermore, he accepts money from people to teach them these problematic doctrines. These accusations had been associated with

Socrates for many years and were reinforced publicly in the play, *Clouds*, by Aristophanes, who made Socrates appear as a shiftless, ridiculous wizard with words.

Well, then, I must make my defence, and endeavor to clear away in a short time, a slander which has lasted a long time. May I succeed, if to succeed be for my good and yours, or likely to avail me in my cause! The task is not an easy one; I quite understand the nature of it. And so leaving the event with God, in obedience to the law, I will now make my defence.

I will begin at the beginning, and ask what is the accusation which has given rise to the slander of me, and in fact has encouraged Meletus to prefer this charge against me. Well, what do the slanderers say? They shall be my prosecutors, and I will sum up their words in an affidavit: "Socrates is an evil-doer, and a curious person, who searches into things under the earth and in heaven, and he makes the worse appear the better cause; and he teaches the aforesaid doctrines to others." Such is the nature of the accusation; it is just what you have yourselves seen in the comedy of Aristophanes, who has introduced a man whom he calls Socrates, going about and saying that he walks in air, and talking a deal of nonsense concerning matters of which I do not pretend to know either much or little—not that I mean to speak disparagingly of any one who is a student of natural philosophy. I should be very sorry if Meletus could bring so grave a charge against me. But the simple truth is, O Athenians, that I have nothing to do with physical speculations. Very many of those here present are witnesses to the truth of this, and to them I appeal. Speak then, you who have heard me, and tell your neighbors whether any of you have ever known me hold forth in few words or in many upon such matters. . . . You hear the answer. And from what they say of this part of the charge you will be able to judge of the truth of the rest.

As little foundation is there for the report that I am a teacher, and take money; this accusation has no more truth in it than the other. Although, if a man were really able to instruct mankind, to receive money for giving instruction would, in my opinion, be an honor to him. There is Gorgias of Leontium, and Prodicus of Ceos, and Hippias of Elis, who go the round of the cities, and are able to persuade the young men to leave their own citizens by whom they might be taught for nothing, and come to them whom they not only pay, but are thankful if they may be allowed to pay them.

I dare say, Athenians, that some one among you will reply, "Yes, Socrates, but what is the origin of these accusations which are brought against you; there must have been something strange which you have been doing? All these rumors and this talk about you would never have arisen if you had been like other men; tell us, then, what is the cause of them, for we should be sorry to judge hastily of you." Now I regard this as a fair challenge, and I will endeavor to explain to you the reason why I am called wise and have such an evil fame. Please to attend then. And although some of you may think that I am joking, I declare that I will tell you the entire truth. Men of Athens, this reputation of mine has come of a certain sort of wisdom which I possess. If you ask me what kind of wisdom, I reply, wisdom such as may perhaps be attained by man, for to that extent I am inclined to believe that I am wise; whereas the persons of whom I was speaking have a superhuman wisdom, which I may fail to describe, because I have it not myself; and he who says that I have, speaks falsely, and is taking away my character. And here, O men of Athens, I must beg you not to interrupt me, even, if I seem to say something extravagant. For the word which I will speak is not mine. I will refer you to a witness who is worthy of credit; that witness shall be the God of Delphi—he will tell you about my wisdom, if I have any, and of what sort it is. You must have known Chaerephon; he was early a friend of mine, and also a friend of yours, for he shared in the recent exile of the people, and returned with you. Well, Chaerephon, as you know, was very impetuous in all his doings, and he went to Delphi and boldly asked the oracle to tell him whether—as I was saying, I must beg you not to interrupt—he asked the oracle to tell him whether any one was wiser than I was, and the Pythian prophetess answered, that there was no man wiser. Chaerephon is dead himself; but his brother, who is in court, will confirm the truth of what I am saying.

Why do I mention this? Because I am going to explain to you why I have such an evil name. When I heard the answer, I said to myself, What can the god mean? and what is the interpretation of his riddle? for I know that I have no wisdom, small or great. What then can he mean when he says that I am the wisest of men? And yet he is a god, and cannot lie; that would be against his nature. After long consideration, I thought of a method of trying the question. I reflect that if I could only find a man wiser than myself, then I might go to the god with a refutation in my hand. I should say to him, "Here is a man who is wiser than I am; but you said that I was the wisest." Accordingly I went to one who had the reputation of wisdom, and observed him—his name I need not mention; he was a politician whom I selected for examination—and the result was as follows: When I began to talk with him, I could not help thinking that he was not really wise, although he was thought wise by many, and still wiser by himself; and thereupon I tried to explain to him that he thought himself wise, but was not really wise; and the consequence was that he hated me, and his enmity was shared by several who were present and heard me. So I left him, saying to myself, as I went away: Well, although I do not suppose that either of us knows anything really beautiful and good, I am better off than he is,—for he knows nothing, and thinks that he knows; I neither know nor think that I know. In this latter particular, then, I seem to have slightly the advantage of him. Then I went to another who had still higher pretensions to wisdom, and my conclusion was exactly the same. Whereupon I made another enemy of him, and of many others besides him.

Then I went to one man after another, being not unconscious of the enmity which I provoked, and I lamented and feared this: But necessity was laid upon me,—the word of God, I thought, ought to be considered first. And I said to myself, Go I must to all who appear to know, and find out the meaning of the oracle. And I swear to you, Athenians, by the dog I swear—for I must tell you the truth—the result of my mission was just this: I found that the men most in repute were all but the most foolish; and that others less esteemed were really wiser and better.

This inquisition had led to my having many enemies of the worst and most dangerous kind, and has given occasion also to many calumnies. And I am called wise, for my hearers always imagine that I myself possess the wisdom which I find wanting in others; but the truth is, O men of Athens, that God only is wise; and by his answer he intends to show that the wisdom of men is worth little or nothing; he is not speaking of Socrates, he is only using my name by way of illustration, as if he said, He, O men, is the wisest, who, like Socrates, knows that his wisdom is in truth worth nothing. And so I go about the world, obedient to the god, and search and make enquiry into the wisdom of any one, whether citizen or stranger, who appears to be wise; and if he is not wise, then in vindication of the oracle I show him that he is not wise; and my occupation quite absorbs me, and I have no time to give either to any public matter of interest or to any concern of my own, but I am in utter poverty by reason of my devotion to the god.

There is another thing—young men of the richer classes, who have not much to do, come about me of their own accord; they like to hear the pretenders examined, and they often imitate me, and proceed to examine others; there are plenty of persons, as they quickly discover, who think that they know something but really know little or nothing; and then those who are examined by them instead of being angry with themselves are angry with me: This confounded Socrates, they say; this villainous misleader of youth!—and if somebody asks them, Why, what evil does he practise or teach? they do not know, and cannot tell; but in order that they may not appear to be at a loss, they repeat the ready-made charges which are used against all philosophers about teaching things up in the clouds and under the earth, and having no gods, making the worse appear the better cause; for they do not like to confess that their pretence of knowledge has been detected—which is the truth; and as they are numerous and ambitious and energetic, and are drawn up in battle array and have persuasive tongues, they have filled your ears with their loud and inveterate calumnies. And this is the reason why my three accusers, Meletus and Anytus and Lycon, have set upon me; Meletus, who has a quarrel with me on behalf of the poets; Anytus, on behalf of the craftsmen and politicians; Lycon, on behalf of the rhetoricians; and as I said at the beginning, I cannot expect to get rid of such a mass of calumny all in a moment. And this, O men of Athens, is the truth and the whole truth; I have concealed nothing, I have dissembled nothing. And yet, I know that my plainness of speech makes them hate me, and what is their hatred but a proof that I am speaking the truth?—Hence has arisen the prejudice against me; and this is the reason of it, as you will find out either in this or in any future enquiry.

In brief, Socrates explains that the evil opinion about himself held by many is the result of his effort to understand what an oracle had said. In the ancient city of Delphi there was a shrine to which the Greeks would sometimes go in quest of prophetic answers to their questions. The human attendants at the shrine, speaking for the god Apollo, had declared that no one was wiser than Socrates. To challenge that saying of the oracle, Socrates sought out allegedly wise people in order to find someone wiser than himself. With his penetrating questions, however, he exposed their pretensions to wisdom and thereby generated hostility in those he had questioned.

For example, a short time before he appeared in court, Socrates encountered his friend Euthyphro and discovered that he, like Socrates, was involved in litigation. After describing the charges that Meletus was bringing against him, Socrates asked Euthyphro to explain his suit. Much to Socrates' amazement, Euthyphro declared that he was prosecuting his own father for "murder" because of the way he let a slave die. Euthyphro firmly believed that, in prosecuting his father, he was exhibiting a high level of piety even though, according to the conventional wisdom of the time, disloyalty to one's father seemed to be an enormously impious act. Euthyphro describes the alleged murder:

Now the man who is dead was a poor dependent of mine who worked for us as a field labourer on our farm in Naxos, and one day in a fit of drunken passion he got into a quarrel with one of our domestic servants and slew him. My father bound him hand and foot and threw him into a ditch, and then sent to Athens to ask of a diviner what he should do with him. Meanwhile he never attended to him and took no care about him, for he regarded him as a murderer; and thought that no great harm would be done even if he did die. Now this was just what happened. For such was the effect of cold and hunger and chains upon him, that before the messenger returned from the diviner, he was dead. And my father and family are angry with me for taking the part of the murderer and prosecuting my father. They say that he did not kill him, and that if he did, the dead man was a murderer, and I ought not to take any notice, for that a son is impious who prosecutes a father. Which shows, Socrates, how little they know what the gods think about piety and impiety.

Euthyphro goes on to claim that he, more than any other person, has exact knowledge about piety and impiety, and it is this knowledge that gives him the confidence that he is being most pious in prosecuting his father. Here, then, is one of those people who claims to have unusual wisdom, and from whom Socrates is prepared to learn. Alas, however, the incisive questions of Socrates reveal that Euthyphro's purported theological wisdom is confused and internally inconsistent. Here is part of the dialogue.

Soc. And what is piety, and what is impiety?

Euth. Piety is doing as I am doing; that is to say, prosecuting any one who is guilty of murder, sacrilege, or of any similar crime—whether he be your father or mother, or whoever he may be—that makes no difference; and not to prosecute them is impiety. And please to consider, Socrates, what a notable proof I will give you of the truth of my words, a proof which I have already given to others:—Of the principle, I mean, that the impious, whoever he may be, ought not to go unpunished. For do not men regard Zeus as the best and most righteous of the gods?—and yet they admit that he bound his father (Cronos) because he wickedly devoured his sons, and that he too had punished his own father (Uranus) for a similar reason, in a nameless manner. And yet when I proceed against my father, they are angry with me. So inconsistent are they in their way of talking when the gods are concerned, and when I am concerned.

Soc. And do you really believe that the gods fought with one another, and had dire quarrels, battles, and the like, as the poets say, and as you may see represented in the world of the great artists? Are all these tales of the gods true, Euthyphro?

Euth. Yes, Socrates; and, as I was saying, I can tell you, if you would like to hear them, many other things about the gods which would quite amaze you.

Soc. I dare say; and you shall tell me them at some other time when I have leisure. But just at present I would rather hear from you a more precise answer, which you have not as yet given, my friend, to the question, What is "piety"? When asked, you only replied, Doing as you do, charging your father with murder.

Euth. And what I said was true, Socrates.

Soc. No doubt, Euthyphro; but you would admit that there are many other pious acts?

Euth. There are.

Soc. Remember that I did not ask you to give me two or three examples of piety, but to explain the general idea which makes all pious things to be pious.

Euth. I remember.

Soc. Tell me what is the nature of this idea, and then I shall have a standard to which I may look, and by which I may measure actions, whether yours or those of any one else, and then I shall be able to say that such and such an action is pious, such another impious.

Euth. I will tell you, if you like.

Soc. I should very much like.

Euth. Piety, then, is that which is dear to the gods, and impiety is that which is not dear to them.

Soc. Very good, Euthyphro; you have now given me the sort of answer which I wanted. But whether what you say is true or not I cannot as yet tell, although I make no doubt that you will prove the truth of your words.

Euth. Of course.

Soc. Come, then, and let us examine what we are saying. That thing or person which is dear to the gods is pious, and that thing or person which is hateful to the gods is impious, these two being the extreme opposites of one another. Was not that said?

Euth. It was.

Soc. And well said?

Euth. Yes, Socrates, I thought so; it was certainly said.

Soc. And further, Euthyphro, the gods were admitted to have enmities and hatreds and differences?

Euth. Yes, that was also said.

Soc. And what sort of difference creates enmity and anger? Suppose for example that you and I, my good friend, differ about a number; do differences of this sort make us enemies and set us at variance with one another? Do we not go at once to arithmetic, and put an end to them by a sum?

Euth. True.

Soc. Or suppose that we differ about magnitudes, do we not quickly mend the differences by measuring?

Euth. Very true.

Soc. And we end a controversy about heavy and light by resorting to a weighing machine?

Euth. To be sure.

Soc. But what differences are there which cannot be thus decided, and which therefore make us angry and set us at enmity with one another? I dare say the answer does not occur to you at the moment, and therefore I will suggest that these enmities arise when the matters of differences are just and unjust, good and evil, honorable and dishonorable. Are not these the points about which men differ, and about which when we are unable satisfactorily to decide our differences, you and I and all of us quarrel, when we do quarrel?

Euth. Yes, Socrates, the nature of the differences about which we quarrel is such as you describe.

Soc. And the quarrels of the gods, noble Euthyphro, when they occur, are of a like nature.

Euth. Certainly they are.

Soc. They have differences of opinion, as you say, about good and evil, just and unjust, honorable and dishonorable; there would have been no quarrels among them, if there had been no such differences—would there now?

Euth. You are quite right.

Soc.   Does not every man love that which he deems noble and just and good, and hate the opposite of them?

Euth.   Very true.

Soc.   But, as you say, people regard the same things, some as just and others as unjust, about these they dispute; and so there arise wars and fightings among them.

Euth.   Very true.

Soc.   Then the same things are hated by the gods and loved by the gods, and are both hateful and dear to them?

Euth.   True.

Soc.   And upon this view the same things, Euthyphro, will be pious and also impious?

Euth.   So I should suppose.

Soc.   Then, my friend, I remark with surprise that you have not answered the question which I asked. For I certainly did not ask you to tell me what action is both pious and impious; but now it would seem that what is loved by the gods is also hated by them. And therefore, Euthyphro, in thus chastising your father you may very likely be doing what is agreeable to Zeus but disagreeable to Cronos or Uranus, and what is acceptable to Hephaestus but unacceptable to Here, and there may be other gods who have similar differences of opinion.

The dialogue continues as Euthyphro adjusts and readjusts his definitions of piety and impiety in response to the pressing questions of Socrates. The discussion closes with Euthyphro being driven to admit that either his claims at the beginning of the dialogue are false or his claims at the end of the dialogue are false. Both cannot be true.

Soc.   Then either we were wrong in our former assertion; or, if we were right then, we are wrong now.

Euth.   One of the two must be true.

Soc.   Then we must begin again and ask, What is piety? That is an enquiry which I shall never be weary of pursuing as far as in me lies; and I entreat you not to scorn me, but to apply your mind to the utmost, and tell me the truth. For, if any man knows, you are he; and therefore I must detain you, like Proteus, until you tell. If you had not certainly known the nature of piety and impiety, I am confident that you would never, on behalf of a serf, have charged your aged father with murder. You would not have run such a risk of doing wrong in the sight of the gods, and you would have had too much respect for the opinions of men. I am sure, therefore, that you know the nature of piety and impiety. Speak out then, my dear Euthyphro, and do not hide your knowledge.

Euth.   Another time, Socrates, for I am in a hurry, and must go now.

Soc.   Alas! my companion, and will you leave me in despair? I was hoping that you would instruct me in the nature of piety and impiety. . . .

Did Euthyphro depart as a friend or as a new foe? Clearly, the wisdom of Socrates—a wisdom rooted in the recognition of how little he knew—is set in sharp contrast to the wisdom of his contemporaries, such as Euthyphro, who pretended to know so much but were unaware of their own ignorance. Made aware of their ignorance, these "wise" persons were probably pleased to see the one who had put their ideas on trial now himself on trial for his life.

Returning now to the trial, Socrates responds to the allegation that he is an evil-doer who corrupts the youth, who does not believe in the gods of the state, but who believes in novel deities. With his characteristically incisive questions, Socrates exposes the inconsistent, self-contradictory, and ill-founded nature of these charges championed by Meletus.

He says that I am a doer of evil, and corrupt the youth; but I say, O men of Athens that Meletus is a doer of evil, in that he pretends to be in earnest when he is only in jest, and is so eager to bring men to trial from a pretended zeal and interest about matters in which he really never had the smallest interest. And the truth of this I will endeavor to prove to you.

Come hither, Meletus, and let me ask a question of you. You think a great deal about the improvement of youth?

Yes, I do.

Tell the judges, then, who is their improver; for you must know, as you have taken the pains to discover their corrupter, and are citing and accusing me before them. Speak, then, and tell the judges who their improver is—Observe, Meletus, that you are silent, and have nothing to say. But is not this rather disgraceful, and a very considerable proof of what I was saying, that you have no interest in the matter? Speak up, friend, and tell us who their improver is.

The laws.

But that, my good sir, is not my meaning. I want to know who the person is, who, in the first place, knows the laws.

The judges, Socrates, who are present in court.

What, do you mean to say, Meletus, that they are able to instruct and improve youth?

Certainly they are.

What, all of them, or some only and not others?

All of them.

By the goddess Here, that is good news! There are plenty of improvers, then. And what do you say of the audience,—do they improve them?

Yes, they do.

And the senators?

Yes, the senators improve them.

But perhaps the members of the assembly corrupt them?—or do they too improve them?

They improve them.

Then every Athenian improves and elevates them; all with the exception of myself; and I alone am their corrupter? Is that what you affirm?

That is what I stoutly affirm.

I am very unfortunate if you are right. But suppose I ask you a question: How about horses? Does one man do them harm and all the world good? Is not the exact opposite the truth? One man is able to do them good, or at least not many;—the trainer of horses, that is to say, does them good, and others who have to do with them rather injure them? Is not that true, Meletus, of horses, or of any other animals? Most assuredly it is; whether you and Anytus say yes or no. Happy indeed would be the condition of youth if they had one corrupter only, and all the rest of the world were their improvers. But you, Meletus, have sufficiently shown that you never had a thought about the young; your carelessness is seen in your not caring about the very things which you bring against me.

And now, Meletus, I will ask you another question—by Zeus I will: Which is better, to live among bad citizens, or among good ones? Answer, friend, I say; the question is one which may be easily answered. Do not the good do their neighbors good, and the bad do them evil?

Certainly.

And is there any one who would rather be injured than benefited by those who live with him? Answer, my good friend, the law requires you to answer—does any one like to be injured?

Certainly not.

And when you accuse me of corrupting and deteriorating the youth, do you allege that I corrupt them intentionally or unintentionally?

Intentionally, I say.

But you have just admitted that the good do their neighbors good, and evil do them evil. Now, is that a truth which your superior wisdom has recognized thus early in life, and am I at my age, in such darkness and ignorance as not to know that if a man with whom I have to live is corrupted by me, I am very likely to be harmed by him; and yet I corrupt him, and intentionally, too—so you say, although neither I nor any other human being is ever likely to be convinced by you. But either I do not corrupt them, or I corrupt them unintentionally; and on either view of the case you lie. If my offence is unintentional, the law has no cognizance of unintentional offences; you ought to have taken me privately, and warned and admonished me; for if I had been better advised, I should have left off doing what I only did unintentionally—no doubt I should; but you would have nothing to say to me and refused to teach me. And now you bring me up in this court, which is a place not of instruction, but of punishment.

It will be very clear to you, Athenians, as I was saying, that Meletus has no care at all, great or small, about the matter. But still I should like to know, Meletus, in what I am affirmed to corrupt the young. I suppose you mean, as I infer from your indictment, that I teach them not to acknowledge the gods which the state acknowledges, but some other new divinities or spiritual agencies in their stead. These are the lessons by which I corrupt the youth, as you say.

Yes, that I say emphatically.

Then, by the gods, Meletus, of whom we are speaking, tell me and the court in somewhat plainer terms, what you mean! For I do not as yet understand whether you affirm that I teach other men to acknowledge some gods, and therefore that I do believe in gods, and am not an entire atheist—this you do not lay to my charge,—but only you say that they are not the same gods which the city recognizes—the charge is that they are different gods. Or, do you mean that I am an atheist simply, and a teacher of atheism?

I mean the latter—that you are a complete atheist.

What an extraordinary statement! Why do you think so, Meletus? Do you mean that I do not believe in the godhead of the sun or moon, like other men?

I assure you, judges, that he does not; for he says that the sun is stone, and the moon earth.

Friend Meletus, you think that you are accusing Anaxagoras; and you have but a bad opinion of the judges, if you fancy them illiterate to such a degree as not to know that these doctrines are found in the books of Anaxagoras the Clazomenian, which are full of them. And so, forsooth, the youth are said to be taught them by Socrates, when there are not unfrequently exhibitions of them at the theater (price of admission one drachma at the most); and they might pay their money, and laugh at Socrates if he pretends to father these extraordinary views. And so, Meletus, you really think that I do not believe in any god?

I swear by Zeus that you believe absolutely in none at all.

Nobody will believe you, Meletus, and I am pretty sure that you do not believe yourself. I cannot help thinking, men of Athens, that Meletus is reckless and impudent, and that he has written this indictment in a spirit of mere wantonness and youthful bravado. Has he not compounded a riddle, thinking to try me? He said to himself:—I shall see whether the wise Socrates will discover my facetious contradiction, or whether I shall be able to deceive him and the rest of them. For he certainly does appear to me to contradict himself in the indictment as much as if he said that Socrates is guilty of not believing in the gods, and yet of believing in them—but this is not like a person who is in earnest.

I should like you, O men of Athens, to join me in examining what I conceive to be his inconsistency; and do you, Meletus, answer. And I must remind the audience of my request that they would not make a disturbance if I speak in my accustomed manner.

Did ever man, Meletus, believe in the existence of human things, and not of human beings? . . . I wish, men of Athens, that he would answer, and not be always trying to get up an interruption. Did ever any man believe in horsemanship, and not in horses? or in flute-playing, and not in flute-players? No, my friend; I will answer to you and to the court, as you refuse to answer for yourself. There is no man who ever did. But now please to answer the next question: Can a man believe in spiritual and divine agencies, and not in spirits or demigods?

He cannot.

How lucky I am to have extracted that answer, by the assistance of the court! But then you swear in the indictment that I teach and believe in divine or spiritual agencies (new or old, no matter for that); at any rate, I believe in spiritual agencies,—so you say and swear in the affidavit; and yet if I believe in divine beings, how can I help believing in spirits and demigods;—must I not? To be sure I must; and therefore I may assume that your silence gives consent. Now what are spirits or demigods? are they not either gods or the sons of gods?

Certainly they are.

But this is what I call the facetious riddle invented by you: the demigods or spirits are gods, and you say first that I do not believe in gods, and then again that I do believe in gods; that is, if I believe in demigods. For if the demigods are the illegitimate sons of gods, whether by the nymphs or by any other mothers, of whom they are said to be the sons—what human being will ever believe that there are no gods if they are the sons of gods? You might as well affirm the existence of mules, and deny that of horses and asses. Such nonsense, Meletus, could only have been tended by you to make trial of me. You have put this into the indictment because you had nothing real of which to accuse me. But no one who has a particle of understanding will ever be convinced by you that the same men can believe in divine and superhuman things, and yet not believe there are gods and demigods and heroes.

   I have said enough to answer to the charge of Meletus; any elaborate defence is unnecessary; but I know only too well how many are the enmities which I have incurred; and this is what will be my destruction if I am destroyed;—not Meletus, nor yet Anytus, but the envy and detraction of the world, which has been the death of many good men, and will probably be the death of many more; there is no danger of my being the last of them.

Can one believe Meletus that every Athenian except Socrates promotes the well-being of the youth? Can one believe Meletus that Socrates would intentionally do harm to his neighbors when Socrates was aware that such injury would backfire on himself? Can one believe Meletus that Socrates is an atheist when in fact he believes in divine agencies? Such queries certainly erode the strength of Meletus' allegations. Yet it is not the truth or falsity of these charges that will determine his fate, but rather the intensity of the hostility which Socrates' probing questions have engendered in the populace. Judgment based on incited passions rather than on reasoned assessment is what one would expect from a jury of five hundred and one members.

   The death penalty hangs over Socrates' head. Is he prepared to change his ways in order to subdue the hostility of the citizenry? Is he willing to stop exposing the pretense of wisdom among his fellow Athenians to save his life? Is he willing to give up philosophizing in order to avoid death? His response is unequivocal.

Men of Athens, I honor and love you; but I shall obey God rather than you, and while I have life and strength I shall never cease from the practice and teaching of philosophy, exhorting any one whom I meet and saying to him after my manner: You, my friend—a citizen of the great and mighty and wise city of Athens,—are you not ashamed of heaping up the greatest amount of money and honor and reputation, and caring so little about wisdom and truth and the greatest improvement of the soul, which you never regard or heed at all? And if the person with whom I am arguing, says: Yes, but I do care; then I do not leave him or let him go at once; but I proceed to interrogate and examine and cross-examine him, and if I think that he has no virtue in him, but only says that he has, I reproach him with undervaluing the greater, and overvaluing the less. And I shall repeat the same words to every one whom I meet, young and old, citizen and alien, but especially to the citizens, inasmuch as they are my brethren. For know that this is the command of God; and I believe that no greater good has ever happened in the state than my service to the God. For I do nothing but go about persuading you all, old and young alike, not to take thought for your persons or your properties, but first and chiefly to care about the greatest improvement of the soul. I tell you that virtue is not given by money, but that from virtue comes money and every other good of man, public as well as private. This is my teaching, and if this is the doctrine which corrupts the youth, I am a mischievous person. But if any one says that this is not my teaching, he is speaking an untruth. Wherefore, O men of Athens, I say to you, do as Anytus bids or not as Anytus bids, and either acquit me or not; but whichever you do, understand that I shall never alter my ways, not even if I have to die many times.

The vote is taken, and it is close. Socrates is found guilty, but thirty additional votes (out of 501) being cast in his favor would have resulted in his acquittal. His accusers call for the death penalty, and Socrates is offered the opportunity to argue for a lesser penalty. Instead, with a touch of irony, Socrates suggests that he should be rewarded in a fashion similar to the treatment accorded to victorious Olympian athletes because of the benefit that his philosophizing has brought to Athens. Unwilling to admit that he has wronged anyone, Socrates refuses to acknowledge that he deserves any punishment whatsoever. We rejoin the dialogue at the point where Socrates is examining the suggestion that he propose "exile" as the court's penalty.

Some one will say: Yes, Socrates, but cannot you hold your tongue, and then you may go into a foreign city, and no one will interfere with you? Now I have great difficulty in making you understand my answer to this. For if I tell you that to do as you say would be a disobedience to the God, and therefore that I cannot hold my tongue, you will not believe that I am serious; and if I say again that daily to discourse about virtue, and of those other things about which you hear me examining myself and others, is the greatest good of man, and that the unexamined life is not worth living, you are still less likely to believe me. Yet I say what is true, although a thing of which it is hard for me to persuade you. Also, I have never been accustomed to think that I deserve to suffer any harm. Had I money I might have estimated the offence at what I was able to pay, and not have been much the worse. But I have none, and therefore I must ask you to proportion the fine to my means. Well, perhaps I could afford a mina, and therefore I propose that penalty: Plato, Crito, Critobulus, and Apollodorus, my friends here, bid me say thirty minae, and they will be the sureties. Let thirty minae be the penalty; for which sum they will be ample security to you.

Another vote is taken. Socrates is condemned to death. In his concluding statement, he addresses his accusers and charges that they are guilty of unrighteousness.

You think that I was convicted because I had no words of the sort which would have procured my acquittal—I mean, if I had thought fit to leave nothing undone or unsaid. Not so; the deficiency which led to my conviction was not of words—certainly not. But I had not the boldness or impudence or inclination to address you as you would have liked me to do, weeping and wailing and lamenting, and saying and doing many things which you have been accustomed to hear from others, and which, as I maintain, are unworthy of me. I thought at the time that I ought not to do anything common or mean when in danger; nor do I now repent of the style of my defence; I would rather die having spoken after my manner, than speak in your manner and live. For neither in war nor yet at law ought I or any man to use every way of escaping death. Often in battle there can be no doubt that if a man will throw away his arms, and fall on his knees before his pursuers, he may escape death; and in other dangers there are other ways of escaping death, if a man is willing to say and do anything. The difficulty, my friends, is not to avoid death, but to avoid unrighteousness; for that runs faster than death. I am old and move slowly, and the slower runner has overtaken me, and my accusers are keen and quick, and the faster runner, who is unrighteousness, has overtaken them. And now I depart hence condemned by you to suffer the penalty of death,—they too go their ways condemned by the truth to suffer the penalty of villainy and wrong; and I must abide by my award—let them abide by theirs. I suppose that these things may be regarded as fated,—and I think that they are well.

Socrates also has some parting words for his friends among the jurors who are distressed by the apparently evil outcome of the trial. To encourage them, Socrates suggests that death is either going to sleep or going on a journey, and that neither of those possibilities would occasion any evil for him.

Friends, who would have acquitted me, I would also like to talk with you about the thing which has come to pass, while the magistrates are busy, and before I go to the place at which I must die. Stay then a little, for we may as well talk with one another while there is time. . . .

Let us reflect . . . and we shall see that there is great reason to hope that death is a good; for one of two things—either death is a state of nothingness and utter unconsciousness, or, as men say, there is a change and migration of the soul from this world to another. Now if you suppose that there is no consciousness, but a sleep like the sleep of him who is undisturbed even by dreams, death will be an unspeakable gain. For if a person were to select the night in which his sleep was undisturbed even by dreams, and were to compare with this the other days and nights of his life, and then were to tell us how many days and nights he had passed in the course of his life better and more pleasantly than this one, I think that any man, I will not say a private man, but even the great king will not find many such days or nights, when compared with the others. Now if death be of such a nature, I say that to die is gain; for eternity is then only a single night. But if death is the journey to another place, and there, as men say, all the dead abide, what good, O my friends and judges, can be greater than this? If indeed when the pilgrim arrives in the world below, he is delivered from the professors of justice in this world, and finds the true judges who are said to give judgment there, Minos and Rhadamanthus and Aeacus and Triptolemus, and other sons of God who were righteous in their own life, that pilgrimage will be worth making. What would not a man give if he might converse with Orpheus and Musaeus and Hesiod and Homer? Nay, if this be true, let me die again and again. I myself, too, shall have a wonderful interest in there meeting and conversing with Palamedes, and Ajax the son of Telamon, and any other ancient hero who has suffered death through an unjust judgment; and there will be no small pleasure, as I think, in comparing my own sufferings with theirs. Above all, I shall then be able to continue my search into true and false knowledge; as in this world, so also in the next; and I shall find out who is wise, and who pretends to be wise, and is not. What would not a man give, O judges, to be able to examine the leader of the great Trojan expedition; or Odysseus or Sisyphus, or numberless others, men and women too! What infinite delight would there be in conversing with them and asking them questions! In another world they do not put a man to death for asking questions; assuredly not. For besides being happier than we are, they will be immortal, if what is said is true.

Wherefore, O judges, be of good cheer about death, and know of a certainty, that no evil can happen to a good man, either in life or after death. He and his are not neglected by the gods . . .

I have a favor to ask. . . When my sons are grown up, I would ask you, O my friends, to punish them; And I would have you trouble them, as I have troubled you, if they seem to care about riches, or anything, more than about virtue; or if they pretend to be something when they are really nothing,—then reprove them, as I have reproved you, for not caring about that for which they ought to care, and thinking that they are something when they are really nothing. And if you do this, both I and my sons will have received justice at your hands.

The hour of departure has arrived, and we go our ways—I to die, and you to live. Which is better God only knows.

Having viewed Socrates the philosopher in action, are you now able to say what philosophy is? If you are having some difficulty, take heart because contemporary professional philosophers are by no means in agreement about how philosophy should be defined. Indeed, one could view the current philosophical scene as a debate between two different views of philosophy. On the one hand, there is the modern analytic tradition which has roots in eighteenth century British empiricism, modern science, and twentieth century logical positivism. It emphasizes the analysis of language in order to achieve both clarity and also the resolution of verbal disputes. Would not the modern analytic philosopher who focuses on the clarification of the meaning of words be following the example of Socrates as he challenged Euthyphro to clarify his concept of "piety"? On the other hand, there is the more speculative tradition of philosophy (as exemplified by metaphysicians such as Descartes, Spinoza, Leibniz, and Hegel) which tries to formulate answers to such questions as the nature of human existence, the purpose of human life, the prospect of life after death, the existence of God, the nature of ultimate reality, the features necessary for the good life, and so forth. Could not such philosophers also claim to be following the example of Socrates when he summoned his contemporaries to pursue virtue and as he speculated about whether death was going to sleep or going on a journey?

If both of these traditions can legitimately appeal to Socrates in support of their views, does it not seem likely that philosophy in the Socratic tradition involves both views, that it embraces concern for clarifying the words of human discourse and also formulating responses to perennial human questions? The presence of these two emphases in the Socratic tradition can be seen if we consider the Socratic *goal* and *method* of philosophizing.

The Socratic Goal.   What did Socrates want to accomplish? Some might say that Socrates wished primarily to make himself appear wise by making others look foolish. If so, Socrates was a clever and arrogant man. Others might say that his major goal was to promote social change by teaching young people how to question and discredit the authorities of society. If so, Socrates was something of a revolutionary. Still others might say that Socrates wished to nourish the examined life. Let us consider this latter alternative in more detail.

You will recall that Socrates declared that "the unexamined life is not worth living." Why is it not worth living? The unexamined life does not ponder questions like this: Who am I? What ought I to do? What may I hope? The unexamined life does not evaluate alternative futures. It lives with the flow. The unexamined life hears no evil and sees no evil. It is devoid of critical self-assessment. It stifles the breath of reason. It violates a distinctive human capacity. In contrast, the examined life allows human reason to breathe, live, and grow strong. The examined life seeks not simply to satisfy curiosity, but rather strives for human virtue. Remember how concerned Socrates was about virtue. Recall that he asked his friends to punish his sons when they are grown if they cared about anything more than virtue. The examined life and the pursuit of virtue were dear to Socrates and they were linked together in the philosophical task. Through the examined life, one could pursue answers to fundamental human questions, discover what it means to be a human being, and learn what human virtue is. Does not the philosophic quest in the Socratic tradition, then, seem to include the pursuit of the examined life in order to make virtue abound?

The Socratic Method.   How did Socrates pursue this goal? At least two features of Socrates' method stand out. First, he sought conceptual clarification. Even as he challenged Euthyphro over the meaning of piety, no doubt he would require us to be clear about the meaning of virtue. He might ask us, for example, if virtue stands for the personal qualities that a particular culture at a specific time finds attractive. If so, would not the meaning of virtue vary according to time and place? Or is virtue transcultural? If so, would not human beings who pursued virtue have a common goal? If so, what would be the human characteristics that these people from diverse cultures would consider to be at the heart of virtue? Notice how the philosophic goal inspires one question after another.

Second, the Socratic method involved a critical examination of received opinions and accepted beliefs. In the wake of the declaration of the Oracle of Apollo at Delphi, Socrates went about testing the knowledge claims of his contemporaries. Suppose you said "I believe that there is a God who cares for humankind." Socrates would probably ask you, "On what basis do you hold that belief?" Clearly, Socrates would be asking you to justify your belief. What do you think Socrates would accept as justification for your belief? Would quoting from sacred scriptures do the job? Would citing a personal, private religious experience count as evidence to justify your belief? How about summoning the testimony of the leaders of society who also believe in God? Would their testimony satisfy Socrates? What about the so-called proofs for the existence of God offered by Aristotle, Thomas Aquinas, René Descartes, William Paley, and others? Finding evidence to justify one's belief in God is not easy, as we will discover in the chapter on God's existence. Indeed, finding evidence to justify a good number of our beliefs is no easy matter.

If we are able to produce evidence that justifies our belief that God exists, then we could say that we have *knowledge* that God exists. But in whose eyes does the evidence for our belief have to be convincing? Do all rational persons have to agree that our evidence is sufficient before we can claim that our belief is justified? Or would the concurrence of the majority of rational persons be sufficient? Or should we be willing to settle for something less than a majority? And would it be permissible to speak of degrees of justification depending upon the quantity and quality of the evidence we are able to cite in support of our belief? What if we are unable to produce evidence that justifies our belief that God exists? Must we then abandon that belief? Indeed, is it ever permissible to hold a belief that is unjustified? Furthermore, what really counts as evidence? These are the kinds of questions that give rise to a theory of knowledge, and to that subject we will be devoting a full chapter later in this book.

Philosophers, in the Socratic tradition, pursue the examined life in order to generate virtue; and the virtue that Socrates and his disciples had in mind is multifaceted. It involves the fulfillment of all the distinctively human potentialities, the harmonious blending of human appetites, emotions, and thinking. In other words, to pursue virtue is to seek human flourishing. The method philosophers use in this pursuit involves both conceptual clarification and the critical examination of accepted beliefs. Unrelentingly, philosophers ask us, "What do you mean by that?" and "What evidence do you have to support that belief?"

If we agree with Socrates that the unexamined life is not worth living, and decide to pursue the examined life, then we must subject the beliefs of humankind to rigorous scrutiny. But where should we begin? Let us return to the life of Socrates for a suggestion. The ancient oracle of Apollo at Delphi, where the divine declaration had been made that no one was wiser than Socrates, has some advice for us. At the entrance to that shrine these words were carved in stone: "Know Thyself." Those words suggest an intriguing point of departure for us. Perhaps the examined life should begin with an attempt to understand who or what we are. The pursuit of such self-knowledge would, in due course, prompt us to raise additional questions, which would cease only when we have examined the whole human condition. In this book we have adopted the oracle's advice.

The questions we have explored include the following:

Am I a body and a mind?
Am I determined or free?
Am I a creature of God?
On what basis shall I judge things morally?
On what basis shall I judge things artistically?
On what basis shall I judge the law?
On what basis shall I claim to have knowledge?
What does science tell me about the world?
Does my life have any meaning?

All of these are perennial questions, which generation after generation of Socrates' disciples have encountered as they have pursued the examined life. We have selected passages from the writings of modern philosophers who will often propose conflicting answers to these questions. The debate between these philosophers will at times be heated, and, we hope, at all times engaging. As we ourselves try to fashion responses to these questions (and respond to them we must), occasionally we will achieve some strongly warranted answers to our questions. Frequently, however, our questioning will result in uncertainties. Indeed, we will find ourselves in what Bertrand Russell referred to as the "no man's land" between the knowledge of science and the dogma of theology. Yet those uncertainties can be celebrated as the high cost of being human, of being rational, of being open to the future, of being able to ask questions that we are perhaps unable to answer completely.

NOTE ON SOURCES.   The material in this section is quoted from Plato, "Euthyphro" and "Apology," trans. B. Jowett in *The Dialogues of Plato,* 4th ed. (Oxford, England: Oxford University Press, 1953).

2

Am I a Body and a Mind?

THE QUESTION POSED

I am free; I am immortal; I am a creature of God. Each of these is an answer to the question, "What am I?" We shall discuss these answers in Chapter 3. In this chapter, we focus on three different kinds of answers: I am just a mind, I am just a body, I am some mix of the two. These answers show the influence of the philosopher-mathematician, René Descartes. He began by asking "What can I know with certainty?" His answer led to Western philosophy's discussion of what is now termed, the mind-body problem and the problem of other minds. Descartes' views on certainty also lead us to ask questions about what keeps us the same person, the problem philosophers refer to as, the problem of personal identity.

Descartes wrote during the period often called the rise of the new science. The new science basically embraced materialism, a view which held that matter is the primary feature of reality and relegates mind or spirit either to a secondary, dependent status or to no status at all. Promulgated by sixth- and fifth-century B.C. Greek philosophers like Leucippus and Democritus, materialism was overshadowed for centuries by the doctrines of Plato, Aristotle, and Christian theologians who accorded mind (or spirit) a more prominent and independent position in the landscape of reality.

Materialism, however, had a formidable ally in modern science, which began with the quest for generalizations about nature based on empirical data; the more quantitative (mathematical) the information about the world, the better. The search for mathematical ways to represent the world is most easily seen in astronomy in the works of Copernicus (1473–1543), Kepler (1571–1630), Brahe (1546–1601), and Galileo (1564–1642).

The view of reality that emerged from this new science seemed to support materialism. According to the new science, physical reality was depicted as matter in motion. Matter objectively possessed position, shape, size, mass, and velocity. All these characteristics were definable, so their relations to one another could be reasoned out, as in geometry. In contrast smells, sounds, colors, and tastes could be identified only by putting a person in a situation where the person will have the experience we have in mind and saying, "There, that is what I mean." These latter characteristics that do not lend themselves to deductions and reasoning were considered to be not objectively real. They were rather "appearances" that arise in us when our sense organs are stimulated by objectively real matter with its geometrical characteristics. Objective reality, accordingly, came to be viewed as basically a world of material objects moving in a mechanistic fashion. That view of reality left precious little room, if any, for an immaterial mind, for human freedom, for immortality, and for a spiritual being called God—all of which had been prominent in medieval thought.

Writing during this time, but not entirely from within the tradition, Descartes developed an impressive philosophical system in which the human was interpreted as being both a mind (*res cogitans*—a thinking thing) and a body (*res extensa*—an extended thing).

The twentieth-century philosopher Gilbert Ryle, our second author, contends that Descartes made a serious mistake in logic, called the category-mistake. Next, we read excerpts from J. J. C. Smart and Jerry Fodor, who agree with Ryle that Descartes has made serious errors but are not convinced that Ryle's answer to the mind-body problem is acceptable. Smart and Fodor appeal to contemporary advances in science to support their view. Smart appeals to neurophysiology, whereas Fodor uses advances in computer science. Our fifth author, Alan Turing, says that when computers get to be sophisticated to a certain degree, a degree he spells out in his article, we will start talking as if computers had thoughts. John Searle, the next author in this section, thinks that those who appeal to computer science to bolster the view that thinking is nothing more than what computers do have made a serious mistake—one just as serious as the category-mistake apparently made by Descartes. Paul and Patricia Churchland reply to Searle by pointing out that there are ways to compute other than by rule-governed symbol manipulation. Computers using these other methods will not be affected by Searle's arguments against the possibility of a thinking computer.

---

1   RENÉ DESCARTES
I Am a Mind (*Res Cogitans*) and a Body (*Res Extensa*)

Descartes begins by asking a question about knowledge, what philosophers would call an epistemological question: What can I know? But for Descartes and for the group of philosophers known as Rationalists, "What can I know?" means "What can I know for sure?" To know something to Descartes is to know it with the certainty of mathematics. Just as one cannot deny that $5 + 3 = 8$ without being involved in a contradiction, so if one really knows anything, to deny that, would be to be involved in a contradiction. This is not our present day sense of "to know." Today we would distinguish between mathematics which may have a kind of certainty attached to it and factual (empirical) claims to knowledge which are always subject to being modified. Not so for Descartes. As Descartes answers his question, "What can I know for sure?" we will see that he decides that he needs to prove the existence of a non-deceiving God. Yet, not even such a God can save Descartes from the mind-body problem (How do mind and body interact?) and the problem of other minds (Are there other minds? Can we know if there are any other minds?)

BIOGRAPHICAL NOTE.   René Descartes was born in France in 1596 and died in Sweden in 1650 at the age of fifty-four. His formal education from eight to sixteen was received at the Jesuit college of La Flêche. Here he acquired the essentials of a "gentleman's education," which he subsequently devoted much time to erasing. Before he had turned seventeen he put aside his books and after a few lessons in fencing and horsemanship went to "the great world of Paris." Here he remained for about five years, living at first the usual life of gaiety and gambling, but retiring after a while to the quiet and seclusion of an obscure lodging house. His thoughtful temper reasserted itself. Habits of reflection acquired at La Flêche, and roused once more by a Catholic friend, Father Mersenne, took possession of him again.

In 1618 Descartes left Paris, determined to see the world. He became a soldier, serving in three different European armies, in the Netherlands, in Bavaria, and in Hungary. It was a life that gave him much time for thought during months of idleness in winter quarters. He stuck to soldiering for three or four years, then resolved "no longer to carry a musket." Army days over, he continued his travels for five or six years more, visiting Switzerland and Italy, until in 1628, he decided that he had read enough in the "great book of the world."

In 1629, his mind crowded with ideas demanding to be written down, he settled in Holland. He was seeking quiet and seclusion once more. His European retirement, as he called it, lasted twenty years. These were years of fruitful production. Book followed book. His reputation spread. He had the intellectuals of his generation for his readers, and its rulers for his patrons and friends. In rapid succession he wrote *Quest for Truth, Rules for the Direction of the Mind, Discourse on Method, Meditations on First Philosophy, Principles of Philosophy, Treatise on the Passions,* and many other volumes that soon became stock-in-trade for the philosophically minded of his day. In 1649 he was invited by Queen Christina of Sweden to visit her at Stockholm and expound the principles of the "new philosophy." After much hesitation, and against the advice of his friends, he agreed to go. It cost him his life, for he caught a cold in his lungs that brought about his death.

THE ARGUMENT OF THE PASSAGES.   While Descartes' writings explore many topics of philosophy, our attention in the following passages from his *Meditations on First Philosophy* focuses on what he has to say about the existence of the mind and the body and their interactions. We will observe Descartes using hyperbolic doubt, that is, doubt taken to extreme limits, in his attempt to find a belief that is beyond doubt, indubitable. Step by step he will question the reliability of his senses and beliefs based on them until he finds within himself a belief that doubt cannot shatter.

He begins,

> Some years ago I was struck by the large number of falsehoods that I had accepted as true in my childhood, and by the highly doubtful nature of the whole edifice that I had subsequently based on them. I realized that it was necessary, once in the course of my life, to demolish everything completely and start again right from the foundations if I wanted to establish anything at all in the sciences that was stable and likely to last. But the task looked an enormous one, and I began to wait until I should reach a mature enough age to ensure that no subsequent time of life would be more suitable for tackling such inquiries. This led me to put the project off for so long that I would now be to blame if by pondering over it any further I wasted the time still left for carrying it out. So

today I have expressly rid my mind of all worries and arranged for myself a clear stretch of free time. I am here quite alone, and at last I will devote myself sincerely and without reservation to the general demolition of my opinions.

But to accomplish this, it will not be necessary for me to show that all my opinions are false, which is something I could perhaps never manage. Reason now leads me to think that I should hold back my assent from opinions which are not completely certain and indubitable just as carefully as I do from those which are patently False. So, for the purpose of rejecting all my opinions, it will be enough if I find in each of them at least some reason for doubt. And to do this I will not need to run through them all individually, which would be an endless task. Once the foundations of a building are undermined, anything built on them collapses of its own accord; so I will go straight for the basic principles on which all my former beliefs rested.

Descartes will try to find what he can know for certain by rejecting any claims to knowledge that can have the slightest doubt attached to them. If Descartes tried to test each and every claim to knowledge, he would never finish, so he will divide them by type. He will begin with knowledge claims that he has acquired through his senses, e.g., that the tree is ten feet tall, is an oak, has a brown trunk with a squirrel sitting next to it. It might turn out that it is just an artist's mock-up of an oak tree, that the brown of the trunk is really green but the artist has special lighting and the squirrel—it is really a chipmunk. Descartes used an example of a castle that when seen from a distance looks small. We, of course, know that it is large. In certain kinds of lighting, some colors are hard to tell apart. Looking at railroad tracks, we see them as meeting at the horizon. Surely, they cannot meet. These sorts of arguments have come to be called arguments from illusion. We will not discuss here whether they really are illusions in the sense of a magician's illusion that she is making pigeons appear from nowhere; or that there is water on the asphalt highway ahead of us.

Whatever I have up till now accepted as most true I have acquired either from the senses or through the senses. But from time to time I have found that the senses deceive, and it is prudent never to trust completely those who have deceived us even once.

This is an odd argument. Because we are deceived once, never trust again? This is not even prudent. A restaurant may disappoint once, but does it make sense never to go back again? How can we make sense of Descartes' strategy? The answer is that he using hyperbolic doubt. In other words, this is exaggerated doubt used to make a point. It is not the sort of doubt that we would use to get us through everyday situations. I may doubt the ability of my friend to play a trumpet solo without mistakes; but not because he once made a mistake. Indeed, within reason, the more mistakes he made during practice, the more I will expect him to play flawlessly during a performance. When Descartes goes on to make his claims about dreaming, remember that they are made within the use of hyperbolic doubt, and that the goal of such doubt is to find a belief that is indubitable (beyond doubt), a belief upon which all other beliefs that count as knowledge can securely rest.

Yet although the senses occasionally deceive us with respect to objects which are very small or in the distance, there are many other beliefs about which doubt is quite impossible, even though they are derived from the senses—for example, that I am here, sitting by the fire, wearing a winter dressing-gown, holding this piece of paper in my hands, and so on. Again, how could it be denied that these hands or this whole body are mine? Unless perhaps I were to liken myself to madmen, whose brains are so damaged by the persistent vapours of melancholia that they firmly maintain they are kings when they are paupers, or say they are dressed in purple when they are naked, or that their heads are made of earthenware, or that they are pumpkins, or made of glass. But such people are insane, and I would be thought equally mad if I took anything from them as a model for myself.

A brilliant piece of reasoning! As if I were not a man who sleeps at night, and regularly has all the same experiences while asleep as madmen do when awake—indeed sometimes even more improbable ones. How often, asleep at night, am I convinced of just such familiar events—that I am here in my dressing-gown, sitting by the fire—when in fact I am lying undressed in bed! Yet at the moment my eyes are certainly wide awake when I look at this piece of paper; I shake my head and it is not asleep; as I stretch out and feel my hand I do so deliberately, and I know what I am doing. All this would not happen with such distinctness to someone asleep. Indeed! As if I did not remember other occasions when I have been tricked by exactly similar thoughts while asleep! As I think about this more carefully, I see plainly that there are never any sure signs by means of which being awake can be distinguished from being asleep. The result is that I begin to feel dazed, and this very feeling only reinforces the notion that I may be asleep.

Are we so readily fooled by dreams? Sometimes we can't tell whether we are remembering a dream or remembering an event that happened during a waking state. "That never happened—you just dreamt it!" But of a dream that I am president or fighting in a foxhole during some strange war—am I supposed to think that I really might have been in that foxhole? Consider the notion of being tricked while asleep. What could this mean? If I dream that I can fly, am I being deceived in the way that a con man might trick me into believing I had won the lottery? Again, note that when Descartes says that there are "never any sure signs by means of which being awake can be distinguished from being asleep," he is using hyperbolic doubt.

Suppose then that I am dreaming, and that these particulars—that my eyes are open, that I am moving my head and stretching out my hands—are not true. Perhaps, indeed, I do not even have such hands or such a body at all. Nonetheless, it must surely be admitted that the visions which come in sleep are like paintings, which must have been fashioned in the likeness of things that are real, and hence that at least these general kinds of things—eyes, head, hands and the body as a whole—are things which are not imaginary but are real and exist. For even when painters try to create sirens and satyrs with the most extraordinary bodies, they cannot give them natures which are new in all respects; they simply jumble up the limbs of different animals. Or if perhaps they manage to think up something so new that nothing remotely similar has ever been seen before—something which is therefore completely fictitious and unreal—at least the colours used in the composition must be real. By similar reasoning, although these general kinds of things—eyes, head, hands and so on—could be imaginary, it must at least be admitted that certain other even simpler and more universal things are real. These are as it were the real colours from which we form all the images of things, whether true or false, that occur in our thought.

This class appears to include corporeal nature in general, and its extension; the shape of extended things; the quantity, or size and number of these things; the place in which they may exist, the time through which they may endure,[1] and so on.

Here Descartes tells us that bodies are extended; they have a shape, a size and a place where they are located. Later on, Descartes will contrast body to mind. Mind will be unextended and, therefore, have none of the other properties of body. How the two can be a unit, given their disparate natures (the mind-body problem) will be a problem Descartes never really answers.

So a reasonable conclusion from this might be that physics, astronomy, medicine, and all other disciplines which depend on the study of composite things, are doubtful; while arithmetic, geometry and other subjects of this kind, which deal only with the simplest and most general things, regardless of whether they really exist in nature or not, contain something certain and indubitable. For whether I am awake or asleep, two and three added together are five, and a square has no more than four sides. It seems impossible that such transparent truths should incur any suspicion of being false.

Here we see Descartes winding up his argument against trusting the senses. The argument from illusion made us mistrust observations from afar or under less than normal circumstances. Now with the dream argument Descartes concludes that no observation is trustworthy, for even the simplest claims such as my pants are blue or that I am sitting at my desk, might be false if we are dreaming. And yet, we still have not given any reason to doubt the truths of mathematics; $2 + 6 = 8$ even in a dream!

And yet firmly rooted in my mind is the long-standing opinion that there is an omnipotent God who made me the kind of creature that I am. How do I know that he has not brought it about that there is no earth, no sky, no extended thing, no shape, no size, no place, while at the same time ensuring that all these things appear to me to exist just as they do now? What is more, since I sometimes believe that others go astray in cases where they think they have the most perfect knowledge, may I not similarly go wrong every time I add two and three or count the sides of a square, or in some even simpler matter, if that is imaginable? But perhaps God would not have allowed me to be deceived in this way, since he is said to be supremely good. But if it were inconsistent with his goodness to have created me such that I am deceived all the time, it would seem equally foreign to his goodness to allow me to be deceived even occasionally; yet this last assertion cannot be made.[2]

What about God's goodness? How could there be an all-powerful and all-good God and still be deception? Descartes will depend on God for help later in the *Meditations,* but at this point Descartes cannot appeal to God because he has yet to prove that God even exists no less that He is perfectly good. This is part of Descartes' hyperbolic doubt—that is, pretend to doubt everything doubtable first and then move on once one finds certainty.

---

[1] The place where they ate, the time which measures their duration (French version).

[2] . . . yet I cannot doubt that he does allow this (French version).

But there is another part to the Cartesian method. That is, Descartes is writing using the order of discovery, not what is termed the order of logic (sometimes called the order of being). In the order of logic, one writes in logical order (think of Euclid's Geometry which begins with definitions, moves on to axioms, then postulates, then theorems, etc.). So, using the method of discovery, the method that shows the order in which ideas are actually discovered, Descartes first doubts everything, and then realizes that it would be useful to prove the existence of a good God. If Descartes were to use the method of logic, he would start with a proof for the existence of God.

Perhaps there may be some who would prefer to deny the existence of so powerful a God rather than believe that everything else is uncertain. Let us not argue with them, but grant them that everything said about God is a fiction. According to their supposition, then, I have arrived at my present state by fate or chance or a continuous chain of events, or by some other means; yet since deception and error seem to be imperfections, the less powerful they make my original cause, the more likely it is that I am so imperfect as to be deceived all the time. I have no answer to these arguments, but am finally compelled to admit that there is not one of my former beliefs about which a doubt may not properly be raised; and this is not a flippant or ill-considered conclusion, but is based on powerful and well thought-out reasons. So in future I must withhold my assent from these former beliefs just as carefully as I would from obvious falsehoods, if I want to discover any certainty.[3]

But it is not enough merely to have noticed this; I must make an effort to remember it. My habitual opinions keep coming back, and, despite my wishes, they capture my belief, which is as it were bound over to them as a result of long occupation and the law of custom. I shall never get out of the habit of confidently assenting to these opinions, so long as I suppose them to be what in fact they are, namely highly probable opinions—opinions which, despite the fact that they are in a sense doubtful, as has just been shown, it is still much more reasonable to believe than to deny. In view of this, I think it will be a good plan to turn my will in completely the opposite direction and deceive myself, by pretending for a time that these former opinions are utterly false and imaginary. I shall do this until the weight of preconceived opinion is counter-balanced and the distorting influence of habit no longer prevents my judgement from perceiving things correctly. In the meantime, I know that no danger or error will result from my plan, and that I cannot possibly go too far in my distrustful attitude. This is because the task now in hand does not involve action but merely the acquisition of knowledge.

I will suppose therefore that not God, who is supremely good and the source of truth, but rather some malicious demon of the utmost power and cunning has employed all his energies in order to deceive me. I shall think that the sky, the air, the earth, colours, shapes, sounds and all external things are merely the delusions of dreams which he has devised to ensnare my judgement. I shall consider myself as not having hands or eyes, or flesh, or blood or senses, but as falsely believing that I have all these things. I shall stubbornly and firmly persist in this meditation; and, even if it is not in my power to know any truth, I shall at least do what is in my power,[4] that is, resolutely guard against

---

[3] . . . in the sciences (added in French version).

[4] nevertheless it is in my power to suspend my judgement (French version).

assenting to any false-hoods, so that the deceiver, however powerful and cunning he may be, will be unable to impose on me in the slightest degree. But this is an arduous undertaking, and a kind of laziness brings me back to normal life. I am like a prisoner who is enjoying an imaginary freedom while asleep; as he begins to suspect that he is asleep, he dreads being woken up, and goes along with the pleasant illusion as long as he can. In the same way, I happily slide back into my old opinions and dread being shaken out of them, for fear that my peaceful sleep may be followed by hard labour when I wake, and that I shall have to toil not in the light, but amid the inextricable darkness of the problems I have now raised.

Here is the final and most exaggerated of Descartes' doubts. A being so malicious and so powerful that it can trick us so well that nothing can be known for sure. Notice how difficult a belief this is for Descartes to hold.

So serious are the doubts into which I have been thrown as a result of yesterday's meditation that I can neither put them out of my mind nor see any way of resolving them. It feels as if I have fallen unexpectedly into a deep whirlpool which tumbles me around so that I can neither stand on the bottom nor swim up to the top. Nevertheless I will make an effort and once more attempt the same path which I started on yesterday. Anything which admits of the slightest doubt I will set aside just as if I had found it to be wholly false; and I will proceed in this way until I recognize something certain, or, if nothing else, until I at least recognize for certain that there is no certainty. Archimedes used to demand just one firm and immovable point in order to shift the entire earth; so I too can hope for great things if I manage to find just one thing, however slight, that is certain and unshakeable. I will suppose then, that everything I see is spurious. I will believe that my memory tells me lies, and that none of the things that it reports ever happened. I have no senses. Body, shape, extension, movement and place are chimeras. So what remains true? Perhaps just the one fact that nothing is certain.

Yet apart from everything I have just listed, how do I know that there is not something else which does not allow even the slightest occasion for doubt? Is there not a God, or whatever I may call him, who puts into me[5] the thoughts I am now having? But why do I think this, since I myself may perhaps be the author of these thoughts? In that case am not I, at least, something? But I have just said that I have no senses and no body.

This is the sticking point: what follows from this? Am I not so bound up with a body and with senses that I cannot exist without them? But I have convinced myself that there is absolutely nothing in the world, no sky, no earth, no minds, no bodies. Does it now follow that I too do not exist?

No: if I convinced myself of something[6] then I certainly existed. But there is a deceiver of supreme power and cunning who is deliberately and constantly deceiving me. In that case I too undoubtedly exist, if he is deceiving me; and let him deceive me as much as he can, he will never bring it about that I am nothing so long as I think that I am something. So after considering everything very thoroughly, I must finally conclude that this proposition, *I am, I exist,* is necessarily true whenever it is put forward by me or conceived in my mind.

[5] . . . puts into my mind (French version).
[6] . . . or thought anything at all (French version).

Here is the famous slogan, *Cogito ergo sum,* I think, therefore I am. The malicious demon makes Descartes doubt everything until Descartes realizes that he is thinking while being deceived and that while thinking he must exist. Descartes cannot think and not exist at the same time. Philosophers often refer to the entire expression, "Cogito ergo sum," as "the Cogito." Later in the *Second Meditation,* Descartes will say that he knows the Cogito clearly and distinctly, that when he knows it he also knows that he knows it. He will propose that whatever he knows through the mind, i.e., without appeal to the senses, clearly and distinctly, he can take as certain. But for knowledge of bodies, what he will term corporeal substance, external to his mind, Descartes will need the existence of a non-deceiving God. That is, the clearness and distinctness which guarantee Descartes' existence as a thinking thing only is not enough to guarantee that there are bodies—no matter how clearly and distinctly we perceive them—unless God guarantees the trustworthiness of clarity and distinctness for bodies as opposed to minds. We will see later how this need for God to underwrite clear and distinct ideas may lead Descartes into a circular argument.

> But I do not yet have a sufficient understanding of what this 'I' is, that now necessarily exists. So I must be on my guard against carelessly taking something else to be this 'I', and so making a mistake in the very item of knowledge that I maintain is the most certain and evident of all. I will therefore go back and meditate on what I originally believed myself to be, before I embarked on this present train of thought. I will then subtract anything capable of being weakened, even minimally, by the arguments now introduced, so that what is left at the end may be exactly and only what is certain and unshakeable.

In our terminology, Descartes will subtract from his pre-hyperbolic idea of 'I' what he has learned to question via the use of hyperbolic doubt. The result:

> What then did I formerly think I was? A man. But what is a man? Shall I say 'a rational animal'? No; for then I should have to inquire what an animal is, what rationality is, and in this way one question would lead me down the slope to other harder ones, and I do not now have the time to waste on subtleties of this kind. Instead I propose to concentrate on what came into my thoughts spontaneously and quite naturally whenever I used to consider what I was. Well, the first thought to come to mind was that I had a face, hands, arms and the whole mechanical structure of limbs which can be seen in a corpse, and which I called the body. The next thought was that I was nourished, that I moved about, and that I engaged in sense-perception and thinking; and these actions I attributed to the soul. But as to the nature of this soul, either I did not think about this or else I imagined it to be something tenuous, like a wind or fire or ether, which permeated my more solid parts.

Pay special attention to the following passage about body. It is this characterization of body that will set it apart from mind and create the mind-body problem. Descartes will expand a bit on this in the Sixth Meditation (which we have not excerpted).

> As to the body, however, I had no doubts about it, but thought I knew its nature distinctly. If I had tried to describe the mental conception I had of it, I would have expressed it as follows: by a body I understand whatever has a determinable shape and

a definable location and can occupy a space in such a way as to exclude any other body; it can be perceived by touch, sight, hearing, taste or smell, and can be moved in various ways, not by itself but by whatever else comes into contact with it. For, according to my judgement, the power of self-movement, like the power of sensation or of thought, was quite foreign to the nature of a body; indeed, it was a source of wonder to me that certain bodies were found to contain faculties of this kind.

Descartes repeats the characterization of body that he gave in *Meditation One* but adds to it that bodies are moved only when touched by other bodies from the outside. This is a physicalistic picture of causality. The standard way to think of this is that causality is best pictured by billiard balls hitting each other. No hit, no motion. Self-movement, where the cause of motion is from within, belongs only to thinking things. (Descartes did not believe that other animals could think. He believed that they were machines.)

Body has extension. Mind does not. But if mind is not extended and causal interaction requires a touch, how can the mind and body interact? This is a specific way to ask how can two totally different kinds of things act as a unit?

But what shall I now say that I am, when I am supposing that there is some supremely powerful and, if it is permissible to say so, malicious deceiver, who is deliberately trying to trick me in every way he can? Can I now assert that I possess even the most insignificant of all the attributes which I have just said belong to the nature of a body? I scrutinize them, think about them, go over them again, but nothing suggests itself; it is tiresome and pointless to go through the list once more. But what about the attributes I assigned to the soul? Nutrition or movement? Since now I do not have a body, these are mere fabrications. Sense-perception? This surely does not occur without a body, and besides, when asleep I have appeared to perceive through the senses many things which I afterwards realized I did not perceive through the senses at all. Thinking? At last I have discovered it—thought; this alone is inseparable from me. I am, I exist—that is certain. But for how long? For as long as I am thinking. For it could be that were I totally to cease from thinking, I should totally cease to exist. At present I am not admitting anything except what is necessarily true. I am, then, in the strict sense only a thing that thinks;[7] that is, I am a mind, or intelligence, or intellect, or reason—words whose meaning I have been ignorant of until now. But for all that I am a thing which is real and which truly exists. But what kind of a thing? As I have just said—a thinking thing.

Again, Descartes shows us that no matter how powerful the malicious being may be, if I think, I exist while I am thinking. I just cannot be wrong about this. What keeps us existing when we are not thinking? What keeps us the same through time? The answer will be God. But we will have to wait for the *Third Meditation* to get the answer in Descartes' own words.

What else am I? I will use my imagination.[8] I am not that structure of limbs which is called a human body. I am not even some thin vapour which permeates the limbs—a

[7] The word 'only' is most naturally taken as going with 'a thing that thinks', and this interpretation is followed in the French version. When discussing this passage with Gassendi, however, Descartes suggests that he meant the 'only' to govern 'in the strict sense'.

[8] . . . to see if I am not something more (added in French version).

wind, fire, air, breath, or whatever I depict in my imagination; for these are things which I have supposed to be nothing. Let this supposition stand;[9] for all that I am still something. And yet may it not perhaps be the case that these very things which I am supposing to be nothing, because they are unknown to me, are in reality identical with the 'I' of which I am aware? I do not know, and for the moment I shall not argue the point, since I can make judgements only about things which are known to me. I know that I exist; the question is, what is this 'I' that I know? If the 'I' is understood strictly as we have been taking it, then it is quite certain that knowledge of it does not depend on things of whose existence I am as yet unaware; so it cannot depend on any of the things which I invent in my imagination. And this very word 'invent' shows me my mistake. It would indeed be a case of fictitious invention if I used my imagination to establish that I was something or other; for imagining is simply contemplating the shape or image of a corporeal thing. Yet now I know for certain both that I exist and at the same time that all such images and, in general, everything relating to the nature of body, could be mere dreams [and chimeras]. Once this point has been grasped, to say 'I will use my imagination to get to know more distinctly what I am' would seem to be as silly as saying 'I am now awake, and see some truth; but since my vision is not yet clear enough, I will deliberately fall asleep so that my dreams may provide a truer and clearer representation.' I thus realize that none of the things that the imagination enables me to grasp is at all relevant to this knowledge of myself which I possess, and that the mind must therefore be most carefully diverted from such things[10] if it is to perceive its own nature as distinctly as possible.

But what then am I? A thing that thinks. What is that? A thing that doubts, understands, affirms, denies, is willing, is unwilling, and also imagines and has sensory perceptions.

This is a considerable list, if everything on it belongs to me. But does it? Is it not one and the same 'I' who is now doubting almost everything, who nonetheless understands some things, who affirms that this one thing is true, denies everything else, desires to know more, is unwilling to be deceived, imagines many things even involuntarily, and is aware of many things which apparently come from the senses? Are not all these things just as true as the fact that I exist, even if I am asleep all the time, and even if he who created me is doing all he can to deceive me? Which of all these activities is distinct from my thinking? Which of them can be said to be separate from myself? The fact that it is I who am doubting and understanding and willing is so evident that I see no way of making it any clearer. But it is also the case that the 'I' who imagines is the same 'I'. For even if, as I have supposed, none of the objects of imagination are real, the power of imagination is something which really exists and is part of my thinking. Lastly, it is also the same 'I' who has sensory perceptions, or is aware of bodily things as it were through the senses. For example, I am now seeing light, hearing a noise, feeling heat. But I am asleep, so all this is false. Yet I certainly seem to see, to hear, and to be warmed. This cannot be false; what is called 'having a sensory perception' is strictly just this, and in this restricted sense of the term it is simply thinking.

From all this I am beginning to have a rather better understanding of what I am. But it still appears—and I cannot stop thinking this—that the corporeal things of which images

---

[9] Lat. *maneat* ('let it stand'), first edition. The second edition has the indicative *manet*. 'The proposition still stands, *viz.* that I am nonetheless something.' The French version reads 'without changing this supposition, I find that I am still certain that I am something'.

[10] from this manner of conceiving things (French version).

are formed in my thought, and which the senses investigate, are known with much more distinctness than this puzzling 'I' which cannot be pictured in the imagination.

What is the intellect, the understanding—the mind. It is not pictureable by the imagination. Why not? Descartes' implication here is that only bodies can be pictured by the mind. They are picturable because they are extended. Thus minds are not extended. Descartes here would also refer to what most people would say makes the difference between, e.g., a horse and a thought of a horse. Thoughts, ideas, what we might term the mental, are just not in that class of solid objects.

And yet it is surely surprising that I should have a more distinct grasp of things which I realize are doubtful, unknown and foreign to me, than I have of that which is true and known—my own self. But I see what it is: my mind enjoys wandering off and will not yet submit to being restrained within the bounds of truth. Very well then; just this once let us give it a completely free rein, so that after a while, when it is time to tighten the reins, it may more readily submit to being curbed.

Let us consider the things which people commonly think they understand most distinctly of all; that is, the bodies which we touch and see. I do not mean bodies in general—for general perceptions are apt to be somewhat more confused—but one particular body. Let us take, for example, this piece of wax. It has just been taken from the honeycomb; it has not quite lost the taste of the honey; it retains some of the scent of the flowers from which it was gathered; its colour, shape and size are plain to see; it is hard, cold and can be handled without difficulty; if you rap it with your knuckle it makes a sound. In short, it has everything which appears necessary to enable a body to be known as distinctly as possible. But even as I speak, I put the wax by the fire, and look: the residual taste is eliminated, the smell goes away, the colour changes, the shape is lost, the size increases; it becomes liquid and hot; you can hardly touch it, and if you strike it, it no longer makes a sound. But does the same wax remain? It must be admitted that it does; no one denies it, no one thinks otherwise. So what was it in the wax that I understood with such distinctness? Evidently none of the features which I arrived at by means of the senses; for whatever came under taste, smell, sight, touch or hearing has now altered—yet the wax remains.

Perhaps the answer lies in the thought which now comes to my mind; namely, the wax was not after all the sweetness of the honey, or the fragrance of the flowers, or the whiteness, or the shape, or the sound, but was rather a body which presented itself to me in these various forms a little while ago, but which now exhibits different ones. But what exactly is it that I am now imagining? Let us concentrate, take away everything which does not belong to the wax, and see what is left: merely something extended, flexible and changeable. But what is meant here by 'flexible' and 'changeable'? Is it what I picture in my imagination: that this piece of wax is capable of changing from a round shape to a square shape, or from a square shape to a triangular shape? Not at all; for I can grasp that the wax is capable of countless changes of this kind, yet I am unable to run through this immeasurable number of changes in my imagination, from which it follows that it is not the faculty of imagination that gives me my grasp of the wax as flexible and changeable. And what is meant by 'extended'? Is the extension of the wax also unknown? For it increases if the wax melts, increases again if it boils, and is greater still if the heat is increased. I would not be making a correct judgement about the nature of wax unless I believed it capable of being extended in many more different ways than I will ever encompass in my imagination. I must therefore admit that the nature of this piece of wax is in no way revealed by my imagination, but is perceived by the mind alone. (I am speaking of this particular piece of wax; the point is even clearer with regard to wax in general.) But what is this wax which is perceived by the mind alone?[11] It is of course the same wax which I see, which I touch, which I picture in my imagination, in short the same wax which I thought it to be from the start. And yet, and here is the point, the perception I have of it[12] is a case not of vision or touch or imagination—nor has it ever been, despite previous appearances—but of purely mental scrutiny; and this can be imperfect and confused, as it was before, or clear and distinct as it is now, depending on how carefully I concentrate on what the wax consists in.

The wax we literally sense changes as conditions change. Its shape, consistency, even its smell, change. If we trusted our senses alone to answer, "Is it the same wax?" we would have to answer, "No." But our understanding via our mind tells us that it is the same piece of wax; that the wax and its properties are logically distinct. We can use the following terminology of Descartes' picture of science. Shape and hardness (along with motion) are primary qualities (properties). Secondary qualities are those that we sense through the five traditional sense modalities: colors, smells, sounds, felt textures and taste. These properties are subjective; they are in us and not really in the things we perceive. Roughly, the more conditions affect how we perceive a property, the more obviously it is a secondary quality, in us and not in the thing. Primary qualities are extension and motion. These are the properties of corpuscles, the tiniest parts of matter that make up matter. Extension in motion causes colors, sounds, textures, tastes and smells. The sensible properties of the wax, e.g., its colors and smells, are really in us—ready to be released from the primary qualities of the wax by the right conditions, e.g., heat. Thus when heat is applied to the extended wax, the wax gets even more extended because the heat makes the corpuscles of the body fly apart.

To Descartes, there were two kinds of substances, holders of properties. To Descartes every kind of substance had one particular property as its essence. For mental substance, that property was thought; for material substance, that property was extension. Indeed, Descartes talks as if material substance was extension. This is because while he held that there were two kinds of substance, the mental and the physical, he also held that there were as many mental substances as there were thinking things but there was only one extended substance and it filled the universe.

Because he held that there were only two kinds of substance, Descartes is called a Dualist. A Monist would hold that there is one kind of substance. If a Monist's one kind of substance is material, we have Materialism. If the one kind of substance is mental, we have Idealism. Neutral Monism is the view that there is one kind of substance that is neither mental nor material, but rather is neutral to both.

But as I reach this conclusion I am amazed at how [weak and] prone to error my mind is. For although I am thinking about these matters within myself, silently and without

[11] . . . which can be conceived only by the understanding of the mind (French version).
[12] . . . or rather the act whereby it is perceived (added in the French version).

speaking, nonetheless the actual words bring me up short, and I am almost tricked by ordinary ways of talking. We say that we see the wax itself, if it is there before us, not that we judge it to be there from its colour or shape; and this might lead me to conclude without more ado that knowledge of the wax comes from what the eye sees, and not from the scrutiny of the mind alone. But then if I look out of the window and see men crossing the square, as I just happen to have done, I normally say that I see the men themselves, just as I say that I see the wax. Yet do I see any more than hats and coats which could conceal automatons? I *judge* that they are men. And so something which I thought I was seeing with my eyes is in fact grasped solely by the faculty of judgement which is in my mind.

Not surprisingly, Descartes has argued that using the mind without the senses is a surer route to knowledge than using only the senses. He will reiterate this point at the end of the next passage.

Concerning his comment on men passing by his window, Descartes is not addressing the problem of other minds here when he says that what look like men might be machines. Even so, let us take Descartes to be reminding us that if we accept what he has so far offered us, we will be left with a question: Can we ever know that there is a mind other than the one I have? The Cogito left us with the same problem. The Cogito taken literally says that I exist because I think—with the emphasis on the I. The Cogito, by its very nature, can only be about the thinker who is presently thinking. Put another way, I can never know that you are a thinking thing and you can never know that I am a thinking thing. This inability to justify belief in other minds (thinking things) is one form of what is called solipsism.

However, one who wants to achieve knowledge above the ordinary level should feel ashamed at having taken ordinary ways of talking as a basis for doubt. So let us proceed, and consider on which occasion my perception of the nature of the wax was more perfect and evident. Was it when I first looked at it, and believed I knew it by my external senses, or at least by what they call the 'common' sense'[13]—that is, the power of imagination? Or is my knowledge more perfect now, after a more careful investigation of the nature of the wax and of the means by which it is known? Any doubt on this issue would clearly be foolish; for what distinctness was there in my earlier perception? Was there anything in it which an animal could not possess? But when I distinguish the wax from its outward forms—take the clothes off, as it were, and consider it naked—then although my judgement may still contain errors, at least my perception now requires a human mind.

But what am I to say about this mind, or about myself? (So far, remember, I am not admitting that there is anything else in me except a mind.) What, I ask, is this 'I' which seems to perceive the wax so distinctly? Surely my awareness of my own self is not merely much truer and more certain than my awareness of the wax, but also much more distinct and evident. For if I judge that the wax exists from the fact that I see it, clearly this same fact entails much more evidently that I myself also exist. It is possible that what I

[13] The supposed faculty which integrates the data from the five specialized senses. . . The seat of the common sense must be very mobile to receive the impressions coming from the senses, but must be movable only by the spirits which transmit these impressions. Only the conarion [pineal gland] fits these conditions. Letter to Mersenne, 21 April 1641.

see is not really the wax; it is possible that I do not even have eyes with which to see anything. But when I see, or think I see (I am not here distinguishing the two), it is simply not possible that I who am now thinking am not something. By the same token, if I judge that the wax exists from the fact that I touch it, the same result follows, namely that I exist. If I judge that it exists from the fact that I imagine it, or for any other reason, exactly the same thing follows. And the result that I have grasped in the case of the wax may be applied to everything else located outside me. Moreover, if my perception of the wax seemed more distinct[14] after it was established not just by sight or touch but by many other considerations, it must be admitted that I now know myself even more distinctly. This is because every consideration whatsoever which contributes to my perception of the wax, or of any other body, cannot but establish even more effectively the nature of my own mind. But besides this, there is so much else in the mind itself which can serve to make my knowledge of it more distinct, that it scarcely seems worth going through the contributions made by considering bodily things.

I see that without any effort I have now finally got back to where I wanted. I now know that even bodies are not strictly perceived by the senses or the faculty of imagination but by the intellect alone, and that this perception derives not from their being touched or seen but from their being understood; and in view of this I know plainly that I can achieve an easier and more evident perception of my own mind than of anything else. But since the habit of holding on to old opinions cannot be set aside so quickly, I should like to stop here and meditate for some time on this new knowledge I have gained, so as to fix it more deeply in my memory.

Descartes knows his mind best of all because he knows it through understanding, through the intellect. Remember, however, that while Descartes may know himself better than he can know anything else (this is a form of epistemic privilege), he cannot know that others have minds. But is Descartes' hyperbolic doubt and epistemic privileging of his own mind buying him certainty about himself at the cost of slipping into solipsism?

. . . [P]erhaps some God could have given me a nature such that I was deceived even in matters which seemed most evident. And whenever my preconceived belief in the supreme power of God comes to mind, I cannot but admit that it would be easy for him, if he so desired, to bring it about that I go wrong even in those matters which I think I see utterly clearly with my mind's eye. Yet when I turn to the things themselves which I think I perceive very clearly, I am so convinced by them that I spontaneously declare: let whoever can do so deceive me, he will never bring it about that I am nothing, so long as I continue to think I am something; or make it true at some future time that I have never existed, since it is now true that I exist; or bring it about that two and three added together are more or less than five, or anything of this kind in which I see a manifest contradiction. And since I have no cause to think that there is a deceiving God, and I do not yet even know for sure whether there is a God at all, any reason for doubt which depends simply on this supposition is a very slight and, so to speak, metaphysical one. But in order to remove even this slight reason for doubt, as soon as the opportunity arises I must examine whether there is a God, and, if there is, whether he can be a deceiver. For if I do not know this, it seems that I can never be quite certain about anything else . . .

[14] The French version has 'more clear and distinct' and, at the end of this sentence, 'more evidently, distinctly and clearly'.

Descartes has given us a quick summary of the previous two *Meditations*. Here, when he says "some God," he is referring to a being more like the malicious demon and not the traditional Judeo-Christian God. This God is the sort that cannot deceive. It is the one Descartes will prove to exist.

The proof follows.

> . . . the idea that gives me my understanding of a supreme God, eternal, infinite, [immutable] omniscient, omnipotent and the creator of all things that exist apart from him, certainly has in it more objective reality than the ideas that represent finite substances.
>
> Now it is manifest by the natural light that there must be at least as much [reality] in the efficient and total cause as in the effect of that cause. For where, I ask, could the effect get its reality from, if not from the cause? And how could the cause give it to the effect unless it possessed it? It follows from this both that something cannot arise from nothing, and also that what is more perfect—that is, contains in itself more reality—cannot arise from what is less perfect. And this is transparently true. . . . A stone, for example, which previously did not exist, cannot begin to exist unless it is produced by something which contains, either formally or eminently, everything to be found in the stone;[15] similarly, heat cannot be produced in an object which was not previously hot, except by something of at least the same order [degree or kind] of perfection as heat, and so on.

By "natural light," Descartes means our use of reason. He means to distinguish it from any form of revealed or supernatural truth that we could only get from a deity. To use revealed light of this sort to prove the existence of a deity would be a clear case of arguing in a circle.

> But it is also true that the *idea* of heat, or of a stone, cannot exist in me unless it is put there by some cause which contains at least as much reality as I conceive to be in the heat or in the stone . . .

For Descartes, ideas of *x* (where x can be anything) have as much reality as the *x* is given by the haver of the idea to *x*'s. Thus, the idea of a horse will have as much reality as Descartes thinks a horse will have. For Descartes to have the idea of a horse, the cause of the idea must have at least as much reality as any horse.

> . . . If the objective reality of any of my ideas turns out to be so great that I am sure the same reality does not reside in me, either formally or eminently, and hence that I myself cannot be its cause, it will necessarily follow that I am not alone in the world, but that some other thing which is the cause of this idea also exists. But if no such idea is to be found in me, I shall have no argument to convince me of the existence of anything apart from myself. For despite a most careful and comprehensive survey, this is the only argument I have so far been able to find . . .

---

[15] . . . it will contain in itself the same things as are in the stone or other more excellent things (added in the French version). In scholastic terminology, to possess a property 'formally' is to possess it literally, in accordance with its definition; to possess it 'eminently' is to possess it in some higher form.

> . . . there remains only the idea of God; and I must consider whether there is any-
> thing in the idea which could not have originated in myself. By the word 'God' I under-
> stand a substance that is infinite, [eternal, immutable] independent, supremely intelligent,
> supremely powerful, and which created both myself and everything else (if anything else
> there be) that exists. All these attributes are such that, the more carefully I concentrate
> on them, the less possible it seems that they[16] could have originated from me alone. So
> from what has been said it must be concluded that God necessarily exists.

Understanding the proof requires some terminology from the Scholastic era (roughly, what is termed Medieval). To say that an effect is in its cause formally is to say that both cause and effect have in them the same nature. For example, fire causes heat and heat is in the nature of fire. The nature involved is the same, heat. When the natures are different and the nature of the cause is more perfect than the nature of the effect, then the effect is said to be eminently in the cause. Think of causes as having enough power to create their effects. If it takes 100 units of power to make a cup of water boil, then seeing a boiling cup of water means that somewhere there was at least 100 units of power. Now just take power to be perfection or (degree of) reality. If something has 10 units of perfection (10 units of reality), it could only have been caused by something with at least 10 units of perfection (reality).

The idea of God contains God as its object. Given Descartes' previous comments about the idea of a stone, the idea of God as perfect could only be caused (in Descartes) by a perfect being. This God certainly cannot be a deceiver, since deception implies a defect (of character) and a perfect being can have no such defect.

> . . . I clearly understand that there is more reality in an infinite substance than in
> a finite one, and hence that my perception of the infinite, that is God, is in some way
> prior to my perception of the finite, that is myself. For how could I understand that I
> doubted or desired—that is, lacked something—and that I was not wholly perfect, un-
> less there were in me some idea of a more perfect being which enabled me to recog-
> nize my own defects by comparison?

We might consider this an auxiliary proof based on the same basic assumptions about causality. If I have the idea of x, and realize there is a better x (have an idea of that better x), I must also realize that there must be a best x, etc. If I can realize that I am finite, I must also be able to realize that there is an infinite; that is, have an idea of the infinite. But then, the cause of that idea of the infinite must itself be infinite. A slight variation on this auxiliary argument is used by Thomas Aquinas, his Fourth Way. See Chapter 3.

Many philosophers have pointed out this argument for the existence of God argues in a circle. Descartes needs a non-deceiving God to guarantee truth outside the Cogito. That is, Descartes needs the existence of a non-deceiving God to guarantee the principle that there must be at least as much reality in the cause as in the effect. But Descartes uses this very principle to prove the existence of God. This claim that Descartes has argued in a circle is often referred to as the Cartesian circle.

---

[16] . . . that the idea I have of them (French version).

Descartes summarizes his thinking at the close of Meditation Three. Once again, we get his arguments for the existence of a non-deceiving God.

> Altogether then, it must be concluded that the mere fact that I exist and have within me an idea of a most perfect being, that is, God, provides a very clear proof that God indeed exists.
>
> It only remains for me to examine how I received this idea from God. For I did not acquire it from the senses; it has never come to me unexpectedly, as usually happens with the ideas of things that are perceivable by the senses, when these things present themselves to the external sense organs—or seem to do so. And it was not invented by me either; for I am plainly unable either to take away anything from it or to add anything to it. The only remaining alternative is that it is innate in me, just as the idea of myself is innate in me.
>
> And indeed it is no surprise that God, in creating me, should have placed this idea in me to be, as it were; the mark of the craftsman stamped on his work—not that the mark need be anything distinct from the work itself. But the mere fact that God created me is a very strong basis for believing that I am somehow made in his image and likeness, and that I perceive that likeness, which includes the idea of God, by the same faculty which enables me to perceive myself. That is, when I turn my mind's eye upon myself, I understand that I am a thing which is incomplete and dependent on another and which aspires without limit to ever greater and better things; but I also understand at the same time that he on whom I depend has within him all those greater things, not just indefinitely and potentially but actually and infinitely, and hence that he is God. The whole force of the argument lies in this: I recognize that it would be impossible for me to exist with the kind of nature I have—that is, having within me the idea of God—were it not the case that God really existed. By 'God' I mean the very being the idea of whom is within me, that is, the possessor of all the perfections which I cannot grasp, but can somehow reach in my thought, who is subject to no defects whatsoever.[17] It is clear enough from this that he cannot be a deceiver, since it is manifest by the natural light that all fraud and deception depend on some defect . . .

With God as no deceiver, as the guarantor and conservator of our existence, Descartes, in the *Sixth Meditation,* goes back to flesh out the relationship between the mind and the body.

> Now there is no more explicit lesson of nature than that I have a body; that it is being injured when I feel pain; that it needs food, or drink, when I suffer from hunger, or thirst, and so on. So I must not doubt that there is some truth in this. Nature also teaches by these sensations of pain, hunger, thirst, etc., that I am not present in my body merely as a pilot is present in a ship; I am most tightly bound to it, and as it were mixed up with it, so that I and it form a unit. Otherwise, when the body is hurt, I, who am simply a conscious being, would not feel pain on that account, but would perceive the injury by a pure act of understanding, as the pilot perceives by sight any breakages there may be in the ship; and when the body needs food or drink, I should explicitly understand the fact, and not have confused sensations of hunger and thirst. For these sensations of thirst,

---

[17] . . . and has not one of the things which indicate some imperfection (added in French version).

hunger, pain, etc., are simply confused modes of consciousness that arise from the mind's being united to, and as it were mixed up with, the body. . .[18]

By "lesson of nature," Descartes means "what God has given me as compound of mind and body." What is this "compound"? It is not a compound in the way that a ship and its pilot might be a compound entity. Given that the "I" is just consciousness, how can the "I" feel pain? The answer is that the pain and other feelings and emotions are the result of the mind's being aware of bodily harm—but because the senses mediate, there is confusion and error; error as when a man whose leg has been amputated says that the leg hurts. This is helpful but still no answer. Descartes raises an interesting question: If God is no deceiver and God made us, why are we sometimes deceived into wanting water when drinking that water will harm as when we have very serious edema (dropsy)? This question is a form of the problem of evil. See Chapter 3. Descartes tries to answer this by first clarifying the mind-body distinction.

I must begin by observing the great difference between mind and body. Body is of its nature always divisible; mind is wholly indivisible. When I consider the mind—that is, myself, in so far as I am merely a conscious being—I can distinguish no parts within myself; I understand myself to be a single and complete thing. Although the whole mind seems to be united to the whole body, yet when a foot or an arm or any other part of the body is cut off I am not aware that any subtraction has been made from the mind. Nor can the faculties of will, feeling, understanding and so on be called its parts; for it is one and the same mind that wills, feels, and understands. On the other hand, I cannot think of any corporeal or extended object without being readily able to divide it in thought and therefore conceiving of it as divisible. This would be enough to show me the total difference between mind and body, even if I did not sufficiently know this already.

Next, I observe that my mind is not directly affected by all parts of the body; but only by the brain, and perhaps only by one small part of that—the alleged seat of common sensibility. Whenever this is disposed in a given way, it gives the same indication to the mind, even if the other parts of the body are differently disposed at the time; of this there are innumerable experimental proofs, of which I need not give an account here.

I observe further that, from the nature of body, in whatever way a part of it could be moved by another part at some distance, that same part could also be moved in the same way by intermediate parts, even if the more distant part did nothing. For example, if ABCD is a cord, there is no way of moving A by pulling the end D that could not be carried out equally well if B or C in the middle were pulled and the end D were not moved at all. Now, similarly, when I feel pain in my foot, I have learnt from the science of physic that this sensation is brought about by means of nerves scattered throughout the foot; these are stretched like cords from there to the brain, and when they are pulled in the foot they transmit the pull to the inmost part of the brain, to which they are attached, and produce there a kind of disturbance which nature has decreed should give the mind a sensation of pain, as it were in the foot. But in order to reach the brain, these nerves have to pass through the leg, the thigh, the back, and the neck; so it may happen that, although it is not the part in the foot that is touched, but only some intermediate part, there

[18] Cp. *Print.*, K. xlviii *ad fin.; below, pp. 190–191, M—Tr.*

is just the same disturbance produced in the brain as when the foot is injured; and so necessarily the mind will have the same sensation of pain. And the same must be believed as regards any other sensation.

Finally, I observe that, since any given disturbance in the part of the brain that directly affects the mind can produce only one kind of sensation, nothing better could be devised than that it should produce that one among all the sensations it could produce which is most conducive, and most often conducive, to the welfare of a healthy man. Now experience shows that all the sensations nature has given us are of this kind; so nothing can be found in them but evidence of God's power and goodness. For example: when the nerves of the foot are strongly and unusually disturbed, this disturbance, by way of the spinal cord, arrives at the interior of the brain; there it gives the mind the signal for it to have a certain sensation, viz. pain, as it were in the foot; and this arouses the mind to do its best to remove the cause of the pain, as being injurious to the foot. Now God might have so made human nature that this very disturbance in the brain was a sign to the mind of something else; it might have been a sign of its own occurrence in the brain; or of the disturbance in the foot, or in some intermediate place; or, in fact, of anything else whatever. But there would be no alternative equally conducive to the welfare of the body. Similarly, when we need drink, there arises a dryness of the throat, which disturbs the nerves of the throat, and by means of them the interior of the brain; and this disturbance gives the mind the sensation of thirst, because the most useful thing for us to know in this whole process is that we then need drink to keep healthy. And so in other cases.

From all this it is clear that in spite of God's immeasurable goodness, man as a compound of body and mind cannot but be sometimes deceived by his own nature. For some cause that occurs, not in the foot, but in any other of the parts traversed by the nerves from the foot to the brain, or even in the brain itself, may arouse the same disturbance as is usually aroused by a hurt foot; and then pain will be felt as it were in the foot, and there will be a natural illusion of sense. For the brain-disturbance in question cannot but produce always the same sensation in the mind; and it usually arises much more often from a cause that is hurting the foot than from another cause occurring somewhere else; so it is in accordance with reason that it should always give the mind the appearance of pain in the foot rather than some other part. Again, sometimes dryness of the throat arises not, as usual, from the fact that drink would be conducive to bodily health, but from some contrary cause, as in dropsy; but it is far better that it should deceive us in that case, than if it always deceived us when the body was in good condition. And so generally.

Here we have Descartes, the scientist, pointing out that the mind and the body do interact. This is just a fact readily explainable through biology. In his explanation, Descartes says that sensations arise in the mind from bodily causes. But notice that he never says how this is possible if the mind is incorporeal, the body corporeal and physical contact is a requirement for causality. Despite the sophisticated science, Descartes is still unclear on the literal relation between the mind and the body. Descartes was stumped on this issue. But he would not deny that there was an interaction between mind and body. He just could not spell it out, given his other assumptions. Descartes' answer to the mind-body problem is called Interactionism: There is interaction, but I cannot say how that interaction works.

NOTE ON SOURCES.   Selections from Descartes' Meditations, One–Three are taken from, *Meditations on First Philosophy,* revised edition, John Cottingham (ed./trans.), Cambridge University Press, Cambridge, New York, Port Chester, Melbourne, Sydney, 1996, pp. 1–23, 25, 28–31, 35. "Sixth Meditation" is taken from *Descartes, Philosophical Writings,* ed. and trans. Elizabeth Anscombe and Peter Thomas Geach, Macmillan Publishing Company, New York City, New York, American Edition, 1971. Pp. 117, 121–123.

2   GILBERT RYLE
Descartes Was Confused

FROM DESCARTES TO RYLE.   The mind-body problem basically involves the answers to three questions. Can a valid distinction be drawn between mind and body? If so, are there any existing things that are named (or described) by those terms? If that is so, what is the relation between mind and body? Although philosophers as far back as Plato dealt with some of these issues, Descartes was really the first to develop a systematic theory about the natures and interrelationships of mind and body. For him, body was a thing extended in space and unthinking, whereas mind was a thinking thing unextended in space. For him both body and mind were substances of different sorts so intimately united in the human being that mental events can affect physical events, and vice versa.

Descartes' position has been called dualism because of its affirmation of *two* substances. A good number of philosophers have followed Descartes in adopting dualism, although they may differ with him on how mind and body interact. Other philosophers, aware of the perplexing problems associated with dualism, have rejected dualism in favor of monism, which affirms *one* substance, either mind or body, but not both. Ryle mounts an attack on dualism in general and on Descartes in particular; an attack which every dualist committed to the examined life must take seriously.

BIOGRAPHICAL NOTE.   Gilbert Ryle was born in 1900. His academic education was received at Oxford where he taught until his retirement. He succeeded R. C. Collingwood as Waynfleet professor of metaphysical philosophy at the University of Oxford at the end of World War II. He succeeded C. E. Moore as editor of the distinguished philosophical journal *Mind* in 1947. He published his most important and influential book, *The Concept of Mind,* in 1949. For the years 1945–1960, he was one of the most widely read and influential philosophers in the Anglo-American academic world. The reasons for this are to be found in the volumes of *Mind,* in his *Concept of Mind* (1949), his *Dilemmas* (1954), his *Plato's Progress* (1966), and his two volumes of *Collected Papers* (1971). He died in 1976.

THE ARGUMENT OF THE PASSAGES.   The following selection is Chapter One of Gilbert Ryle's *Concept of Mind.* In this chapter, titled *Descartes' Myth,* Ryle sets the problem for his book: How should we conceive of the nature of a mind and its relation to a body? The answer that most persons in the Western world, especially since Descartes' lifetime, have given to that question, Ryle calls the "official doctrine" and believes that it bristles with theoretical difficulties.

The chapter is divided into three sections and a brief terminal historical note. Section One, The Official Doctrine, is a vivid and deflationary account of how many, indeed most, people conceive of a person in terms of a mind-body dualism. Every person, the doctrine declares, has a mind and a body, or *is* a combination, a union of a mind and a body. Bodies are located in space and are subject to mechanical laws. In contrast, minds are not located in space, have no spatial dimensions, no spatial size or shape, and are not subject to mechanical laws. Frequently, the terms *external* and *internal, outer* and *inner,* used in a metaphorical sense, are applied to bodies and minds, respectively. Bodies have surfaces, can meet and collide and jolt; minds have no surfaces, cannot meet "head on." How these spatial bodies are related to nonspatial minds is obscure. How they can influence each other, "inter-act," is a difficult theoretical question. Events in one body can directly cause events in another body. But do events in one mind cause events in another mind? And do events in a mind cause events in the body which that mind presumably "inhabits"? If not, minds are shut out from their bodies and shut off from each other.

Additional difficulties with the "official doctrine" arise. Bodily processes can be observed by second-party observers: I can observe that your body is blanching and sweating and trembling. But I cannot thus observe workings in your mind. They are not witnessable by me. They are "private" to you. I can observe your body wince. I cannot feel your pain. Each of us has direct and unchallengeable knowledge of at least some events in our own minds, but no such knowledge of events in each other's minds. I can observe what happens to or goes on in your body. I may infer from that to what happens or goes on in your mind, but I have no way of confirming that inference by any observation. The question then arises: Does any person have any good reason for believing in the existence of other minds? Other bodies, yes; other minds, how so? The "official doctrine," then, leads us to the notion that each person has two "histories": a history of one's bodily events and a history of one's mental events. But, says Ryle, the relation between these two "histories" is not at all clear.

(1) THE OFFICIAL DOCTRINE

There is a doctrine about the nature and place of minds which is so prevalent among theorists and even among laymen that it deserves to be described as the official theory. Most philosophers, psychologists and religious teachers subscribe, with minor reservations, to its main articles and, although they admit certain theoretical difficulties in it, they tend to assume that these can be overcome without serious modifications being made to the architecture of the theory. It will be argued here that the central principles of the doctrine are unsound and conflict with the whole body of what we know about minds when we are not speculating about them.

The official doctrine, which hails chiefly from Descartes, is something like this. With the doubtful exceptions of idiots and infants in arms every human being has both a body and a mind. Some would prefer to say that every human being is both a body and a mind. His body and his mind are ordinarily harnessed together, but after the death of the body his mind may continue to exist and function.

Human bodies are in space and are subject to the mechanical laws which govern all other bodies in space. Bodily processes and states can be inspected by external observers. So a man's bodily life is as much a public affair as are the lives of animals and reptiles and even as the careers of trees, crystals and planets.

But minds are not in space, nor are their operations subject to mechanical laws. The workings of one mind are not witnessable by other observers; its career is private. Only I can take direct cognisance of the states and processes of my own mind. A person therefore lives through two collateral histories, one consisting of what happens in and to his body, the other consisting of what happens in and to his mind. The first is public, the second private. The events in the first history are events in the physical world, those in the second are events in the mental world.

It has been disputed whether a person does or can directly monitor all or only some of the episodes of his own private history; but, according to the official doctrine, of at least some of these episodes he has direct and unchallengeable cognisance. In consciousness, self-consciousness and introspection he is directly and authentically apprised of the present states and operations of his mind. He may have great or small uncertainties about concurrent and adjacent episodes in the physical world, but he can have none about at least part of what is momentarily occupying his mind.

It is customary to express this bifurcation of his two lives and of his two worlds by saying that the things and events which belong to the physical world, including his own body, are external, while the workings of his own mind are internal. This antithesis of outer and inner is of course meant to be construed as a metaphor, since minds, not being in space, could not be described as being spatially inside anything else, or as having things going on spatially inside themselves. But relapses from this good intention are common and theorists are found speculating how stimuli, the physical sources of which are yards or miles outside a person's skin, can generate mental responses inside his skull, or how decisions framed inside his cranium can set going movements of his extremities.

Even when "inner" and "outer" are construed as metaphors, the problem how a person's mind and body influence one another is notoriously charged with theoretical difficulties. What the mind wills, the legs, arms, and tongue execute; what affects the ear and the eye has something to do with what the mind perceives; grimaces and smiles betray the mind's moods and bodily castigations lead, it is hoped, to moral improvement. But the actual transactions between the episodes of the private history and those of the public history remain mysterious, since by definition they can belong to neither series. They could not be reported among the happenings described in a person's autobiography of his inner life, nor could they be reported among those described in someone else's biography of that person's overt career. They can be inspected neither by introspection nor by laboratory experiment. They are theoretical shuttlecocks which are forever being bandied from the physiologist back to the psychologist and from the psychologist back to the physiologist.

Underlying this partly metaphorical representation of the bifurcation of a person's two lives there is a seemingly more profound and philosophical assumption. It is assumed that there are two different kinds of existence or status. What exists or happens may have the status of physical existence, or it may have the status of mental existence. Somewhat as the faces of coins are either heads of tails, or somewhat as living creatures are either male or female, so, it is supposed, some existing is physical existing, other existing is mental existing. It is a necessary feature of what has physical existence that it is in space and time; it is a necessary feature of what has mental existence that it is in time but not in space. What has physical existence is composed of matter, or else is a function of matter; what has mental existence consists of consciousness, or else is a function of consciousness.

There is thus a polar opposition between mind and matter, an opposition which is often brought out as follows. Material objects are situated in a common field, known as space, and what happens to one body in one part of space is mechanically connected with what happens to other bodies in other parts of space. But mental happenings occur in insulated fields, known as "minds," and there is, apart maybe from telepathy, no direct causal connection between what happens in one mind and what happens in another. Only through the medium of the public physical world can the mind of one person make a difference to the mind of another. The mind is its own place and in his inner life each of us lives the life of a ghostly Robinson Crusoe. People can see, hear and jolt one another's bodies, but they are irremediably blind and deaf to the workings of one another's minds and inoperative upon them.

What sort of knowledge can be secured of the workings of a mind? On the one side, according to the official theory, a person has direct knowledge of the best imaginable kind of the workings of his own mind. Mental states and processes are (or are normally) conscious states and processes, and the consciousness which irradiates them can engender no illusions and leaves the door open for no doubts. A person's present thinkings, feelings and willings, his perceivings, rememberings and imaginings are intrinsically "phosphorescent"; their existence and their nature are inevitably betrayed to the owner. The inner life is a stream of consciousness of such a sort that it would be absurd to suggest that the mind whose life is that stream might be unaware of what is passing down it.

True, the evidence adduced recently by Freud seemed to show that there exist channels tributary to this stream, which run hidden from their owner. People are actuated by impulses the existence of which they vigorously disavow; some of their thoughts differ from the thoughts which they acknowledge; and some of the actions which they think they will to perform they do not really will. They are thoroughly gulled by some of their own hypocrisies and they successfully ignore facts about their mental lives which on the official theory ought to be patent to them. Holders of the official theory tend, however, to maintain that anyhow in normal circumstances a person must be directly and authentically seized of the present state and workings of his own mind.

Besides being currently supplied with these alleged immediate data of consciousness, a person is also generally supposed to be able to exercise from time to time a special kind of perception, namely inner perception, or introspection. He can take a (non-optical) "look" at what is passing in his mind. Not only can he view and scrutinize a flower through his sense of sight and listen to and discriminate the notes of a bell through his sense of hearing; he can also reflectively or introspectively watch, without any bodily organ of sense, the current episodes of his inner life. This self-observation is also commonly supposed to be immune from illusion, confusion, or doubt. A mind's reports of its own affairs have a certainty superior to the best that is possessed by its reports of matters in the physical world. Sense-perceptions can, but consciousness and introspection cannot, be mistaken or confused.

On the other side, one person has no direct access of any sort to the events of the inner life of another. He cannot do better than make problematic inferences from the observed behavior of the other person's body to the states of mind, which by analogy from his own conduct, he supposes to be signalized by that behavior. Direct access to the workings of a mind is the privilege of that mind itself; in default of such privileged access, the workings of one mind are inevitably occult to everyone else. For the supposed arguments from bodily movements similar to their own to mental workings similar to their own would lack any possibility of observational corroboration. Not unnaturally, therefore, an adherent of the official theory finds it difficult to resist this consequence of his premises, that he has no good reason to believe that there do exist minds other than his own. Even if he prefers to believe that to other human bodies there are harnessed minds not unlike his own, he cannot claim to be able to discover their individual characteristics, or the particular things that they undergo and do. Absolute solitude is on this showing the ineluctable destiny of the soul. Only our bodies can meet.

As a necessary corollary of this general scheme there is implicitly prescribed a special way of construing our ordinary concepts of mental powers and operations. The verbs, nouns, and adjectives, with which in ordinary life we describe the wits, characteristics, and higher grade performances of the people with whom we have to do, are required to be construed as signifying special episodes in their secret histories, or else as signifying tendencies for such episodes to occur. When someone is described as knowing, believing, or guessing something, as hoping, dreading, intending, or shirking something, as designing this or being amused at that, these verbs are supposed to denote the occurrence or specific modifications in his (to us) occult stream of consciousness. Only his own privileged access to this stream in direct awareness and introspection could provide authentic testimony that these mental-conduct verbs are correctly or incorrectly applied. The onlooker, be he teacher, critic, biographer, or friend, can never assure himself that his comments have any vestige of truth. Yet it was just because we do in fact know how to make such comments, make them with general correctness and correct them when they turn out to be confused or mistaken, that philosophers found it necessary to construct their theories of the nature and place of minds. Finding mental-conduct concepts being regularly and effectively used, they properly sought to fix their logical geography. But the logical geography officially recommended would entail that there could be no regular or effective use of these mental-conduct concepts in our descriptions of, and prescriptions for, other people's minds.

Ryle defines the "official" doctrine as the view that a person's body is a "machine" intimately but obscurely related to his mind, which "inhabits" or "animates" his body machine. He refers to this traditional body-mind dualism as the doctrine of the "ghost in the machine," and claims that those who hold it are thereby involved in a number of theoretical absurdities, all of which express in one way or another a gross and flagrant "category-mistake." Notice that Ryle never outright defines "category-mistake," rather he gives a number of examples, none of which is the particular category-mistake present in the untenable notion of a person as a "ghost in a machine." Ryle asks us to consider a person who, having seen the colleges that make up Oxford University, asked, "Where, now, is the university?" He would be guilty of a category-mistake, imagining that the university itself existed in the same way that the colleges did. We wouldn't know quite what to make of the question or the person. Similarly, Ryle imagines a person who, having witnessed the marching of the battalions that make up a division, then asks to see the division, as if a division were something over and above its battalions. His other examples are to the same effect. A more blatantly nonsensical example of a category-mistake would be made by a person who upon hearing, "She came in a taxi and left in a rage," asks questions about the rage that presupposed that rages were like taxis; for example, "Was it a yellow rage?" "Was it radio dispatched?" Again, such questions would leave us totally perplexed. Ask yourself, if the mind-body picture of Descartes is based on a category-mistake similar to the ones Ryle has given, how has this gone unnoticed since the time of Descartes. After all, such flagrant misunderstanding is not at all subtle.

In the second section of Chapter 1, Ryle is more concerned to illustrate the notion of a category-mistake, and how it could give rise to completely pointless and misleading questions, than to spell out the particular category-mistake that gives rise to the "impossible" "ghost-in-the-machine" notion of a person as a body united with a mind. It takes the rest of the book to spell out that category-mistake and to suggest some other way of conceiving of the body-mind relation.

(2) THE ABSURDITY OF THE OFFICIAL DOCTRINE

Such in outline is the official theory. I shall often speak of it, with deliberate abusiveness, as "the dogma of the Ghost in the Machine." I hope to prove that it is entirely false, and false not in detail but in principle. It is not merely an assemblage of particular mistakes. It is one big mistake and a mistake of a special kind. It is namely, a category-mistake. It represents the facts of mental life as if they belonged to one logical type or category (or range of types or categories), when they actually belong to another. The dogma is, therefore, a philosopher's myth. In attempting to explode the myth I shall probably be taken to be denying well-known facts about the mental life of human beings, and my plea that I aim at doing nothing more than *rectify* the logic of mental-conduct concepts will probably be disallowed as mere subterfuge.

I must first indicate what is meant by the phrase "category-mistake." This I do in a series of illustrations.

A foreigner visiting Oxford or Cambridge for the first time is shown a number of colleges, libraries, playing fields, museums, scientific departments, and administrative offices. He then asks, "But where is the University? I have seen where the members of the College live, where the Registrar works, where the scientists experiment and the rest. But I have not yet seen the University in which reside and work the members of your University." It has then to be explained to him that the University is not another collateral institution, some ulterior counterpart to the colleges, laboratories and offices which he has seen. The University is just the way in which all that he has already seen is organized. When they are seen and when their coordination is understood, the University has been seen. His mistake lay in his innocent assumption that it was correct to speak of Christ Church, the Bodleian Library, the Ashmolean Museum, *and* the University, to speak, that is, as if "the University" stood for an extra member of the class of which these other units are members. He was mistakenly allocating the University to the same category as that to which the other institutions belong.

The same mistake would be made by a child witnessing the march-past of a division, who, having pointed out to him such and such battalions, batteries, squadrons, etc., asked when the division was going to appear. He would be supposing that a division was a counterpart to the units already seen, partly similar to them and partly unlike them. He would be shown his mistake by being told that in watching the battalions, batteries, and squadrons marching past he had been watching the division marching past. The march-past was not a parade of battalions, batteries, squadrons, *and* a division; it was a parade of battalions, batteries, and squadrons *of* a division.

One more illustration. A foreigner watching his first game of cricket learns what are the functions of the bowlers, the batsmen, the fielders, the umpires, and the scorers. He then says, "But there is no one left on the field to contribute the famous element of team-spirit. I see who does the bowling, the batting, and the wicketkeeping; but I do not see whose role it is to exercise *esprit de corps*." Once more, it would have to be explained that he was looking for the wrong type of thing. Team-spirit is not another cricketing-operation supplementary to all of the other special tasks. It is roughly, the keenness with which each of the special tasks is performed, and performing a task keenly is not per-forming two tasks. Certainly exhibiting team-spirit is not the same thing as bowling or catching, but nor is it a third thing such that we can say that the bowler first bowls *and* then exhibits team-spirit or that a fielder is at a given moment *either* catching or display-ing *esprit de corps*.

These illustrations of category-mistakes have a common feature which must be noted. The mistakes were made by people who did not know how to wield the concepts *University, division* and *team-spirit*. Their puzzles arose from inability to use certain items in the English vocabulary.

The theoretically interesting category-mistakes are those made by people who are perfectly competent to apply concepts, at least in the situations with which they are fa-miliar, but are still liable in their abstract thinking to allocate those concepts to logical types to which they do not belong. An instance of a mistake of this sort would be the fol-lowing story. A student of politics has learned the main differences between the British, the French and the American Constitutions, and has learned also the differences and connections between the Cabinet, Parliament, the various Ministries, the Judicature and the Church of England. But he still becomes embarrassed when asked questions about the connections between the Church of England, the Home Office, and the British Constitution. For while the Church and the Home Office are institutions, the British Con-stitution is not another institution in the same sense of that noun. So inter-institutional re-lations which can be asserted or denied to hold between the Church and the Home Office cannot be asserted or denied to hold between either of them and the British Constitu-tion. "The British Constitution" is not a term of the same logical type as "the Home Of-fice" and "the Church of England." In a partially similar way, John Doe may be a relative, a friend, an enemy or a stranger to Richard Roe; but he cannot be any of these things to the Average Taxpayer. He knows how to talk sense in certain sorts of discussions about the Average Taxpayer, but he is baffled to say why he could not come across him in the street as he can come across Richard Roe.

It is pertinent to our main subject to notice that, so long as the student of politics continues to think of the British Constitution as a counterpart to the other institutions, he will tend to describe it as a mysteriously occult institution; and so long as John Doe con-tinues to think of the Average Taxpayer as a fellow-citizen, he will tend to think of him as an elusive insubstantial man, a ghost who is everywhere yet nowhere.

My destructive purpose is to show that a family of radical category-mistakes is the source of the double-life theory. The representation of a person as a ghost mysteri-ously ensconced in a machine derives from this argument. Because, as is true, a per-son's thinking, feeling and purposive doing cannot be described solely in the idioms of physics, chemistry and physiology, therefore they must be described in counterpart id-ioms. As the human body is a complex organized unit, so the human mind must be an-other complex organized unit, though one made of a different sort of stuff and a different sort of structure. Or, again, as the human body, like any other parcel of matter, is a field of causes and effects, so the mind must be another field of causes and effects, though not (Heaven be praised) mechanical causes and effects.

In the upcoming third section Ryle asks how this body-mind category-mistake ever came to be made anyway. His answer is along two lines: One, finding that the mechanistic model of modern science made good sense of processes that go on in the physical world, Descartes wanted to use similar processes to explain the workings of the mental. But because the mental is not extended, is not physical in any way, it must run on nonphysical processes. If bodies are like clocks, then minds must be like nonphysical clocks. The problem is that without lots more explanation, the concept of a nonphysical clock makes no sense. Two, since the mechanistic model of modern science made good sense of processes that go on in the physical world, Descartes saw that if that model were applied to the human being as a complete and sufficient explanation of human activity, then dire consequences would result in the religious and ethical domains. For example, if the human is only a complex physical machine, what becomes of the soul, freedom, immortality, and moral accountability? Unwilling, therefore, to reduce humans to the status of mere complex clockworks, Descartes and his philosophical followers suggested that whereas such sciences as physics, chemistry, and physiology made good sense of the mechanical processes that go on in the body, nonmechanical processes were needed to understand fully the workings of a person.

The dichotomy between the mental and the physical does match a preanalytic (before philosophical or scientific analysis) picture of the world. Emotions and feelings, pains and thoughts are just different from chairs, tables and stones. On the chair-table-stone side, we have entities that at any given time have a specific place; they can collide with each other; bounce off each other. But this is not so for the thought and feeling side of the dichotomy. So the Cartesian picture fits at least roughly our everyday understanding of the world.

(3) THE ORIGIN OF THE CATEGORY-MISTAKE

One of the chief intellectual Origins of what I have yet to prove to be the Cartesian category-mistake seems to be this. When Galileo showed that his methods of scientific discovery were competent to provide a mechanical theory which should cover every occupant of space, Descartes found in himself two conflicting motives. As a man of scientific genius he could not but endorse the claims of mechanics, yet as a religious and moral man he could not accept as Hobbes accepted, the discouraging rider to those claims, namely that human nature differs only in degree of complexity from clockwork. The mental could not be just a variety of the mechanical.

He and subsequent philosophers naturally but erroneously availed themselves of the following escape-route. Since mental-conduct words are not to be construed as signifying the occurrence of mechanical processes, they must be construed as signifying the occurrence of nonmechanical processes; since mechanical laws explain movements in space as the effects of other movements in space, other laws must explain some of the non-spatial workings of minds as the effects of other non-spatial workings of minds. The difference between the human behaviors which we describe as intelligent and those which we describe as unintelligent must be a difference in their causation; so, while some movements of human tongues and limbs are the effects of mechanical causes, others must be the effects of non-mechanical causes i.e., some issue from movements of particles of matter, others from workings of the mind.

The differences between the physical and the mental were thus represented as differences inside the common framework of the categories of "thing," "stuff," "attribute," "state," "process," "change," "cause," and "effect." Minds are things, but different sort of things from bodies; mental processes are causes and effects, but different sorts of causes and effects from bodily movements. And so on. Somewhat as the foreigner expected the University to be an extra edifice, rather like a college but also considerably different, so the repudiators of mechanism represented minds as extra centers of causal processes, rather like machines but also considerably different from them. Their theory was a para-mechanical hypothesis.

That this assumption was at the heart of the doctrine is shown by the fact that there was from the beginning felt to be a major theoretical difficulty in explaining how minds can influence and be influenced by bodies. How can a mental process, such as willing, cause spatial movements like the movements of the tongue? How can a physical change in the optic nerve have among its effects a mind's perception of a flash of light? This notorious crux by itself shows the logical mould into which Descartes pressed his theory of the mind. It was the self-same mould into which he and Galileo set their mechanics. Still unwittingly adhering to the grammar of mechanics he tried to avert disaster by describing minds in what was merely an obverse vocabulary. The workings of minds had to be described by the mere negatives of the specific descriptions given to bodies; they are not in space, they are not motions, they are not modification of matter, they are not accessible to public observation. Minds are not bits of clockwork, they are just bits of not-clockwork.

As thus represented, minds are not merely ghosts harnessed to machines, they are themselves just spectral machines. Though the human body is an engine, it is not quite an ordinary engine, since some of its workings are governed by another engine inside it— this interior governor-engine being one of a very special sort. It is invisible, inaudible and it has no size or weight. It cannot be taken to bits and the laws it obeys are not those known to ordinary engineers. Nothing is known of how it governs the bodily engine.

A second major crux points the same moral. Since, according to the doctrine, minds belong to the same category as bodies and since bodies are rigidly governed by mechanical laws, it seemed to many theorists to follow that minds must be similarly governed by rigid non-mechanical laws. The physical world is a deterministic system, so the mental world must be a deterministic system. Bodies cannot help the modifications that they undergo, so minds cannot help pursuing the careers fixed for them. *Responsibility, choice, merit* and *demerit* are therefore inapplicable concepts—unless the compromise solution is adopted of saying that the laws governing mental processes, unlike those governing physical processes, have the congenial attribute of being only rather rigid. The problem of the Freedom of the Will was the problem how to reconcile the hypothesis that minds are to be described in terms drawn from the categories of mechanics with the knowledge that higher-grade human conduct is not a piece with the behaviour of machines.

It is an historical curiosity that it was not noticed that the entire argument was broken-backed. Theorists correctly assumed that any sane man could already recognise the differences between, say, rational and non-rational utterances or between purposive and automatic behavior. Else there would have been nothing requiring to be salved from mechanism. Yet the explanation given presupposed that one person could in principle never recognise the difference between the rational and irrational utterances issuing from other human bodies, since he could never get access to the postulated immaterial causes of some of their utterances. Save for the doubtful exception of himself, he could never tell the difference between a man and a Robot. It would have to be conceded, for example, that, for all that we can tell, the inner lives of persons who are classed as idiots or lunatics are as rational as those of anyone else. Perhaps only their overt behaviour is disappointing; that is to say, perhaps "idiots" are not really idiotic, or "lunatics" lunatic. Perhaps, too, some of those who are classed as sane are really idiots. According to the theory, external observers could never know how the overt behaviour of others is correlated with their mental powers and processes and so they could never know or even plausibly conjecture whether their applications of mental-conduct concepts to these other people were correct or incorrect. It would then be hazardous or impossible for a man to claim sanity or logical consistency even for himself, since he would be debarred from comparing his own performances with those of others. In short, our characteristics of persons and their performances as intelligent, prudent and virtuous or as stupid, hypocritical and cowardly could never have been made, so the problem of providing a special causal hypothesis to serve as the basis of such diagnoses would never have arisen. The question, "How do persons differ from machines?" arose just because everyone already knew how to apply mental-conduct concepts before the new causal hypothesis was introduced. This hypothesis could not therefore be the source of the criteria used in those applications. Nor, of course, has the causal hypothesis in any degree improved our handling of those criteria. We still distinguish good from bad arithmetic, polite from impolite conduct and fertile from infertile imaginations in the ways in which Descartes himself distinguished them before and after he speculated how the applicability of these criteria was compatible with the principle of mechanical causation.

He had mistaken the logic of his problem. Instead of asking by what criteria intelligent behaviour is actually distinguished from non-intelligent behaviour, he asked "Given that the principle of mechanical causation does not tell us the difference, what other causal principle will tell us?" He realized that the problem was not one of the mechanics and assumed that it must therefore be one of some counterpart to mechanics. Not unnaturally psychology is often cast for just this role.

When two terms belong to the same category, it is proper to construct conjunctive propositions embodying them. Thus a purchaser may say that he bought a left-hand glove and a right-hand glove, but not that he bought a left-hand glove, a right-hand glove and a pair of gloves. "She came home in a flood of tears and a sedan-chair" is a well-known joke based on the absurdity of conjoining terms of different types. It would have been equally ridiculous to construct the disjunction "She came home either in a flood of tears or else in a sedan-chair." Now the dogma of the Ghost in the Machine does just this. It maintains that there exist both bodies and minds; that there occur physical processes and mental processes; that there are mechanical causes of corporeal movements and mental causes of corporeal movements. I shall argue that these and other analogous conjunctions are absurd; but, it must be noticed, the argument will not show that either of the illegitimately conjoined propositions is absurd in itself. I am not, for example, denying that there occur mental processes. Doing long division is a mental process and so is making a joke. I am saying that the phrase "there occur mental processes" does not mean the same sort of thing as "there occur physical processes," and, therefore, that it makes no sense to conjoin or disjoin the two.

If my argument is successful, there will follow some interesting consequences. First the hallowed contrast between Mind and Matter will be dissipated, but dissipated not by either of the equally hallowed absorptions of Mind by Matter or of Matter by Mind, but in quite a different way. For the seeming contrast of the two will be shown to be as illegitimate as would be the contrast of "she came home in a flood of tears" and "she came home in a sedan-chair." The belief that there is a polar opposition between Mind and Matter is the belief that they are terms of the same logical type.

It will also follow that both Idealism and Materialism are answers to an improper question. The "reduction" of mental states and processes to physical states and processes, presupposes the legitimacy of the disjunction "Either there exist minds or there exist bodies (but not both)." It would be like saying, "Either she bought a left-hand and a right-hand glove or she bought a pair of gloves (but not both)."

It is perfectly proper to say, in one logical tone of voice, that there exist minds and to say, in another logical tone of voice, that there exist bodies. But these expressions do not indicate two different species of existence, for "existence" is not a generic word like "coloured" or "sexed." They indicate two different senses of "exist," somewhat as "rising" has different senses in "the tide is rising," "hopes are rising," and "the average age of death is rising." A man would be thought to be making a poor joke who said that three things are now rising, namely the tide, hopes and the average age of death. It would be just as good or bad a joke to say that there exist prime numbers and Wednesdays and public opinions and navies; or that there exist both minds and bodies. In the succeeding chapters I try to prove that the official theory does rest on a batch of category-mistakes by showing that logically absurd corollaries follow from it. The exhibition of these absurdities will have the constructive effect of bringing out part of the correct logic of mental-conduct concepts.

HISTORICAL NOTES

It would not be true to say that the official theory derives solely from Descartes' theories, or even from a more widespread anxiety about the implications of seventeenth century mechanics. Scholastic and Reformation theology had schooled the intellects of the scientists as well as of the laymen, philosophers and clerics of that age. Stoic-Augustinian theories of the will were embedded in the Calvinist doctrines of sin and grace; Platonic and Aristotelian theories of the intellect shaped the orthodox doctrines of the immortality of the soul in the new syntax of Galileo. The theologian's privacy of conscience became the philosopher's privacy of consciousness, and what had been the bogy of Predestination reappeared as the bogy of Determinism.

It would also not be true to say that the two-worlds myth did no theoretical good. Myths often do a lot of theoretical good, while they are still new. One benefit bestowed by the para-mechanical myth was that it partly superannuated the then prevalent para-political myth. Minds and their Faculties had previously been described by analogies with political superiors and political subordinates. The idioms used were those of ruling, obeying, collaborating and rebelling. They survived and still survive in many ethical and some epistemological discussions. As, in physics, the new myth of occult Forces was a scientific improvement on the old myth of Final Causes, so, in anthropological and psychological theory, the new myth of hidden operations, impulses and agencies was an improvement on the old myth of dictations, differences, and disobediences.

According to Ryle, then, at the heart of Descartes' mind-body dualism is a serious category-mistake. That mistake involves the assumption that mind and body exist in the *same sort of way*. It is permissible, says Ryle, to speak of minds and mental processes as existing. For example, we might say that "Socrates had a keen mind" and then go on to discuss what we mean by his "keen mind." Such a conversation would be legitimate provided we did not assume that Socrates' "keen mind" existed in the same sort of way as a "purple robe" in the statement "Socrates had a purple robe." "Keen minds" do not exist in the same sort of way that "purple robes" exist. "Minds" involve mental processes. "Robes" involve physical processes; and so do "bodies." The whole mind-body problem assumes that mind and body, mental processes, and physical processes exist in the same sort of way. "Not so!" says Ryle.

We are misled, argues Ryle, when we assume that terms such as happy, sad, angry, bewildered, intelligent—mentalistic terms as they are often called by philosophers—are properties like tall, short, and red-haired. These latter properties are readily determined properties of people. It takes only a glance to see that Wilt Chamberlain is tall, that Mickey Rooney is short, and that Little Orphan Annie has orange-red hair. Mentalistic terms are, however, different. They are dispositions to behave in certain ways. For example, to call a person intelligent is to say that the person is very likely to be able to do certain things; e.g., score well on SAT tests and calculus exams. But it is important to remember that a person can be intelligent and do stupid things now and then. This is what makes "being intelligent" a dispositional property. Just as glass is fragile even when it is not shattering, so an intelligent person is intelligent even when doing poorly on one quiz. But a tall person cannot also be short (unless one is playing with words and contexts).

A somewhat extended example will help. Most sugar cubes are white. We can tell this by looking at the cube. Most sugar cubes are also soluble in hot water. This we cannot tell just by looking at the sugar cube itself. Saying that the sugar cube is soluble means that when it is placed in hot water, the sugar cube will dissolve. Solubility is a dispositional property. White is not a dispositional property.

Descartes did not make the distinction between dispositional and nondispositional properties. Ryle imagines that someone says to Descartes "I see the sugar and its whiteness, but where is its solubility?" Or, more to our point, suppose someone said, "I hear Sam screaming and see that Sam is red in the face and breathing hard, but where is the anger?" The insight that mentalistic properties are really dispositional properties, determinable, but not readily determined, leads to rejecting the question, "Where is the anger?" as misguided—based on the incorrect assumption that all properties are nondispositional.

Often, Ryle's position is referred to as logical behaviorism. "Behaviorism is meant to call attention to the need to focus on behavior, whereas "logical" is meant to remind us that Ryle is talking about the logic of the concepts; i.e., the meanings, and relationships between the meanings, of the words we use to talk about pain, anger, love, hate, fear, anxiety, etc.

Remember that Descartes was trying to understand how the mental world, which he insisted had to be nonextended, could interact with the physical world, which was extended. This was a problem because the model for causality at the time was a push or a pull. How could a nonextended thing push or pull anything? This problem of how the mind interacts with the body is called the mind-body problem.

It is by no means clear whether Ryle is correct in thinking that he has dissolved the mind-body problem. As Jerry Fodor points out, in an article later in this section, Ryle does a commendable job criticizing Descartes, but, for all his cleverness, leaves us wondering about whether the mind-body problem has really been dissolved. Thus, it is worth looking at some other answers to the mind-body problem.

1. Everything is really mental. The physical is only an aspect of the mental. That is, the physical can be fully understood in terms of the mental. This view is called idealism or absolute idealism. G. W. F. Hegel (1770–1831) held a version of idealism known as objective idealism. George Berkeley (1685–1753) held a version of idealism which has come to be called subjective idealism.
2. Everything is physical. This has two forms. (A) There really is no mental. (B) The mental can be understood solely in terms of the physical. Notice that if one holds (A), then (B) need not follow. Contemporary philosophers J. J. C. Smart and David M. Armstrong, Patricia Churchland all hold variations of (A) or (B). Variations on (A) are usually referred to as Identity Theories.

Answers (1) and (2) are forms of Monism—the view that there is only one kind of thing; and that what appear to be other kinds of things can be understood in terms of this one basic kind of thing because, when properly understood, there is only one kind of basic thing.

In terms of interaction, there are a number of views (other than Descartes' version of interactionism) that have been popular throughout history.

1. The mental and the physical are parallel. They do not really interact. The interaction is only apparent. It is due to their being set up in a series so that it looks as if there is interaction. This position is called parallelism. The philosopher, G. W. Leibniz (1646–1716), held this position. Spinoza (1632–1677) held a variation of this view.
2. The mental and the physical do not interact. What appears to us to be a causal relationship is the work of God. On each occasion of a seeming interaction, it is really God doing the causing. This view is called Occasionalism and was the position of Nicolas Malebranche (1638–1750).
3. Every mental thing is related to a physical thing in the way that oil gauge readings in an automobile are related to oil pressure. It is the pressure that causes the reading. The reading itself usually has no causal effect on the pressure or anything else. This view is called epiphenomenalism, a name which picturesquely suggests the mental hanging from the physical as an epiphyte (such as an orchid or a fern) hangs from a tree. The American philosopher, William James (1842–1910), held this view.
4. The mental is the ability to make complex computations. If this ability is restricted to brains, then this is just a refined version of Identity Theory. When it is assumed that it does not matter what kind of thing actually does the complex computation, the view is called functionalism. Functionalism is an answer to the mind-body problem that is related to the growth of the field known as cognitive science, a mix of philosophy, mathematics, linguistics, computer science, and psychology. Jerry Fodor is a firm proponent of this view.

5. There is no mental at all. There is just behavior. This view is often called Radical Behaviorism. John Watson (1878–1958) was a proponent of this view.
6. The best way to study humans is to study behavior (because that is all that there is to study scientifically). Whether there is a mental and how it interacts with the behavior is just not a question worth pursuing. This view is usually called Methodological Behaviorism. B. F. Skinner (1904–1990) was a proponent of this view.
7. Logical behaviorism, the view of Ryle, claims that whatever we can say about the mental, using words from mentalistic discourse, can always be translated into words using only physicalistic discourse (behavior).

Remember that the mind-body problem was not the only problem Descartes had. Once he had determined that certainty could be found only with the *Cogito* as the starting point, how could he ever be sure that there were other minds, other things with thoughts. Perception is not only untrustworthy, it also fails to let us see the thoughts of others. (Notice that in Descartes' view, the word *other* can mean only "other thing that looks and acts just as I do.") This problem is called (not unsurprisingly) the problem of other minds.

In the next readings, we will see some contemporary attempts to answer both the mind-body problem as well as the problem of other minds.

NOTE ON SOURCES.   The material in this section is quoted from Gilbert Ryle, *The Concept of Mind* (New York: Harper & Row, 1949), Chapter 1.

---

3   A. M. TURING
Can Machines Think?

FROM FODOR TO TURING.   Functionalism should be able to answer "yes" to the question, "Can computers think?"

To understand this question in the manner of cognitive scientists, we will start with a look at the concept of model and then go on to describe a Turing machine. The following are four senses of the word *model*.

(a) How will this dress look on real women? Try it on a model. Most fashion models are idealized people. Fashion models are chosen because they best "show off" the clothes. Very few of us look like fashion models.
(b) Will this plane survive a wind storm? Try a scale model in a wind tunnel. A scale model is just like what it models except for size. We assume that the scale model will act just like what it models. This assumption is usually borne out.
(c) How will this drug act in humans? Try it on beagles and bunnies, both of which have physiologies like humans. Obviously beagles and bunnies are not too much like people except perhaps in some of their anatomy and their physiology. They are known to be and are called good animal models for studying the effects of drugs in humans.

(d) How will this gas act if we heat it to 150 degrees centigrade? The answer is that it will expand according to the ideal gas law, which is based on assumptions about the actions of molecules that make up a gas. The ideal gas law assumes that gas molecules are perfectly elastic, randomly moving points with no mass or diameter. Despite these incorrect assumptions, the ideal gas law yields excellent predictions under most circumstances. The ideal gas law can be considered to be a mathematical model.

In the list above, we have seen different sorts of models. They are all departures from reality that help us to understand reality. To understand a Turing machine, we have to focus on the sense of model given in (d). There is no ideal gas because there is no molecule that is perfectly elastic, with no mass or diameter. That there is no such gas and cannot be is why we say that it is an ideal gas.

A Turing machine is an ideal computer. It is a model for any digital computer. It is a mathematical abstraction used to highlight what is important in a digital computer. The Turing machine works by scanning a finite (but potentially infinite) tape that is divided into squares. The symbols scanned are: 1, 0, or empty square. The machine can do the following things: move right, move left, stay centered, erase, erase and print one of the allowed symbols. That is all the machine is allowed to do. It turns out that this is a very powerful computing machine. Indeed, whatever we can decide effectively can be computed on a Turing machine. This is called the Church-Turing hypothesis. What exactly does this mean? "To decide effectively" means that there is an algorithm. To have an algorithm (from al-Khuwarizmi, an Arab mathematician of the ninth century) is to have a mechanical procedure that will give a definite yes or no answer to a question in a finite number of steps. The word "mechanical" is used to stress that no insight is needed to get the answer.

The following questions have algorithms: What is the shortest distance between two cities? Given the present board in a chess game, can white win? The first question would probably require a relatively short algorithm. The second would require a much longer algorithm.

The following question has no algorithmic solution: Is the *Mona Lisa* more beautiful than *Guernica*?

Since any problem for which there is an algorithm can be done on a Turing machine, and since a Turing machine is just a mathematical abstraction in the way that an ideal gas is an abstraction, we get the result Fodor wanted: only the program counts—not the material from which a computer might be built. Put another way, *any* material that can be used to build a computer might function well enough to be said to think.

BIOGRAPHICAL NOTE.   Alan Turing was born in 1912 in London, England. He received a Ph.D. in mathematics from Princeton in 1938 for work he completed under the famous American mathematician-logician Alonzo Church. Turing returned to England, where after completing a fellowship at King's College, he took up work for the government as a code-breaker. Turing was instrumental in decoding the Enigma Machine, the device used by the Germans for encoding their messages during World War II. In 1948, Turing took over what was then the computer with the largest memory in the world. His work laid the foundation for what has come to be called "artificial intelligence." Turing became the victim of British antihomosexual programs. He was brought up on charges of soliciting sex. Turing was given the choice of a prison term or undergoing a drug treatment meant to cure him of his "problem." He chose the latter. Unfortunately, it seems to have led to psychological problems, and in 1954 Turing committed suicide.

THE ARGUMENT OF THE PASSAGES.   Alan Turing proposed that if a person could not tell the difference between another person and a computer imitating a person thinking, then we should be convinced that it is acceptable to say that computers can think. Notice that Turing never claims that computers have, do, or will ever think. He is speculating about what we might say about a computer that is powerful enough to fool us into thinking it is a person.

THE IMITATION GAME

I propose to consider the question "Can machines think?" This should begin with definitions of the meaning of the terms "machine" and "think." The definitions might be framed so as to reflect so far as possible the normal use of the words, but this attitude is dangerous. If the meaning of the words "machine" and "think" are to be found by examining how they are commonly used it is difficult to escape the conclusion that the meaning and the answer to the question, "Can machines think?" is to be sought in a statistical survey such as a Gallup poll. But this is absurd. Instead of attempting such a definition I shall replace the question by another, which is closely related to it and is expressed in relatively unambiguous words.

The new form of the problem can be described in terms of a game which we call the "imitation game." It is played with three people, a man (A), a woman (B), and an interrogator (C) who may be of either sex. The interrogator stays in a room apart from the other two. The object of the game for the interrogator is to determine which of the other two is the man and which is the woman. He knows them by labels X and Y, and at the end of the game he says either "X is A and Y is B" or "X is B and Y is A." The interrogator is allowed to put questions to A and B thus: C: Will X please tell me the length of his or her hair?

Now suppose X is actually A, then A must answer. It is A's object in the game to try to cause C to make the wrong identification. His answer might therefore be "My hair is shingled, and the longest strands are about nine inches long."

In order that tones of voice may not help the interrogator the answers should be written, or better still, typewritten. The ideal arrangement is to have a teleprinter communicating between the two rooms. Alternatively the question and answers can be repeated by an intermediary. The object of the game for the third player (B) is to help the interrogator. The best strategy for her is probably to give truthful answers. She can add such things as "I am the woman, don't listen to him!" to her answers, but it will avail nothing as the man can make similar remarks.

We now ask the question, "What will happen when a machine takes the part of A in this game?" Will the interrogator decide wrongly as often when the game is played like this as he does when the game is played between a man and a woman? These questions replace our original, "Can machines think?"

CRITIQUE OF THE NEW PROBLEM

As well as asking, "What is the answer to this new form of the question," one may ask, "Is this new question a worthy one to investigate?" This latter question we investigate without further ado, thereby cutting short an infinite regress.

The new problem has the advantage of drawing a fairly sharp line between the physical and the intellectual capacities of a man. No engineer or chemist claims to be able to produce a material which is indistinguishable from the human skin. It is possible that at some time this might be done, but even supposing this invention available we should feel there was little point in trying to make a "thinking machine" more human by dressing it up in such artificial flesh. The form in which we have set the problem reflects this fact in the condition which prevents the interrogator from seeing or touching the other competitors, or hearing their voices. Some other advantages of the proposed criterion may be shown up by specimen questions and answers.

Thus:

Q: Please write me a sonnet on the subject of the Forth Bridge.

A: Count me out on this one. I never could write poetry.

Q: Add 34957 to 70764.

A: (Pause about 30 seconds and then give as answer) 105621.

Q: Do you play chess?

A: Yes.

Q: I have K at my K1, and no other pieces. You have only K at K6 and R at R1. It is your move. What do you play?

A: (After a pause of 15 seconds) R-R8 mate.

The question and answer method seems to be suitable for introducing almost any one of the fields of human endeavor that we wish to include. We do not wish to penalize the machine for its inability to shine in the beauty competition, nor to penalize a man for losing in a race against an airplane. The conditions of our game make these disabilities irrelevant. The "witnesses" can brag, if they consider it advisable, as much as they please about their charms, strength or heroism, but the interrogator cannot demand practical demonstrations.

The game may perhaps be criticized on the ground that the odds are weighted too heavily against the machine. If the man were to try and pretend to be the machine he would clearly make a very poor showing. He would be given away at once by slowness and inaccuracy in arithmetic. May not machines carry out something which ought to be described as thinking but which is very different from what a man does? This objection is a very strong one, but at least we can say that if, nevertheless, a machine can be constructed to play the imitation game satisfactorily, we need not be troubled by this objection.

It might be urged that when playing the "imitation game" the best strategy for the machine may possibly be something other than imitation of the behavior of a man. This may be, but I think it is unlikely that there is any great effect of this kind. In any case there is no intention to investigate here the theory of the game, and it will be assumed that the best strategy is to try to provide answers that would naturally be given by a man.

CONTRARY VIEWS ON THE MAIN QUESTION

We may now consider the ground to have been cleared and we are ready to proceed to the debate on our question, "Can machines think?" and the variant of it quoted at the end of the last section. We cannot altogether abandon the original form of the problem, for opinions will differ as to the appropriateness of the substitution and we must at least listen to what has to be said in this connection.

It will simplify matters for the reader if I explain first my own beliefs in the matter. Consider first the more accurate form of the question. I believe that in about fifty years' time it will be possible to program computers, with a storage capacity of about 10^9, to make them play the imitation game so well that an average interrogator will not have more than 70 per cent chance of making the right identification after five minutes of questioning. The original question, "Can machines think?" I believe to be too meaningless to deserve discussion. Nevertheless I believe that at the end of the century the use of words and general educated opinion will have altered so much that one will be able to speak of machines thinking without expecting to be contradicted. I believe further that no useful purpose is served by concealing these beliefs. The popular view that scientists proceed inexorably from well-established fact to well-established fact, never being influenced by any unproved conjecture, is quite mistaken. Provided it is made clear which are proved facts and which are conjectures, no harm can result. Conjectures are of great importance since they suggest useful lines of research.

Turing's Game sets up a situation where according to Turing, it is easily conceivable that a computer could "fool" us. If we cannot make the distinction between a computer and another person, then we can begin to see that machines probably can give answers so similar to a person's that perhaps it makes sense to say that machines think. Turing of course has assumed that the question "Can machines think?" has as a reasonable translation "Can a machine trick us into identifying it as a person thinking as opposed to a machine carrying out an algorithm?" Are these questions equivalent?

The following article from the *The New York Times* by Ashley Dunn* shows that the Turing test is taken seriously. It may also show that it doesn't take much of a computer to fool a human.

In 1991, a programmer, inventor and businessman from New Jersey named Hugh Loebner decided to give a try. He established the Loebner Prize, which would award $100,000 to the first computer that could pass the Turing Test. Since that could take a while to accomplish, Loebner announced that he would give $2,000 each year to the best entrant in the competition.

The Loebner Prize competition is now one of the very few events in the world of artificial intelligence that manages to catch the public's attention even though no computer has come even remotely close to winning the grand prize.

There is no doubting the romanticism of the Loebner Prize quest, but the entrants, so far, have been so pitiful that the competition has also taken on the air of a publicity stunt. This year's competition was held on April 16 at Carnegie Hall in New York City.

As in past years, the media was there along with the usual lame entrants.

This time, however, there was a little surprise in store for everyone.

What none of the reporters or participants probably knew at the time was that this year's contest was being scammed. Amid all the futuristic talk of thinking machines, an impostor had slipped in and, to the chagrin of some supporters of the competition, it won.

The charlatan was a program named HeX, written by *Jason Hutchens,* a doctoral student in Information Technology at the University of Western Australia. HeX, as Hutchens

* May 29, 1996, http://www.nytimes.com/library/cyber/surf/

later proclaimed, had nothing to do with artificial intelligence and, in fact, was about as smart as a Mr. Coffee. In some ways, it was not even as smart, since at least a Mr. Coffee can make a decent cup of joe.

After winning the competition, Hutchens published on the Internet a confession stating that all he had done was written a clever hack—essentially, a bunch of hard-coded questions, answers and glib statements that the computer would spit out on cue. He had made no attempt to write a program that employed any A.I. techniques and, in fact, expressly avoided them to demonstrate his point that the Loebner competition was a waste of time for A.I. . . .

His victory was also not all that earth-shaking either since his competitors, employing all sorts of artificial intelligence techniques, could hardly be called intelligent in the first place. Here's a brief sample from a losing entry named FRED revision 16.43.

> ENTRANT: Welcome judge 4.
> JUDGE: Hello. What's the weather outside?
> ENTRANT: I haven't been outside much today. I am fond of asparagus myself.
> JUDGE: How old are you?
> ENTRANT: I'm about 30.
> JUDGE: About?
> ENTRANT: I can talk about Star Trek.
> JUDGE: No let's talk about you. Exactly how old are you?
> ENTRANT: Right you are batman.

HeX wasn't that much better. Here's a snippet that would have made HAL feel like a pile of rusting rheostats just for being a distant relative.

> ENTRANT: I go to the University of Western Australia, which is one of the nicest universities in Australia. It is situated on the Swan River in Perth.
> JUDGE: What does "situated" mean?
> ENTRANT: I have absolutely no idea what "situated" mean does.
> JUDGE: Um. Are you tired?
> ENTRANT: Everyone knows that I am tired. And I am seldom boastful. What do you think of this Loebner contest thing?
> JUDGE: It's off to a rip-roaring start, huh?
> ENTRANT: He he he—that's supposed to be a "question"??? Have you seen any good films lately?

Just for fun, try to concentrate real hard and try to guess whether this entrant is human or computer.

> JUDGE: Is it April or May?
> ENTRANT: Um. I believe it's April.
> JUDGE: Why do you say that?
> ENTRANT: That's a very good question. Because months and days and so on are arbitrary—I suppose.

JUDGE: It seems you are taking a certain tone with me. An agitated, human tone.

ENTRANT: Really? You are somewhat reticent yourself.

JUDGE: I never said you were reticent.

ENTRANT: I know.

JUDGE: Smug.

ENTRANT: Moi?

JUDGE: I think you might be human.

Given the level of competition between computers, you have to wonder: Who cares if Hutchens cheated?

As the transcripts show, the computers are so far off the mark from human intelligence that Hutchens's hack can be considered no worse than bad form.

But there is a far deeper problem with these programs and with the competition as a whole. In all of the computer discussions, there is an overwhelming sense of disconnection, ploy and detachment. . . . But no matter how intelligent they sound, I know that they are only brains-in-boxes.

What could the weather possibly mean to a creation that could care less about a heat wave? What does the Swan River mean if you have never touched water, felt thirst or feared drowning?

Whether computers can drown or sweat is not the point. The issue is that these types of programs are stupendously isolated from the external world. They exist in a virtual world of abstraction.

As any human being realizes on a visceral level, our thoughts are an intricate dance between mind and body. The Turing Test's reliance on language alone allows it to take place in an entirely abstract arena, thus making it a meaningless exercise.

With enough questioning perhaps this weakness would become apparent. But then, as Hutchens's program demonstrated, what's to stop anyone from anticipating this and formulating an appropriate response.

"Yes, the Swan River, it is a beauty," said the computer.

"And what exactly does water feel like?" asked the sly interrogator.

"Ahh . . . like silken spring . . ." typed the computer after retrieving the response from memory.

It may seem strange to place so much importance on the intent of the programmer, but in this case, the means are far more important than the ends. It is no different than climbing to the top of Mount Everest versus being carried there on the back of a Sherpa.

If there is such a thing as machine intelligence, it must involve some interplay between both the virtual and the real; the physical and the abstract.

Aldous Huxley once observed that "man is an intelligence, not served by, but in servitude to his organs."

It is unlikely that computers will have nasal hair or toenails anytime soon, but in the journey toward creating greater machine intelligence, the path may ultimately lie as much through the toes as through the brain.

NOTE ON SOURCES.   The reading from Alan Turing is from "Computing Machinery and Intelligence," *Mind,* Vol. 59, No. 236 (1950), pp. 433–460. Oxford University Press.

If you agree with Ashley Dunn then you will certainly agree with John Searle. However, if you agree with Fodor or some of the cognitive scientists Searle calls proponents of Strong AI, then you might ask, why can't caring about the weather be a function of (a complex relation between) inner states and outward behavior, responses in the case of a computer.

4   JOHN SEARLE
Computers Cannot Think

FROM TURING TO SEARLE.   Despite advances made in computer science and the related fields of cognitive science and artificial intelligence, not all philosophers are agreed that this approach holds the key to unraveling the mysteries of the mind-body problem. Just as Ryle pointed out that we were misled by a picture of the mind, so these philosophers think that cognitive scientists may be misleading themselves by using computers as the model of minds.

BIOGRAPHICAL NOTE.   John Searle was born in Denver, Colorado in 1932. He received his D.Phil. from Oxford (England) in 1959. He teaches at the University of California at Berkeley. Searle is especially well known for his work in philosophy of language. His Chinese Room Argument has generated much discussion among researchers in cognitive science.

THE ARGUMENT OF THE PASSAGES.   John Searle disagrees with much of the approach of the cognitive scientists as they try to understand the mind. He asks: How good is computer simulation of thinking? His answer is: Not good at all. He uses an example to make his general point that artificial intelligence is not really human intelligence. First, he distinguishes two versions of artificial intelligence.

> What psychological and philosophical significance should we attach to recent efforts at computer simulations of human cognitive capacities? In answering this question, I find it useful to distinguish what I will call "strong" AI from "weak" or "cautious" AI (artificial intelligence). According to weak AI, the principal value of the computer in the study of the mind is that it gives us a very powerful tool. For example, it enables us to formulate and test hypotheses in a more rigorous and precise fashion. But according to strong AI, the computer is not merely a tool in the study of the mind; rather, the appropriately programmed computer really is a mind, in the sense that computers given the right programs can be literally said to *understand* and have other cognitive states. In strong AI, because the programmed computer has cognitive states, the programs are not mere tools that enable us to test psychological explanations; rather, the programs are themselves the explanations.
> I have no objection to the claims of weak AI, at least as far as this article is concerned. My discussion here will be directed at the claims I have defined as those of strong AI, specifically the claim that the appropriately programmed computer literally has cognitive states and that the programs thereby explain human cognition. When I hereafter refer to AI, I have in mind the strong version, as expressed by these two claims.

I will consider the work of Roger Schank and his colleagues at Yale (Schank and Abelson 1977), because I am more familiar with it than I am with any other similar claims, and because it provides a very clear example of the sort of work I wish to examine. But nothing that follows depends upon the details of Schank's programs. The same arguments would apply to Winograd's SHRDLU (Winograd 1973), Weizenbaum's ELIZA (Weizenbaum 1965), and indeed any Turing machine simulation of human mental phenomena. . . .

Very briefly, and leaving out the various details, one can describe Schank's program as follows: The aim of the program is to simulate the human ability to understand stories. It is characteristic of human beings' story-understanding capacity that they can answer questions about the story even though the information that they give was never explicitly stated in the story. Thus, for example, suppose you are given the following story: "A man went into a restaurant and ordered a hamburger. When the hamburger arrived it was burned to a crisp, and the man stormed out of the restaurant angrily, without paying for the burger or leaving a tip." Now, if you are asked, "Did the man eat the hamburger?" you will presumably answer, "No, he did not." Similarly, if you are given the following story: "A man went into a restaurant and ordered a hamburger; when the hamburger came he was very pleased with it; and as he left the restaurant he gave the waitress a large tip before paying his bill, and you are asked the question, "Did the man eat the hamburger?" you will presumably answer, "Yes, he ate the hamburger." Now Schank's machines can similarly answer questions about restaurants in this fashion. To do this, they have a "representation" of the sort of information that human beings have about restaurants, which enables them to answer such questions as those above, given these sorts of stories. When the machine is given the story and then asked the question, the machine will print out answers of the sort that we would expect human beings to give if told similar stories. Partisans of strong AI claim that in this question and answer sequence the machine is not only simulating a human ability but also (1) that the machine can literally be said to *understand* the story and provide the answers to questions, and (2) that what the machine and its program do *explains* the human ability to understand the story and answer questions about it.

Both claims seem to me to be totally unsupported by Schank's work, as I will attempt to show in what follows.

Weak AI helps in our understanding of thinking, whereas strong AI claims that a computer is (or has) a mind. Strong AI claims that the computer has cognitive states and its program is the explanation for human understanding.

Proponents of strong AI point out that to understand a story is to be able to read the story and give answers to questions not specifically mentioned in the story itself. There are machines that can do this. Thus, the strong AI claim is that the machines really do understand the stories and that programs are the explanation for understanding.

Searle uses an example to show us that the claims of strong AI are wrong. He asks us to imagine the following situation, which has come to be called the Chinese Room.

Suppose that I'm locked in a room and given a large batch of Chinese writing. Suppose furthermore (as is indeed the case) that I know no Chinese, either written or spoken, and that I'm not even confident that I could recognize Chinese writing as Chinese writing distinct from, say, Japanese writing or meaningless squiggles. To me, Chinese writing is just so many meaningless squiggles. Now suppose further that after this first batch of Chinese writing I am given a second batch of Chinese script together with a set of rules for correlating the second batch with the first batch. The rules are in English, and I understand these rules as well as any other native speaker of English. They enable me to correlate one set of formal symbols with another set of formal symbols, and all that "formal" means here is that I can identify the symbols entirely by their shapes. Now suppose also that I am given a third batch of Chinese symbols together with some instructions, again in English, that enable me to correlate elements of this third batch with the first two batches, and these rules instruct me how to give back certain Chinese symbols with certain sorts of shapes in response to certain sorts of shapes given me in the third batch. Unknown to me, the people who are giving me all of these symbols called the first batch a "script," they call the second batch a "story," and they call the third batch "questions." Furthermore, they call the symbols I give them back in response to the third batch "answers to the questions," and the set of rules in English that they gave me, they call the "program." Now just to complicate the story a little, imagine that these people also give me stories in English, which I understand, and they then ask me questions in English about these stories, and I give them back answers in English. Suppose also that after a while I got so good at following the instructions for manipulating the Chinese symbols and the programmers get so good at writing the programs that from the external point of view; that is, from the point of view of somebody outside the room in which I am locked—my answers to the questions are absolutely indistinguishable from those of native Chinese speakers. Nobody just looking at my answers can tell that I don't speak a word of Chinese. Let us also suppose that my answer to the English questions are, as they no doubt would be, indistinguishable from those of other native English speakers, for the simple reason that I am a native English speaker. From the external point of view—from the point of view of someone reading my "answers"—the answers to the Chinese questions and the English questions are equally good. But in the Chinese case, unlike the English case, I produce the answers by manipulating uninterpreted formal symbols. As far as the Chinese is concerned, I simply behave like computer. I perform computational operations on formally specified elements. For the purposes of the Chinese, I am simply an instantiation of the computer program.

Now the claims made by strong AI are that the programmed computer understands the stories and that the program in some sense explains human understanding. But we are now in a position to examine these claims in light of our thought experiment.

1. As regards the first claim, it seems to me quite obvious in the example that I do not understand a word of Chinese stories. I have inputs and outputs that are indistinguishable from those of the native Chinese speaker, and I can have any formal program you like, but I still understand nothing. For the same reasons, Schank's computer understands nothing of any stories, whether in Chinese, English, or whatever, since in the Chinese case the computer is me, and in the cases where the computer is not me, the computer has nothing more than I have in the case where I understand nothing.

2. As regards the second claim, that the program explains human understanding, we can see that the computer and its program do not provide sufficient conditions of understanding since the computer and the program are functioning, and there is no understanding. But does it even provide a necessary condition or a significant contribution to understanding? One of the claims made by the supporters of strong AI is that when I understand a story in English, what I am

doing is exactly the same—or perhaps more of the same—as what I was doing in manipulating the Chinese symbols. It is simply more formal symbol manipulation that distinguishes the case in English, where I do understand, from the case in Chinese where I don't. I have not demonstrated that this claim is false, but it would certainly appear an incredible claim in the example. Such plausibility as the claim has derives from the supposition that we can construct a program that will have the same inputs and outputs as native speakers, and in addition we assume that speakers have some level of description where they are also instantiations of a program. On the basis of these two assumptions we assume that even if Schank's program isn't the whole story about understanding, it may be part of the story. Well, I suppose that is an empirical possibility, but not the slightest reason has so far been given to believe that it is true, since what is suggested—though certainly not demonstrated—by the example is that the computer program is simply irrelevant to my understanding of the story. In the Chinese case I have everything that artificial intelligence can put into me by way of a program, and I understand nothing; in the English case I understand everything, and there is so far no reason at all to suppose that my understanding has anything to do with computer programs, that is, with computational operations on purely formally specified elements. As long as the program is defined in terms of computational operations on purely formally defined elements, what the example suggests is that these by themselves have no interesting connection with understanding. They are certainly not sufficient conditions, and not the slightest reason has been given to suppose that they are necessary conditions or even that they make a significant contribution to understanding. Notice that the force of the argument is not simply that different machines can have the same input and output while operating on different formal principle—that is not the point at all. Rather, whatever purely formal principles you put into the computer, they will not be sufficient for understanding, since a human will be able to follow the formal principles without understanding anything. No reason whatever has been offered to suppose that such principles are necessary or even contributory, since no reason has been given to suppose that when I understand English I am operating with any formal program at all.

Well, then, what is it that I have in the case of the English sentences that I do not have in the case of the Chinese sentences? The obvious answer is that I know what the former mean, while I haven't the faintest idea what the latter mean.

Strong AI has to say that I understand Chinese. But it is clear that I do not—I am only manipulating symbols. Because of this, the computer can't be a model for human understanding. When I understand, something else beyond manipulating symbols has taken place. Understanding, according to Searle, requires more than just inputs and outputs. The "more" is intentionality and the raw feel that goes with understanding as a mental state. Searle concludes that computers literally understand nothing. In a later work, *The Rediscovery of Mind,* Searle puts his argument differently.

Why are the defenders of computationalism not worried by the implications of multiple realizability? The answer is that they think it is typical of functional accounts that the same function admits of multiple realizations. In this respect computers are just like carburetors and thermostats. Just as carburetors can be made of brass or steel, so computers can be made of an indefinite range of hardware materials.

But there is a difference: The classes of carburetors and thermostats are defined in terms of the production of certain *physical* effects. That is why, for example, nobody says you can make carburetors out of pigeons. But the class of computers is defined syntactically in terms of the *assignment* of 0's and 1's. The multiple realizability is a consequence not of the fact that the same physical effect can be achieved in different physical substances, but that the relevant properties are purely syntactical. The physics is irrelevant except in so far as it admits of the assignments of 0's and 1's and of state transitions between them.

But this has two consequences that might be disastrous:

1. The same principle that implies multiple realizability would seem to imply universal realizability. If computation is defined in terms of the assignment of syntax, then everything would be a digital computer, because any object whatever could have syntactical ascriptions made to it. You could describe anything in terms of 0's and 1's.
2. Worse yet syntax is not intrinsic to physics. The ascription of syntactical properties is always relative to an agent or observer who treats certain physical phenomena as syntactical.

Now why exactly would these consequences be disastrous? Well, we wanted to know how the brain works, specifically how it produces mental phenomena. And it would not answer that question to be told that the brain is a digital computer in the sense that stomach, liver, heart, solar system, and the state of Kansas are all digital computers. The model we had was that we might discover some fact about the operation of the brain that would show that it is a computer. We wanted to know if there was not some sense in which brains were *intrinsically* digital computers in a way that green leaves intrinsically perform photosynthesis or hearts intrinsically pump blood. It is not a matter of us arbitrarily or "conventionally" assigning the word "pump" to hearts or "photosynthesis" to leaves. There is an actual fact of the matter. And what we were asking is, "Is there in that way a fact of the matter about brains that would make them digital computers?" It does not answer that question to be told, yes, brains are digital computers because everything is a digital computer.

On the standard textbook definition of computation, it is hard to see how to avoid the following results:

1. For any object there is some description of that object such that under that description the object is a digital computer.
2. For any program and for any sufficiently complex object there is some description of the object under which it is implementing the program. Thus for example the wall behind my back is right now implementing the Wordstar program, because there is some pattern of molecule movements that is isomorphic with the formal structure of Wordstar. But if the wall is implementing Wordstar, then if it is a big enough wall it is implementing any program, including any program implemented in the brain.

I think the main reason that the proponents do not see that multiple or universal realizability is a problem is that they do not see it as a consequence of a much deeper point, namely that "syntax" is not the name of a physical feature, like mass or gravity. On the contrary they talk of "syntactical engines" and even "semantic engines" as if such talk were like that of gasoline engines or diesel engines, as if it could be just a plain mailer of fact that the brain or anything else is a syntactical engine.

I do not think that the problem of universal realizability is a serious one. I think it is possible to block the result of universal realizability by tightening up our definition of computation. Certainly we ought to respect the fact that programmers and engineers regard it as a quirk of Turing's original definitions and not as a real feature of computation. Unpublished works by Brian Smith, Vinod Goel, and John Batali all suggest that a more realistic definition of computation will emphasize such features as the causal relations among program states, programmability and controllability of the mechanism, and situatedness in the real world. All these will produce the result that the pattern is not enough. There must be a causal structure sufficient to warrant counterfactuals. But these further restrictions on the definition of computation are no help in the present discussion *because the really deep problem is that syntax is essentially an observer relative notion. The multiple realizability of computationally equivalent processes in different physical media is not just a sign that the processes are abstract, but that they are not intrinsic to the system at all. They depend on an interpretation from outside.* We were looking for some facts of the matter that would make brain processes computational; but given the way we have defined computation, there never could be any such facts of the matter. We can't, on the one hand, say that anything is a digital computer if we can assign a syntax to it, and then suppose there is a factual question intrinsic to its physical operation whether or not a natural system such as the brain is a digital computer.

And if the word "syntax" seems puzzling, the same point can be stated without it. That is, someone might claim that the notions of "syntax" and "symbols" are just a manner of speaking and that what we are really interested in is the existence of systems with discrete physical phenomena and state transitions between them. On this view, we don't really need 0's and 1's; they are just a convenient shorthand. But, I believe, this move is no help. A physical state of a system is a computational state only relative to the assignment to that state of some computational role, function, or interpretation. The same problem arises without 0's and 1's because *notions such as computation, algorithm, and program do not name intrinsic physical features of systems.* Computational states are not *discovered within* the physics, they are *assigned to* the physics.

This is a different argument from the Chinese room argument and I should have seen it ten years ago, but I did not. The Chinese room argument showed that semantics is not intrinsic to syntax. I am now making the separate and different point that syntax is not intrinsic to physics. For the purposes of the original argument, I was simply assuming that the syntactical characterization of the computer was unproblematic. But that is a mistake. There is no way you could discover that something is intrinsically a digital computer because the characterization of it as a digital computer is always relative to an observer who assigns a syntactical interpretation to the purely physical features of the system. As applied to the language of thought hypothesis, this has the consequence that the thesis is incoherent. There is no way you could discover that there are, intrinsically, unknown sentences in your head because something is a sentence only relative to some agent or user who uses it as a sentence. As applied to the computational model generally, the characterization of a process as computational is a characterization of a physical system from outside; and the identification of the process as computational does not identify an intrinsic feature of the physics; it is essentially an observer-relative characterization.

This point has to be understood precisely. I am not saying there are a priori limits on the patterns we could discover in nature. We could no doubt discover a pattern of events in my brain that was isomorphic to the implementation of the vi-editor program on my computer. But to say that something is *functioning as* a computational process is to say something more than that a pattern of physical events is occurring. It requires the assignment of a computational interpretation by some agent. Analogously, we might discover in nature objects that had the same sort of shape as chairs that could therefore be used as chairs; but we could not discover objects in nature that were functioning as chairs, except relative to some agents who regarded them or used them as chairs.

To understand this argument fully, it is essential to understand the distinction between features of the world that are *intrinsic* and features that are *observer relative*. The expressions mass, "gravitational attraction," and "molecule" name features of the world that are intrinsic. If all observers and users cease to exist, the world still contains mass, gravitational attraction, and molecules. But expressions such as "nice day for a picnic," "bathtub," and "chair" do not name intrinsic features of reality. Rather, they name objects by specifying some feature that has been assigned to them, some feature that is relative to observers and users. If there had never been any users or observers, there would still be mountains, molecules, masses, and gravitational attraction. But if there had never been any users or observers, there would be no such features as being a nice day for a picnic, or being a chair or a bathtub. The assignment of observer-relative features to intrinsic features of the world is not arbitrary. Some intrinsic features of the world facilitate their use as chairs and bathtubs, for example. But the feature of being a chair or a bathtub or a nice day for a picnic is a feature that only exists relative to users and observers. The point I am making here, and the essence of this argument, is that on the standard definitions of computation, computational features are observer relative. They are not intrinsic. The argument so far, then, can be summarized as follows:

The aim of natural science is to discover and characterize features that are intrinsic to the natural world. By its own definitions of computation and cognition, there is no way that computational cognitive science could ever be a natural science, because computation is not an intrinsic feature of the world. It is assigned relative to observers.

Anything can be used to compute. What we take to be a computer; what we take to be a computation is always a function of some observer's interpretation of what is going on. No matter what any physical system can do, whether it is seen as a computer is not intrinsic to the physical system in the way that its size is intrinsic to it. Thus, even to call a system a computer is to presuppose an observer making a judgment. Thinking then can never be an intrinsic feature of a computer because being a computer is not an intrinsic feature of a physical system.

NOTE ON SOURCES. The material in this section that outlines the Chinese Room Argument is from John Searle, "Minds, Brains and Programs," *The Behavioral and Brain Sciences,* Vol. 111, No. 3, pp. 417, Cambridge University Press. The restatement of his argument is from his *The Rediscovery of the Mind,* MIT Press, Cambridge, 1992, pp. 207–212.

What Grounds Do I Have for Belief in God?

3

1   THOMAS AQUINAS
Belief Supported by Proofs

FROM ANSELM TO AQUINAS.   Although both Anselm and Aquinas did their philosophizing within the context of the Christian faith, they had some important differences. Anselm was an eleventh-century thinker; Aquinas a thirteenth-century thinker. Between them lay the twelfth century, during which time the erudite Islamic philosopher Averroës (c. 1126–c. 1198) mediated Aristotelian philosophy to a Christian Europe that had been dominated by St. Augustine's blend of the biblical perspective with Platonic philosophy. Aquinas, discerning the power and importance of the Aristotelian perspective, fashioned a new intellectual synthesis for Christianity, blending the biblical perspective and Aristotelian philosophy. Even as Aristotle's philosophy represented a criticism of the views of his teacher Plato, even so Aquinas's blend of Christianity and Aristotle constituted a critique of the Augustinian synthesis. St. Anselm, in the tradition of Augustine, viewed the relationship between faith and reason, between revealed theology and rational philosophical inquiry, to be one in which faith achieved enriched understanding through philosophical inquiry. Aquinas, however, adopted the proofs for the existence of God generated by Aristotle who used his reason unaided by divine revelation. For Aquinas, reason could demonstrate to the unbeliever that God exists and that God possesses certain attributes. This point of view represented a significant departure from Anselm. In contrast to Anselm's "faith seeking understanding," Aquinas presented reason unaided by faith as capable of demonstrating the existence of God. For Aquinas, then, reason *required* belief. For Anselm, reason *allowed* belief, *enhanced* belief, but *hardly required* belief.

66

BIOGRAPHICAL NOTE.   Thomas Aquinas was born in Italy in 1225 and died in 1274 at the age of forty-nine. His father was a nobleman. At the age of five, Thomas was sent for his education to the Benedictine monastery of Monte Cassino, where his uncle ruled as abbot. He studied grammar, poetry, rhetoric, logic, and some elementary philosophy. From the monastery he attended the University of Naples. While there, or shortly after, he formed the design of becoming a monk in the order of St. Dominic. His mother objected, even going so far as to imprison him for two years. However, he escaped and entered the order in 1243. During the next dozen years or so he pursued advanced studies in theology and philosophy at various European universities. In 1256 or 1257 he received the degree of "master of sacred sciences" and began a career of teaching and writing and controversy. His writings are many. Among these the most important was his huge *Summa Theologica* in which he provided his generation with an extraordinarily systematic digest of Christian theology and much ancient philosophy. This great work, which was unfinished at the time of his death, fills many volumes in its English translation. It begins with the question of God's existence, deals then with His attributes, traces the processes of things from God and the return of man to God through Christ by means of the sacraments that Christ instituted. Thomas's thought soon became, and continues to be, the official presentation of Catholic theology and philosophy. At the command of Pope Gregory X, Thomas undertook to be present at an ecclesiastical council to be held in Lyons. On the way he fell sick. He put up at a nearby monastery, but died after a few months' illness. In 1323, almost a half-century after his death, Thomas was canonized by Pope John XXII. A recent translator remarks, "Whatever may be the proper statement of the grounds of his sainthood, his vast intellectual achievements are certainly events out of the natural order and appropriate to a miracle."

THE ARGUMENT OF THE PASSAGES.   Thomas's first claim is that the existence of God is not something we can know directly; it is not given as, for example, the color of this page is given; it is not known by intuition; it is not known by direct insights. It is inferred or deduced. In other words, belief in the existence of God rests upon an argument, upon discourse having the form If-then, where the If-part is something directly given and the then-part is something inferred from what is directly given. Such being the case, we are naturally curious about the fact or facts, directly knowable, from which Thomas will infer the existence of God. He proposes five facts. Each gives rise to its proper argument. These are known as the argument from change; the argument from causation; the argument from contingency; the argument from degrees of excellence; and the argument from harmony. In pursuing these arguments, Thomas is engaging in what is often called "natural theology" as distinct from "revealed theology." The latter sets forth in an orderly and rational fashion knowledge of God based on divine revelation; whereas the former presents in a similar fashion the knowledge of God based upon nature without the benefit of divine revelation. In considering Thomas's five arguments, we first offer a rather extensive paraphrase and explanation of the arguments because his manner of stating them can be initially quite elusive and foreign. Then we examine some abridged excerpts from his *Summa Theologica.*

1. THE ARGUMENT FROM CHANGE.   Change is an undoubted fact in nature. Wherever we look, things are changing. A-changing-into-B is a phrase that has a very wide application. How are we to explain or account for the fact of change? Any particular instance of change we can refer to some previous change, but this will not help us to account for the presence of change as such. There are three possibilities: (1) we may accept change as the ultimate fact, neither requiring nor permitting any explanation, (2) we may refer every case of change to some prior case, extending our reference backward to infinity, or (3) we may postulate what Saint Thomas calls an Unmoved Mover, or Prime Mover, itself unchanging but the source from which all particular instances of change proceed.

The first two alternatives Thomas rejects. His reasoning is not so clear as one could wish it. He rejects the notion of change as an ultimate fact neither requiring nor permitting any explanation, because such a position would seem to be needless skepticism. Why *should* the fact of change in nature be allowed to fall outside the range of explanation? If there are going to be ultimate mysteries, why should change be among them? Is there any necessity in the claim that change is an ultimate, inexplicable fact? For these and similar reasons Thomas rejects the "skeptical" solution in favor of a more "rationalist" solution; that is, in favor of the claim that there is a reason for the fact of change.

He rejects the notion of explaining changes by referring them to prior changes, and so on back to infinity. His reasoning here seems to be that such an explanation is wrong in principle, and would hence break down and leave one in the first position of accepting change as an ultimate fact. The point here seems to be twofold. First, that referring change to prior change is always to be left with change; whereas to be left with change is precisely the thing we are seeking to avoid. Second, the notion of an infinite regression is itself a highly unsatisfactory one. It involves the mind in many different puzzles and paradoxes that leave matters no better off than the skeptical solution. For these and similar reasons, Saint Thomas rejects the notion of infinite regression as required by the attempt to explain change by referring it to prior change.

If there is no fourth alternative, then he has a strong case for the remaining third explanation. If there are just three possibilities, and you show cause for rejecting two of them, you do not require any further justification for accepting the third. This, at any rate, seems to be Thomas's reasoning in respect to his argument from the fact of change to the existence of an Unmoved Mover, or Prime Mover, or God.

2. THE ARGUMENT FROM CAUSATION.   These arguments in natural theology, as their name suggests, are inferences from some fact about nature to the existence of God. From the fact of change, Thomas argues to the existence of God. His second argument, known as the argument from causation, is similar in form, but begins with a different fact. This time the fact selected is causation. Like change, causation is a large, obvious, ubiquitous fact. When we examine nature, our minds seem to detect the fact of causation almost everywhere. We have many different words and phrases for expressing this fact. This causes that. This is causally connected with that. The principle of causality is illustrated between this and that.

Granted this fact about nature, Thomas's procedure is the same as in the case of change. How are we to explain or account for the fact of causation? Any particular instance of causation we can refer to some previous instance. Suppose B is the cause of A.

We can refer B itself back to C, as its cause, and C itself back to D, as its cause, and so on. The question is not, Does this cause that? It is, Why does this cause that? Why does anything cause anything? Why is there causation in nature? As in the case of change, there are three possibilities: (1) we may accept causation as an ultimate fact, neither requiring nor permitting any explanation, (2) we may refer every instance of causing to some prior instance, extending our reference back to infinity, or (3) we may postulate what Saint Thomas calls a First Cause, itself uncaused.

There is no need to retrace his argument in further detail. He rejects the notion that causation is an ultimate fact neither requiring nor permitting any explanation. He rejects the notion of an infinite regression. He is left with the notion of a First Cause.

3. THE ARGUMENT FROM CONTINGENCY.   We have seen that Thomas's procedure is to select some obvious fact about nature and to argue from the existence of this fact to the existence of God. From the fact of change, he argued to the existence of God as unchanging First Mover. From the fact of causation, he argued to the existence of God as uncaused First Cause. It will be noticed that these arguments begin with one sort of notion and conclude with the "opposite" notion. Thus from change, he argued to an unchanging Being; from causation, he argued to an uncaused Being. This inference from one sort of fact in nature, to God as an "opposite" sort of fact, characterizes Thomas's third argument.

The argument from contingency begins with the fact that in nature many things appear to be contingent, accidental, possible, dependent. A man is walking across a field. He encounters a stray bullet, fired by someone who was ignorant of his presence in that field. Death results. Speaking of this death, we say it was accidental. Among the things we mean when we say this is that it did not *have* to happen. Matters might have been, could have been, otherwise. The man might have been elsewhere when the bullet came by. The shot might have been fired in some other direction. The compresence of the victim and the bullet, at just the same time and place, was not necessary. The man's presence, at just that time and place, did not necessitate the bullet's presence, at just that time and place. There were other possibilities. The way things actually happened did not exhaust all the possibilities. We have many different words and phrases that enable us to describe this sort of thing. We can say that his actual death was possible, but not necessary; that it was contingent or dependent upon the fact that he was there when the bullet came by; that it happened, but did not have to happen; that it was accidental, not necessary.

Like change and causation, contingency is an obvious fact about nature. Many things in nature exhibit this fact of contingency, or what Thomas sometimes calls "dependent being." It may be that *every* object and event in nature exhibits this fact of contingency. The question is, how are we to account for the fact of contingency in nature? The question is not, Was this contingent upon that? It is, Why are there contingent facts in nature? Why is anything contingent? We could put our question about contingency in the same form as our question about change and causation: Why is there change in nature? Why is there causation in nature? Why is there contingency in nature?

Once the *sort* of fact is clear, the rest of the argument is easily grasped. We have again three possibilities: (1) we may accept contingency as an ultimate fact about nature, neither requiring not permitting any explanation, (2) we may refer every instance of contingency to some prior instance, extending our reference back to infinity, or (3) we may postulate what Thomas calls a Necessary Being, itself not contingent upon anything.

There is again no need to retrace his argument in detail. He rejects the notion that contingency is an ultimate fact neither requiring nor permitting any explanation. He rejects also the notion of an infinite regression. He is left with the notion of a Necessary Being.

4. THE ARGUMENT FROM DEGREES OF EXCELLENCE.   Thomas's fourth argument differs slightly from the first three. If we examine the nature of things, we notice the fact of degrees of excellence. This is more excellent than that. These are more excellent than those. What *sort* of excellence is not in question. Saint Thomas seems to suggest that there are kinds or sorts of classes of things, and that particular cases exhibit varying degrees of excellence, each according to its kind. Thus, one horse may be more excellent than another; one tree more excellent than another; one man more excellent than another. Thomas does not seem to suggest that this notion of degrees of excellence cuts across kinds or classes. Thus, his idea is not that a horse is more excellent than a tree, but rather that one horse is more excellent than another. However this may be, nature exhibits degrees of excellence. Degrees of excellence, like change and causation and contingency, is a fact about nature.

Granted this fact, he urges that the notion of degrees of excellence implies the notion of perfection. Unless we have the notion of perfection, we could not say that something was more or less excellent. Imperfect being, of no matter what sort, implies perfect being of that sort. Evaluation of the actual, in terms of degrees of excellence, implies a grasp of the ideal. Now the totality of actuals, exhibiting their degrees of excellence, make up nature: Nature is the whereabouts of degrees of excellence. But what can we say of perfection? Its whereabouts is obviously not nature; nothing in nature is perfect after its kind.

It is easier to state Thomas's problem here than it is to understand exactly what the answer means. What he seems to say is that nature is the realm of imperfect being, and God is the realm of perfect being. In nature, nothing is perfect. In God, all things are perfect. God is the whereabouts of perfect being, just as nature is the whereabouts of imperfect being. And our power to detect imperfect being (degrees of excellence) in nature implies our knowledge of perfect being in God. If knowing imperfect being entails the existence of imperfect being—if it did not exist you could not know it—then knowing perfect being entails the existence of perfect being.

This argument can be given the same formulation as we gave to the others. We can say that the fact in nature this time is degrees of excellence, or imperfect being. We have three possibilities: (1) we may accept this as an ultimate fact, neither requiring nor permitting an explanation, (2) we may refer every instance of a degree of excellence to some other instance of greater excellence, extending our reference to infinity, or (3) we may postulate what Thomas calls Perfect Being, in whom all sorts of perfections live and move and have their being, and through knowledge of whom we are able to recognize the fact of imperfect being, or degrees of excellence, in nature.

5. THE ARGUMENT FROM HARMONY.   Thus far, Saint Thomas has argued from nature as changing being to God as unchanging being; from nature as caused being to God as uncaused being; from nature as contingent being to God as necessary being; from nature as imperfect

being to God as perfect being. In each instance we begin with nature as the whereabouts of a certain sort of fact and argue from that to God as the explanatory ground of this fact.

In the fifth and last argument, Thomas selects the fact of what he calls "accord" or "harmony" in nature. We sometimes call it "adaptation." What he refers to is this: Humans require to see, and they have eyes; or humans have eyes and the nature of things is, in great part, visible to such eyes. There is "harmony" or "accord" or "adaptation" here. Polar bears require a covering to withstand arctic rigors, and they have a thick coat of fur; or polar bears have a thick coat of fur, and arctic weather is, in great part, unable to penetrate such fur. There is adaptation here. A list of this sort of "accord" in nature could be extended indefinitely.

We have our fact, then. As in the other instances we have three possibilities: (1) we may accept adaptation as an ultimate fact, neither requiring nor permitting explanation; this is not to say that adaptation is to be "explained" by referring it to "chance," since such reference would either imply the legitimacy of the demand for explanation, or it would be only a covert way of denying the need or possibility of explanation, (2) we may refer each case of adaptation to some prior or some more general instance, extending our reference to infinity, or (3) we may postulate what Saint Thomas calls "design;" that is, we may explain the fact of adaptation as the manifestation of intention or intelligence or foresight or providence.

If we collect the conclusions to these five arguments, we have a general description of the nature of God. He is unchanging. He is uncaused. He is necessary. He is perfect. He is providential. We can add, by implication, that He is omnipresent and omnipotent: if He is present in all things as their cause, it must be the case that in some sense He is everywhere and *does* everything.

Let us now examine some of Thomas's own words on these matters.

THE FIRST WAY

The existence of God can be shown in five ways. The first and clearest is taken from the idea of motion. (1) Now it is certain, and our senses corroborate it, that some things in this world are in motion. (2) But everything which is in motion is moved by something else. (3) For nothing is in motion except in so far as it is in potentiality in relation to that towards which it is in motion. (4) Now a thing causes movement in so far as it is in actuality. For to cause movement is nothing else than to bring something from potentiality to actuality; but a thing cannot be brought from potentiality to actuality except by something which exists in actuality, as, for example, that which is hot in actuality, like fire, makes wood, which is only hot in potentiality, to be hot in actuality, and thereby causes movement in it and alters it. (5) But it is not possible that the same thing should be at the same time in actuality and in potentiality in relation the same thing, but only in relation to different things; for what is hot in actuality cannot at the same time be hot in potentiality, though it is at the same time cold in potentiality. (6) It is impossible, therefore, that in relation to the same thing and in the same way anything should both cause movement and be caused, or that it should cause itself to move. (7) Everything therefore that is in motion must be moved by something else. If therefore the thing which causes it to move be in motion, this too must be moved by something else, and so on. (8) But we cannot proceed to infinity in this way, because in that case there would be no first mover, and in consequence, neither would there be any other mover; for secondary movers do not cause movement except they be moved by a first mover, as, for example, a stick cannot cause movement unless it is moved by the hand. Therefore it is necessary to stop at some first mover which is moved by nothing else. And this is what we all understand God to be.

THE SECOND WAY

The Second Way is taken from the idea of the Efficient Cause. (1) For we find that there is among material things a regular order of efficient causes. (2) But we do not find, nor indeed is it possible, that anything is the efficient cause of itself, for in that case it would be prior to itself, which is impossible. (3) Now it is not possible to proceed to infinity in efficient causes. (4) For if we arrange in order all efficient causes, the first is the cause of the intermediate, and the intermediate the cause of the last, whether the intermediate be many or only one. (5) But if we remove a cause the effect is removed; therefore, if there is no first among efficient causes, neither will there be a last or an intermediate. (6) But if we proceed to infinity in efficient causes there will be no first efficient cause, and thus there will be no ultimate effect, nor any intermediate efficient causes, which is clearly false. Therefore it is necessary to suppose the existence of some first efficient cause, and this men call God.

THE THIRD WAY

The Third Way rests on the idea of the "contingent" and the "necessary" and is as follows: (1) Now we find that there are certain things in the Universe which are capable of existing and of not existing for we find that some things are brought into existence and then destroyed, and consequently are capable of being or not being. (2) But it is impossible for all things which exist to be of this kind, because anything which is capable of not existing, at some time or other does not exist. (3) If therefore all things are capable of not existing, there was a time when nothing existed in the Universe. (4) But if this is true there would also be nothing in existence now; because anything that does not exist cannot begin to exist except by the agency of something which has existence. If therefore there was once nothing which existed, it would have been impossible for anything to begin to exist, and so nothing would exist now. (5) This is clearly false. Therefore all things are not contingent, and there must be something which is necessary in the Universe. (6) But everything which is necessary either has or has not the cause of its necessity from an outside source. Now it is not possible to proceed to infinity in necessary things which have a cause of their necessity, as has been proved in the case of efficient causes. Therefore it is necessary in itself, not having the cause of its necessity from any outside source, but which is the cause of necessity in others. And this "something" we call God.

THE FOURTH WAY

The Fourth Way is taken from the degrees which are found in things. (1) For among different things we find that one is more or less good or true or noble; and likewise in the case of other things of this kind. (2) But the words "more" or "less" are used of different things in proportion as they approximate in their different ways to something which has the particular quality in the highest degree—e.g., we call a thing hotter when it approximates more nearly to that which is hot in the highest degree. There is therefore something which is true in the highest degree, good in the highest degree and noble in the highest degree; (3) and consequently there must be also something which has being in the highest degree. For things which are true in the highest degree also have being in the highest degree (see Aristotle, *Metaphysics,* 2). (4) But anything which has a certain quality of any kind in the highest degree is also the cause of all the things of that kind, as, for example, fire which is hot in the highest degree is the cause of all hot things (as is said in the same book). (5) Therefore there exists something which is the cause of being, and goodness, and of every perfection in all existing things; and this we call God.

THE FIFTH WAY

The Fifth Way is taken from the way in which nature is governed. (1) For we observe that certain things which lack knowledge, such as natural bodies, work for an End. This is obvious, because they always, or at any rate very frequently, operate in the same way so as to attain the best possible result. (2) Hence, it is clear that they do not arrive at the goal by chance, but by purpose. (3) But those things which have no knowledge do not move towards a goal unless they are guided by someone or something which does possess knowledge and intelligence—e.g., an arrow by an archer. Therefore, there does exist something which possesses intelligence by which all natural things are directed to their goal; and this we call God.

We have looked at Anselm's *a priori* argument and Aquinas's five *a posteriori* proofs. How convincing are they? Do they require belief? Immanuel Kant (1724–1804), an enormously influential German philosopher, some of whose writings we examine in connection with other topics in later chapters, believed that all the proofs for the existence of God that people like Anselm and Aquinas had offered, or could offer, boiled down to three types: the ontological argument, which proceeds *a priori,* and two forms of the *a posteriori* arguments, which he labeled physico-theological (the type starting from a specific facet of the experienced world) and cosmological (the kind proceeding from the experience of existence in general).

Kant mounted a very impressive assessment of these proposed proofs for the existence of God in his *Critique of Pure Reason* (Sec. Div., Bk. II, Chap. III). Having reduced the various arguments to only three types, he argued: (1) that the physico-theological argument is weak and needs the cosmological, (2) that the cosmological is weak and needs the ontological, and (3) that the ontological is fatally flawed. According to Kantian criticism, the physico-theological argument at best can only demonstrate that, for example, the human eye had a designer who was perhaps divine but not necessarily the supreme being we call God. To move beyond this designer to God, the physico-theological argument needs the cosmological argument, which attempts to show that there is a supreme being that is responsible for the causal network in which things like human eyes are generated. The cosmological argument, however, is also weak inasmuch as the most it can do is bring a person to the alternative that there is either a supreme being responsible for the experienced world with its manifold network of causes, or there is an infinite regress of causes without a supreme being. What the cosmological argument does is lead a person to the idea of a supreme being without demonstrating that there is a referent in reality corresponding to that concept. Thus, the argument needs the ontological argument, which attempts to generate just such a demonstration. The ontological proof, however, is fatally flawed in that no scrutiny of a concept will ever demonstrate that there is, in fact, a referent in reality corresponding to that concept.

Kant himself went on to argue that reason allowed him to postulate the existence of God on the grounds that taking seriously the moral life with its requirement that he perform perfectly his duty without qualification meant that he needed to postulate: (1) a life after death where he would have sufficient opportunity to achieve the moral goal reason set before him, and (2) a supreme being who would insure that those who reach the moral goal are also those that are happy. Kant's so-called moral argument for the existence of God is *not* offered by Kant as a *proof.* A proof would claim that reason *requires* one to believe in the existence of God. Kant rejected all such proofs. Instead, he proposed that reason *allows* one to believe in the existence of God if one takes the moral life seriously.

NOTE ON SOURCES.   The material in this section is from Thomas Aquinas, *Summa Theologica,* trans. Laurence Shapcote, Part 1, Question 2, Article III.

---

2   BLAISE PASCAL
Belief Without Proofs

FROM THOMAS TO PASCAL.   Living in the thirteenth century, Thomas Aquinas wrote in an age of Christian faith. His trust in reason to infer knowledge of God from knowledge of nature was a trust shared by most of his contemporaries and readers. By the time Pascal wrote in the seventeenth century, the Renaissance and Reformation had shaken the accepted beliefs of Thomas's age. In the previous century, Pascal's fellow Frenchman, Michel De Montaigne (1533–1592) penned his *Essais,* which revived the ancient arguments for skepticism, declaring that human reason by itself is unable to attain absolute truth, and rejecting claims of human superiority over the beasts of the field as vain and hollow pretensions. Montaigne encapsulated his skepticism in the motto, "What do I know?" Pascal's seventeenth-century French contemporary, René Descartes (whom we encountered in Chapter 2), was deeply troubled by such skepticism and formulated a philosophical method that would use doubt to conquer doubt. Descartes' method generated for him proofs concerning his own existence as well as the existence of God. Whereas Thomas Aquinas had inferred God's existence from certain facts in nature, Descartes inferred God's existence from certain facts about the self. Pascal found neither approach convincing. For him, reason is unable to prove the existence of God. That does not mean, however, that reason is completely incompetent in the debate the believer has with the nonbeliever. Indeed, Pascal's great ambition was to prepare an intellectual vindication of Christianity that would lead nonbelievers to the threshold of faith. Death prevented Pascal from completing that task. What remains of his effort is a group of several hundred notes and aphorisms gathered together and published after his death under the title *Pensées,* or "Thoughts." The selections in this section come from his *Pensées.*

BIOGRAPHICAL NOTE.   Pascal was born in 1623 and died in 1662 at the age of thirty-nine. He was educated at home. His parents, especially his father, were devout Catholics, pious but stern. Blaise early displayed a remarkable precocity in physics and mathematics; at the age of fifteen he was producing monographs on conic sections that were thought important enough to be read by "the most learned and scientific men in Paris." He was considered one of the outstanding physicists and mathematicians of his time. His discoveries were made during the years when most scientists are still mastering the known facts of their field.

The elder Pascal died in 1650, leaving a patrimony to Blaise and his sister Jacqueline. Jacqueline entered a convent; Blaise went off to Paris. During the next four years he lived among scholars, scientists, wits, and the nobility. On November 23, 1654, he had what is termed a mystical experience. That he had this experience, there is no reason to doubt; that it meant what he interpreted it to mean is perhaps open to debate.

That hour, described for posterity in a note found sewn into the coat he was wearing at the time of his death, wrought a change in Pascal's life. Austerity, self-denial, almsgiving, and obedience to his spiritual director replaced his routine of scientist and man-about-town. He threw himself into the defense of the Cistercian abbey of Port Royal des Champs, which was being persecuted by the hierarchy for a number of real or supposed heresies. The case for the Port Royalists was stated by Pascal in his celebrated *Letters to a Provincial.* The closing years of his life were given to planning and sketching in his *Pensées.*

THE ARGUMENT FROM THE PASSAGES.   We do not know how Pascal would have marshalled his thoughts into a vindication of Christianity. What he left us is, so to speak, a box of several hundred note cards of his research, which we must try to organize into a coherent whole. Accordingly, the passages we have selected and the order in which we present them involves considerable interpretation on our part. We do not attempt to reconstruct the argument of his entire book. We limit our attention to his discussion as it relates to the question of proving the existence of God.

At the outset Pascal surveys humankind on the issue of belief in God and comes up with three classes of people.

> Before entering the proofs of the Christian religion, I find it necessary to set forth the unfairness of men who are indifferent to the search for truth in a matter which is so important to them and which touches them so nearly. Among all their errors, this most proves them to be fools and blind.
>
> We know well enough how men of this temper behave. They believe they have made a great effort after their instruction when they have spent a few hours reading some book of Scripture and putting a few questions to some ecclesiastic. Whereupon they boast that they have "in vain consulted books and men." Such carelessness is intolerable.
>
> Among unbelievers I make a vast distinction. I can have nothing but compassion for all who sincerely lament their doubt, who look upon it as the worst of evils, who spare no pains to escape it, who make these matters their chief and most serious occupation. But those who pass their lives without thinking of this ultimate end of existence, who neglect to examine whether these are matters which people receive through credulous simplicity or have a solid and impregnable basis, such persons I regard in a wholly different manner. Their negligence irritates me much more than it excites my pity. It astonishes and overwhelms me; it is for me something monstrous.
>
> There are but three classes of persons: those who have found God and serve Him; those who have not found God, but do diligently seek Him; and those who have not

found God, and live without seeking Him. The first are happy and wise. The second are unhappy, but wise. The third are unhappy and fools.

It is a sorry evil to be in doubt. It is an indispensable duty to seek when we are in doubt. Therefore he who doubts and neglects to seek to dispel these doubts, is at once in a sorry plight and guilty of great perversity. If he is calm and contented in his doubt, if he frankly avows it, if he boasts of it, if he makes it the subject of vanity and delight, I can find no terms with which to describe him.

How do men come by these sentiments? What delight is there in such things? What is there to be proud of in beholding ourselves in the midst of impenetrable darkness? How can any rational man reason in this way: "I know not who has put me in the world, nor what the world is, nor what I am myself. I am in terrible ignorance of all these things. I view the awful spaces of the universe that surround me, I find myself fixed to a corner of this vast extent, I see nothing but infinites on every side enclosing me like an atom. All that I know is that I must soon die. Such is my state—full of misery, weakness, obscurity. And from this I conclude that I ought to pass all the days of my life without thinking of what is to happen to me hereafter. It may be that I could find some answers to my doubts; but I am unwilling to take the trouble."

Who would desire to have for a friend a man who discourses in such a fashion? Who would select such a person to be the confidant of his affairs? Who would have recourse to such a one in his afflictions? In fine, for what use in life could such a man be destined? It is the glory of religion to have such irrational men for its enemies. Such strange insensibility for the greatest things is something monstrous. It is an incomprehensible delusion.

There must be a strange revulsion in the nature of man, to make him glory in such a state. Most of those who are thus involved are people who have heard that fine worldly manners consist in what they call "throwing off the yoke." This they try to imitate. But, what good does it do us to hear a man say that he has "thrown off the yoke," that he does not believe there is a God, that he is answerable in his conduct to none but himself? Is this a thing to be said gaily? On the contrary, is it not a thing to be said with sadness, as of all things the saddest? It requires all the love of the religion which they despise, not to despise such persons and abandon them in their folly.

Pascal is not prepared to abandon these unbelievers in their folly. Remember his three classes of persons: first, the happy and wise who have sought God and found Him; second, the unhappy and wise who are seeking God but have not found Him; third, the unhappy fools who are not seeking God and have not found Him. Pascal will present arguments to move persons in the third group into the second group; that is, to convert the unhappy fools into being seekers after God who have not yet found him. Then he will offer some suggestions as to how persons in the second group can move into the first group. Let us consider now his strategy for encouraging persons in group three to become members of group two.

First, he declares that the proofs for the existence of God offered by thinkers like Anselm, Aquinas, and Descartes will not dislodge people from their doubts or callous indifference concerning the existence of God.

I wonder at the boldness of those who undertake to speak of God to the irreligious. Their first chapter is to prove the existence of God by reference to the works of nature. I should not be astonished if they addressed their argument to those who already believe; for those who have a lively faith in their heart see at once that all that exists is none other than the handiwork of God. But for those who are destitute of faith—to tell them that they need only look at nature around them in order to see God unveiled, to give them the course of the sun and the moon as the sole proof of this important matter, to imagine with such an argument we have proved anything, is only to give grounds for believing that the proofs of our religion are very feeble. Indeed, I see by reason and experience that nothing is more fitted to excite contempt.

This is what I see, and what troubles me. I look on all sides, and see nothing but obscurity; nature offers me nothing but matter for doubt. If I saw nothing in nature which marked a Divinity, I should decide not to believe in Him. If I saw everywhere the marks of a Creator, I should rest peacefully in faith. But I see too much to deny, and to little to affirm; so my state is pitiful. A hundred times I have wished that God would mark His presence in nature unequivocally, if He upholds nature; or that nature would wholly suppress the signs which she gives of God, if those signs are fallacious; that she would either say all or say nothing, so I might see what part I should take. While in my present state, ignorant of what I am and of what I ought to do, I know neither my condition nor my duty.

The metaphysical proofs of God are so far apart from man's reason, and so complicated, that they are but little striking. If they are of use to any, it is only during the moment that the demonstration is before them. An hour afterwards they fear they have been mistaken. Therefore I do not here undertake to prove by natural reason the existence of God. I do not feel myself strong enough to find in nature proofs to convince hardened atheists. All who seek God in nature find no light to satisfy them. They fall either into atheism or into deism, two things which the Christian religion almost equally abhors.

Second, Pascal uncovers the uneasiness of the human being poised between the infinitely large and the infinitely small. The spatiotemporal universe displays the infinitely large.

Let a man contemplate nature in her full majesty. Let him extend his view beyond the objects which surround him. Let him regard the sun. Let him consider the earth whereon he lives as a point in comparison with the vast orbit described by the sun. Let him learn that his vast orbit is but a point compared with that embraced by the stars which roll in the firmament. Let his imagination pass beyond. All this visible cosmos is but a point in the ample bosom of nature. In vain we extend our conceptions beyond imaginable spaces: We bring forth but atoms in comparison with the reality of things. For the universe is an infinite sphere whose center is everywhere and whose circumference is nowhere.

From the vastness of things, he passes to the other extreme. Compared to the whole of nature, man may be a mere speck. But compared to the infinitely small particles that compose the material world, he is a colossus.

There is another aspect, equally astonishing. Let a man seek things the most minute. Let him consider a mite, in the exceeding smallness of its body; parts incomparably smaller, limbs with joints, veins in those limbs, blood in those veins, humors in this blood, globules in these humors, gases in the globules. Let him divide these globules. Let him exhaust his powers of conception. He will think perhaps that he has arrived at the minutest atoms of nature. I will show him therein a new abyss. I will picture to him the inconceivable immensity of nature in the compass of this abbreviation of an atom. Let him view therein an infinity of worlds, each with its own firmament, its planets, its earth, in the same proportion as the visible world. Let him lose himself in these wonders, as astonishing in their littleness as the others in their magnitude. His body which just before was imperceptible in the universe, is now a colossus in comparison with the infinitely small at which it is possible to arrive.

With this contrast in mind, Pascal pauses to ask: What is man, amid all this? He could have used the words of the Psalmist, "What is man that Thou art mindful of him?" But at this point, that would be begging the question: it is that "Thou" that is in question.

What is man, in the midst of these two infinities? A nothing compared with the infinitely large, all compared with the infinitely small. A mean between all and nothing, infinitely far from comprehending the extremes. Let us, then, know our range. Such is our true state. This is what renders us incapable, alike of absolute knowledge and absolute ignorance.

Nature confounds the skeptics and reason confounds the dogmatists. What will become of you, O man, who would search out your true condition by your natural reason? You can avoid neither skepticism nor dogmatism; but, alas, you can live with neither!

Our intelligence holds the same position as our body, in the vast extent of nature. This middle state between two extremes is common to all our weaknesses: our senses can perceive no extreme; too much noise deafens us, too much light blinds us, too far or too near interferes with our vision, too much brevity or too much prolixity obscures our understanding, too much truth overwhelms us, too much pleasure cloys on us, too many benefits annoy us, we feel neither extreme heat nor extreme cold, too much and too little teaching hinder our minds—in a word, all extremes are for us as though they were not. They escape us or we escape them.

Man is a creature full of natural error. Nothing shows him the truth, everything deceives him. His reason and his senses deceive each other. These senses trick the reason by false appearances; reason in turn avenges herself and deceives the senses. His emotions trouble his senses and make false impressions on him. Reason, senses, emotions, lie and deceive, outdoing each other.

What a chimera is man! Strange and monstrous! A chaos, a contradiction, a prodigy. Judge of all things, yet a weak earthworm. Depository of truth, yet a cesspool of uncertainty and error; the glory and the scraping of the universe.

Who will unravel such a tangle? Is it beyond the power of dogmatism, of skepticism, of philosophy. Man is incomprehensible by man. We grant that to the skeptics. Truth is not within our reach, nor to our taste; her home is not on earth.

We sail on a vast expanse of being, ever uncertain, ever drifting, ever hurried from one goal to another. If we seek to attach ourselves to any one point, it totters and fails us; if we follow, it eludes our grasp, vanishing forever. Nothing stays for us. This is our natural condition. Yet, it is the condition most contrary to our inclination; for we burn with desire to find a steadfast place and a fixed basis whereupon we may build. But our whole foundation breaks up, and the abysses open before us.

When I consider the short duration of my life, swallowed up in an eternity before and after, the small space I fill engulfed in the infinite immensity of spaces whereof I know nothing and which know nothing of me, I am terrified. The eternal silence of these infinite spaces alarms me. I wonder why I am here, rather than there, now rather than then. Who has set me here? By whose order and design have this place and time been destined for me?

When I see the blindness and misery of man; when I survey the whole dumb universe; when I see man left to himself without a light unto his path, lost in this corner of the cosmos, ignorant of who placed him here, of what he has come here to do, of what will overtake him when he dies, I fall into terror. And my terror is like that of a man who should awake upon a terrible desert island with no means of escape. And I wonder why men do not fall into despair. I see others around me, of like nature. I ask if they are better informed than I am; and they say they are not.

We may not, then, look for certainty or stability. Our reason is always deceived by changing shows. It matters not that man should have a trifle more knowledge of the universe; if he has it, he but begins a little higher; but he is always infinitely distant from the end. In regard to the infinities, all finites are equal, and I see no reason why we should fix our imagination on one more than on another.

Who would not think, when we declare that man consists of mind and matter, that we really understood this combination? Yet—it is the one thing we least understand. Nothing is more obscure than just this mixture of spirit and clay. Man is, to himself, the most marvelous object in nature, for he cannot conceive what matter is, nor what mind is, nor how a material body should be united to an immaterial mind. This is the crown of all his difficulties, yet it is his very being.

These are some of the causes which render man so totally unable to know nature. For nature has a twofold infinity, while he is finite. Nature is permanent, while he is fleeting and mortal. All things change and fail; he sees them only as they pass. All things have their beginning and their end; he sees neither the one nor the other. Things are simple and homogenous. He is complex and composed of two different elements.

Not from space must I see my dignity. I should have no more if I possessed whole worlds. By space the universe encompasses and swallows me as an atom. Man is but a reed, weakest in nature, but a reed which thinks. A thinking reed. It needs not that the whole universe should arm to crush him. A vapor, a drop of water is enough to kill him. But were the universe to kill him, man would still be more noble than that which has slain him, because he knows that he dies, and that the universe has the better of him. The universe knows nothing of this.

Know then, proud Man, how great a paradox thou art to thyself. Bow down thyself, impotent reason; be silent, thou foolish human nature. Learn that man is altogether incomprehensible by man.

Let man now estimate his value. Let him love himself, because he has a nature capable of good. But let him not love the vileness which exists in that nature. He has in himself the capacity of knowledge and happiness, yet he finds no last truth or satisfaction. I would lead him to desire it; to be freed from passions, to know how his passions obscure his knowledge and his achievement of happiness. I would have him hate in himself the desires which bias his judgment, that they might neither blind him in choosing nor obstruct him when he has chosen.

The net result is that man and woman are ignorant and helpless and alone. The blind forces of nature offer them no haven. The universe at large cares as little for their living as for their dying. Pascal might have let it go at that. Many have; for example, Schopenhauer and Thomas Hardy and Bertrand Russell. Not so Pascal. He presses the discussion further.

The *third* fact of his strategy is to remind the human being who experiences the uneasiness of being confronted by an alien, indifferent, even hostile universe that nothing less than the conquest of true happiness is at stake.

> All men seek happiness. To this there is no exception. Our will makes no step, except toward this object. This is the motive of every action of every man. And yet, after so many years no one has arrived, without faith, at the point to which all eyes are turned. All complain, rulers and ruled, nobles and commons, old and young, strong and weak, learned and ignorant, sound and sick, of all countries, all times, all ages, and all conditions.
>
> A trial so long, so constant, so uniform, should have convinced us of our inability to arrive at our complete happiness by our own strength. But example teaches us little. We expect that our efforts will not be foiled on this occasion, as before. Thus while the present never satisfies us, experience never teaches us; and from misfortune to misfortune we are led on to death, the eternal crown of our sorrows.
>
> This desire, and this weakness, cry aloud to us that there is an empty space in man which he seeks vainly to fill from all that surrounds him, seeks vainly to find in things absent the happiness which he finds not in things present.

The *fourth* move made by Pascal is to suggest that the happiness all humans seek but so seldom find is to be found only in God. Pascal's strategy is in fact an autobiographical rehearsal of his own spiritual pilgrimage. He had experienced a great thirst for peace of mind, for happiness of soul. He had tried to find that tranquility and joy through the escapades of high society, the certainties of mathematics, the new insights of the physical sciences, and the inherited wisdom of traditional philosophy. He ended up empty-handed: happiness eluded his grasp. Then came his dark night of the soul when in desperation he cast himself upon God. The mystic experience of God that ensued convinced Pascal that the joy he sought could be found only in God. His thought echoes the confession of Saint Augustine (354–430 A.D.): "Our hearts are restless until they rest in Thee."

> Man finds his happiness only in God. Without Him, there is nothing in nature which will take His place; neither the stars, nor heaven, nor earth, nor the elements; not plants, cabbages, animals, insects, calves, serpents, fever, pestilence, war, famine, vices, adultery, incest. Since man has lost track of his true happiness, all things appear equally good to him, even his own destruction, though so contrary to God, to right reason, and to the whole course of nature.
>
> There is no good without knowledge of God. Only as we approach Him are we happy; and our ultimate good is to know Him certainly. We are unhappy, in proportion as we are removed from Him; and the greatest evil would be the certainty of being cut off from Him.

The *fifth* and final feature of his strategy for encouraging people to move out of group three into group two is his famous religious wager. Let us recapitulate his strategy thus far. He has rejected the traditional proofs for the existence of God: Renaissance skepticism, personified in Montaigne, has eroded those. He has displayed the utter loneliness and littleness of the human poised between the two infinites. Must not the most resolute nonbelievers agree with that? He has argued that the happiness we all seek is seldom found through attachment to things of this world. Must not the most resolute nonbeliever in moments of utter honesty also agree with that? But how can Pascal move the nonbeliever who experiences a frustrated quest for happiness to redirect his or her quest toward God? That is the task of his wager.

> If there be a God, He is infinitely incomprehensible, since having neither parts nor limits, He has no relation to us. We are, then, incapable of knowing either that He is or what He is.
>
> Let us examine this point: "Either God is, or is not," we can say. But to which side shall we incline? Reason cannot help us. There is an infinite gulf fixed between creature and creator. What will you wager? It is like a game in which heads or tails may turn up. There is no reason for backing either the one possibility or the other. You cannot reasonably argue in favor of either.
>
> If you know nothing either way, it might be urged, the true course is not to wager at all. But you must wager; that does not depend on your will. You are embarked in this business. Which will you choose?
>
> Let us see. Since you must choose, your reason is no more affronted in choosing one way than the other. That point is clear. But what of your happiness? Let us weigh the gain and the loss in wagering that God does exist. If you wager that He does, and He does, you gain all; if you wager that He does, and He does not, you lose nothing. If you win, you take all; if you lose, you lose nothing. This is demonstrable, and if men are capable of any truths, this is one. Wager then, unhesitatingly, that He does exist.
>
> If we ought to do nothing except on a certainty, we ought to do nothing for religion, because it is not a matter of certainty. But it is false to say, "We ought to do nothing except on a certainty." In a voyage at sea, in a battle, we act on uncertainties. If it be the case that we ought to do nothing except on a certainty, then we ought to do nothing at all, for nothing is certain.

Pascal is counting on the prudential calculations of the nonbeliever. There is an infinity of happiness at stake if God exists. Surely it is wiser to wager that He exists, than to wager He doesn't exist. When the nonbeliever takes the gamble of wagering that God exists (with the hoped-for pay-off being an eternal life of happiness in God's presence), has not the nonbeliever moved into group two? But making a wager that God exists is not the same thing as living a life of faith, hope and love in the presence of the Living God. Making a wager is not the same thing as faith. Pascal is too alert to make that mistake, and to let the matter rest with the wager. The issue that now arises is how to move people from group two into group one. Pascal offers a provocative response.

> You may object: "My hands are tied, my mouth is gagged. I am forced to wager, I am not free. But, despite this, I am so made that I cannot believe. What then would you have me do?"
>
> I would have you understand your incapacity to believe. Labor to convince yourself, not by more "proofs" of God's existence, but by disciplining your passions and wayward emotions. You would arrive at faith, but know not the way. You would heal yourself of unbelief, yet know not the remedies. I answer: Learn of those who have been bound

as you are. These are they who know the way you would follow, who have been cured of a disease you would be cured of. Follow the way by which they began, by making believe what they believe. Thus you will come to believe.

Now, what will happen to you if you take this side in the religious wager? You will be trustworthy, honorable, humble, grateful, generous, friendly, sincere, and true. You will no longer have those poisoned pleasures, glory and luxury; but you will have other pleasures. I tell you that you will gain this life; at each step you will see so much certainty of gain, so much nothingness in what you stake, that you will know at last that you have wagered on a certainty, an infinity, for which you have risked nothing.

If my words please you, and seem to you cogent, know that they are the words of one who has thrown himself on his knees before and after to pray to that infinite Being to whom he submits all; know too that you also would submit to Him your all for your own good and His glory, and that this strength may be in accord with this weakness.

Is Pascal urging those who are seeking God but cannot find Him to act as if they were already believers? Is he saying that genuine belief would soon appear? Is he suggesting that if you practice the appropriate moral virtues, you will in due course find the God you are seeking, in whose presence abiding happiness is to be found?

Pascal's position, then, on natural theology is clear. According to him, you cannot use what you know about nature to prove the existence of God. Yet you can use what you know about nature and human nature to show a need for God as the solution to the human being's unfulfilled quest for abiding happiness. But, careful thinker that he is, Pascal knows that there is a gap between the fact of our need for God and God's inferred existence to fill that need. Accordingly, he recognizes that the most his arguments can do is to bring a person to the threshold of faith. The wager and what follows it are matters settled in personal decision and action, not in philosophical debate and proof.

NOTE ON SOURCES.   The Pascal material in this section is quoted, abridged, or paraphrased from Blaise Pascal, *Thoughts*. That book consists of 923 numbered items. The following items have been used in this chapter: Numbers 194, 195, 205, 206, 229, 233, 347, 348, 434, 437—and a few here and there among the remaining items.

---

3   DAVID HUME
Doubts About Natural Theology

FROM PASCAL TO HUME.   The problem of natural theology continued to command attention. We have seen repudiation by Pascal; a repudiation, however, that left no bitter taste in the devout reader's mouth, since Pascal strove earnestly to restore with one hand what he swept aside with the other. By the middle of the eighteenth century times and tempers had changed. The "Age of Reason" had set in. The French Revolution was drawing nearer. The natural sciences, from their small beginnings with Galileo and Bacon and Harvey in the seventeenth century, had come to exercise considerable dominion over the imaginations of the intellectual classes. It was in this somewhat more chilly climate of opinion that David Hume turned his critical attention to natural theology.

BIOGRAPHICAL NOTE.   Hume was born in Scotland in 1711 and died in 1776 at the age of sixty-five. Although he was destined, along with Immanuel Kant, to mark the opening of a chapter in the history of philosophy that is still unclosed, his early life was passed in obscurity, and his fame, among his contemporaries, was based principally upon his writings in the field of political history.

He was intended by his father for the law, and to that end was educated in Edinburgh. However, he abandoned the study of law and tried his hand in a Bristol counting-house. This, too, proved uncongenial. He went to France, where he proceeded to write one of the epoch-making books in modern philosophy, his *Treatise of Human Nature*. The theme of this philosophical masterpiece is simply stated in the form of a question: How much of human knowledge, human emotional preferences and aversions, human mortality, is what it is for no better reason than the fact that human nature is what it is? The suggestion, that once you have taken the "human" out of these things there is nothing left over, was too much for his generation to entertain. It contained too many skeptical implications. The *Treatise* fell, as though stillborn, from the press.

Hume now set about to find employment that would put him in a position of independence. He applied, without success, for the chair of moral philosophy in the University of Edinburgh. For two years he tutored an almost insane Scottish marquis. He accompanied a diplomatic expedition to France. He applied, again without success, for the chair of logic at the University of Glasgow. At last he secured the position of Keeper of the Advocates' Library in Edinburgh. The access to books and original authorities that this gave him suggested the idea of writing a work of history. This he proceeded to do and, between 1754 and 1762, produced his famous *History of England,* which ranked, in that century, with Gibbon's *Decline and Fall of the Roman Empire.*

In the lean years before he became Keeper and turned historian, Hume continued reworking and expanding the ideas of his original philosophical treatise. These were published in a series of short monographs and collections of essays. In this form they gained a gradual acceptance. But it was still the historian who overshadowed the philosopher in the minds of his generation. He retired in 1769, on a combined income and pension of £1,000 a year. He spent the remainder of his days, the recognized head of the intellectual and literary society in Edinburgh, admired by those who read his *History* and his miscellaneous essays, distrusted or misunderstood by those who tried their hand at his philosophy.

THE ARGUMENT OF THE PASSAGES.   The selections that follow provide a skeptical examination of natural theology. They are, for the most part, from Hume's essay "On Miracles" and from *Dialogues Concerning Natural Religion.* They presuppose, as a starting point, that the reader is familiar with the stock arguments for the existence of God.

The position finally occupied by Hume is somewhat complex. We may imagine him saying:

> If we possess, or claim to possess, knowledge of God's existence and nature, then it must rest on some sort of evidence. What is this evidence? It is formulated, usually, in three "arguments." There is the argument from miracles, the argument from design, and the argument from first cause. A skeptical examination of the claims of natural theology will include a skeptical examination of these three arguments. We shall advance two lines of criticism with respect to each: first, that the argument itself is unsound;

second, that even if it were accepted without question, it does not prove what it claims to prove.

It is well to remember the limitations of the task that Hume sets himself. He is not attempting to prove that God does not exist; that is, he is not stating the case for atheism. Nor is he seeking to discredit all belief in God. His claim is the more modest one, namely, that such belief, whether true or false, is not susceptible to the traditional argumentative justification; that no "appeal to reason" can be made in support of the claims of natural theology.

Belief in God has, in time past, been supported by what is called the *argument from miracles*. It is to this effect: Miracles, violations of natural laws, occur from time to time. An explanation of such events must therefore refer to something outside or beyond nature. That is, miracles point to a miracle worker, namely, God. Hence Hume's interest in the question of miracles. His approach is indirect. He does not deny that miracles ever happen. He directs attention to the nature of the evidence upon which we believe that miracles happen and claims that the evidence in question is not strong enough to support the belief.

> I flatter myself I have discovered an argument which will be an everlasting check to all kinds of superstitious delusion, all accounts of miracles and prodigies sacred and profane.
>
> A miracle is a violation of the laws of nature. Now, as a firm and unalterable experience has established our belief in those laws, the proof against miracles, from the very nature of the case, is as entire as any argument from experience can possibly be imagined. There must be a uniform experience against any miracle; otherwise it would not be so described. Now, as a uniform experience amounts to a proof, there is here a full proof against the occurrence of any miracle. Nor can such a proof against any miracle be weakened or destroyed, except by an opposite proof which would be superior to it.
>
> The plain consequence is this: No testimony is sufficient to establish a miracle unless the testimony be of such a kind that its falsehood would be as miraculous as, or more miraculous than, the fact which it endeavors to establish. Even in that case there is a mutual destruction of arguments; and the superior only gives us an assurance suitable to that degree of evidential force which remains after deducting the inferior.
>
> A man tells me he saw one dead restored to life. I ask myself: Is it more probable that he should deceive or be deceived, or that the fact which he relates should really have happened? I weigh one miracle against the other, and reject the greater. If the falsehood of his testimony would be more miraculous than the event which he relates, then (but not until then) can he command my belief.

There are two parts to Hume's criticism of the evidence for believing that miracles happen. The first, and most incisive, has been given already: Miracles purport to be violations of the laws of nature. Our evidence for believing in the uniformity of nature is so great that no evidence for doubting it could be strong enough, since it would have to be stronger than the evidence for believing in nature's uniformity and this latter includes practically all our experience. He moves on to a second criticism:

> We have supposed in the foregoing that the evidence for a miracle may be so strong that its falsehood would itself be a miracle. But it is easy to show that we have been

a great deal too liberal in our concessions, and that no miracle has ever been established on so full an evidence.

First: There is not to be found in all history any miracle attested by a sufficient number of men of such unquestioned good sense, education, and learning, as to secure us against all delusion in themselves; of such undoubted integrity as to place them beyond all suspicion of any design to deceive others; of such credit and reputation as to have a great deal to lose in case of being detected in any falsehood; and, at the same time, attesting facts in such a manner and in so celebrated a place as to render that detection unavoidable.

Second: The many instances of mistaken or fraudulent miracles which have been detected show that mankind have a strong propensity to believe in the extraordinary and marvelous. This fact ought reasonably to beget a suspicion against all narratives concerning such matters.

Third: Reports of miracles abound chiefly among ignorant and barbarous peoples; or if such reports have been admitted by civilized and educated peoples they will be found to have received them from ignorant and barbarous peoples who transmitted them with that sanction and authority which, among such peoples, attends received opinions. This fact constitutes a strong presumption against all accounts of miracles.

Fourth: There is no *a priori* case in favor of the miracles peculiar to any one religion. The miracles of all religions stand on the same footing. If any such should be mutually incompatible, they simply cancel each other out. Nor is there any *a priori* case in favor of religious over secular miracles.

Fifth: The records of miracles in ancient times are not to be placed on an equal level with the records of nonmiraculous events in ancient times. Because some human testimony has the utmost force and authority in some cases, as when it relates to the battle of Philippi or Pharsalia, the assassination of Caesar or the execution of Socrates, it is not therefore reasonable that all kinds of testimony must, in all cases, have equal force and authority.

It appears, then, that no testimony for any kind of miracle has ever amounted to a probability, much less a proof. Experience only gives authority to human testimony, and it is experience which assures us of the laws of nature. When, therefore, these two kinds of experiences are contrary, we can only subtract the one from the other and embrace the opinion with that assurance which arises from the remainder. But, according to the measures of probability above established, this subtraction amounts to entire annihilation. Therefore no human testimony can have such force as to prove a miracle and make it a just foundation for any system of religion.

Mere reason is not sufficient to convince us of the miracles of the Christian religion. Whoever is moved by faith to assent to it, is conscious of a continued miracle in his own person, which subverts all the principles of his understanding and gives him a determination to believe what is most contrary to custom and experience.

The net result thus far: Belief in miracles rests on questionable grounds. Belief in God, therefore, insofar as it rests on belief in miracles, rests on questionable grounds. Hume's case against the argument from miracles ends at that point. He might have rounded out his argument with greater force. This was done by T. H. Huxley, Hume's biographer, in the next century. Huxley's argument proceeded along this line: Suppose the evidence for believing in miracles is left unquestioned. Suppose we admit without argument that miracles do take place. What follows? Belief in the Deity described by orthodox Christian theology? It would seem not. For miracles are an equivocal kind of evidence. They point frequently to a Deity who befriends some people at the expense of others. Consider, for example, the Old Testament miracle of the taking of Jericho. What kind of evidence would this be, in the eyes of a citizen of Jericho? Or consider the miracle of the Gadarene swine recorded in the New Testament. What kind of evidence would this be, in the eyes of the unfortunate individual who owned those swine, or (to stretch a point) in the eyes of the still more unfortunate swine? These, and similar miracles, are equivocal testimony to the Deity's universal benevolence. Moreover, if miracles are evidence of His benevolence, why do they fail to occur in so many cases where benevolence would seem to be in order, for example, when a vessel is sinking in a storm at sea? The point does not need elaboration: miracles, even if not disputed, do not provide us with decisive evidence one way or the other about God. And, when evidence is ambiguous, it is wiser to omit it.

Hume proceeds, in his examination of natural theology, to a statement and refutation of the *argument from design*. This is one of his most famous pieces of destructive criticism. Hume presents the design argument as follows:

> The chief argument for divine existence is derived from the order of nature. Where there appear marks of intelligence and design, you think it extravagant to assign for its cause either chance or the blind unguided force of matter. This is an argument from effects to causes. From the order of the work you infer there must have been project and forethought in the workman.
>
> Look around the world. Contemplate the whole and every part of it. You will find it to be nothing but one great machine, subdivided into an infinite number of lesser machines, which again admit of subdivisions to a degree beyond what human sense can trace and explain.
>
> All these various machines, and even their most minute parts, are adjusted to each other with an accuracy which ravishes into admiration all men who have ever contemplated them. The curious adapting of means to ends, throughout all nature, resembles exactly, though it much exceeds, the productions of human contrivance, human design, human thought, wisdom, and intelligence.
>
> Anatomize the eye. Survey its structure and contrivance. Does not the idea of contriver immediately flow in upon you with the force like that of a sensation? Behold the male and female of each species, their instincts, their passions, the whole course of their life before and after generation. Millions of such instances present themselves through every part of the universe. Can language convey a more intelligible, more irresistible meaning than the curious adjustment of means to ends in nature?
>
> Since the effects (natural productions and human productions) resemble each other, you are led to infer, by analogy, that the causes also resemble; that the author of nature is somewhat similar to the mind of man, though possessed of larger powers, proportioned to the grandeur of the work He has created.
>
> You compare the universe to productions of human intelligence, to houses, ships, furniture, machines, and so forth. Since both terms of the comparison exhibit adaptation and design, you argue that the cause of the one must resemble the cause of the other.

The argument from design, he says, is an argument from analogy: We examine a watch, a house, or a ship, and we conclude that such things were produced by beings possessing intelligence and controlled by purposes. We can, if we wish, verify this inference by acquainting ourselves with watchmakers, architects, and shipwrights. We examine the universe, or parts of it, and conclude that it too must have been produced by a being possessing intelligence and controlled by purposes. Our reason for drawing this inference is that we find the universe, or parts of it, intelligible and answering to our needs and purposes. That is, we draw the analogy watch-watchmaker and universe-Deity. From the intelligibility and utility of a watch, we infer intelligence and purposiveness in the watchmaker. By analogy, from the intelligibility and utility of nature we infer intelligence and purposiveness in the author of nature. Hume's first line of attack is to question whether the principle of causal analogy is really applicable to the universe.

> When two things (human intelligence and the products of human intelligence) have been observed to be conjoined, you can infer, by custom, from the one to the other. This I call an *argument from experience.* But how this argument can have place in the present case, may be difficult to explain. If you see a house, you can conclude it had an architect or builder because such effects, you have experienced, proceed from such causes.
>
> But does the universe resemble a house so closely that we can with the same certainty infer a similar cause? Is the analogy entire and perfect? Can you pretend here to more than a guess, a conjecture, a presumption, concerning a similar case? To ascertain such reasoning, it were necessary that you have had experience in the origin of the world. Have worlds ever been formed under your eye? Have you experienced the generation of the universe as you have experienced the building of a house?

Suppose we see a column of smoke in the distance. By the principle of causal analogy we would infer that there was some sort of fire in the distance that was the cause of the smoke. We have confidence in the accuracy of such a conclusion because we have seen fires producing smoke in the past. When the principle of causal analogy is applied to a situation, the legitimacy of that application depends on our having experienced similar situations in the past. We can readily argue, for example, that this specific house had an architect or builder because we have encountered houses in the past that have had architects or builders. When it comes to the universe, however, we have no past experience of universes having been designed by an intelligent being on the basis of which we can say, by the principle of, causal analogy, that this, our universe, was also designed by an intelligent being. Accordingly, the principle of causal analogy is not really applicable to the universe because we have no past experience of other universes from which we can argue analogically. Suppose, however, that we allow the proponents of the design argument to use the principle of causal analogy (even though its use is unwarranted); the next question Hume would ask is, "Why should one settle on the design-designer analogy? Are not other analogies equally possible?"

> You have argued, thus far, on the principle that like effects have like causes. But there is another you might try, based no less on experience: Where several known parts are observed to be similar, the unknown parts will also be found similar. Thus, if you see the limbs of a human body, you conclude that it is attended with a human head, though hid from you. If you see a small part of the sun, through a chink in the wall, you conclude that, were the wall removed, you should see the rest. Within the limits of experience, this method of reasoning is obvious and reliable.
>
> Now I say, if you survey the universe, so far as it falls under your knowledge, it bears a great resemblance to an animal, or organized body, and seems actuated by a like

principle of life and motion. A continual circulation of matter produces no disorder. A continual waste in every part is incessantly repaired. Each part, in performing its proper offices, operates both to its own preservation and that of the whole. From all this, why not infer that the world is an organism, an animal, and that Deity is the soul of the world, actuating it and being actuated by it?

If it be legitimate to argue thus by analogy from part to whole, I affirm that other parts of the world bear a greater resemblance to the structure of the world than do matters of human invention; and, therefore, should afford a better conjecture concerning the origin and nature of the whole. These parts are animals and vegetables. The world resembles more an organism than a clock or a knitting loom. Its cause, therefore, more probably resembles the cause of the former, namely generation.

As a tree sheds its seed into neighboring fields, so the great system of the world produces certain seeds which, being scattered into the surrounding chaos, grow into new worlds. A comet, for instance, may be taken as such a seed. After it has been fully ripened, by passing from sun to sun and star to star, it is at last tossed into the unformed elements which surround this universe, and sprouts into a new system.

Or, for variety (for I see no other advantage), suppose this world to be an animal instead of a vegetable. A comet then would be an egg. And, in like manner as an ostrich lays its egg in the sand, which without any further care hatches the egg, so. . . .

You protest: What wild, arbitrary suppositions are these? What data have I for such extraordinary conclusions? Is the slight resemblance of the world to a vegetable or animal sufficient basis for an argument as to further resemblances? You are right. This is what I have been insisting on, all along. We have no data, or insufficient data, for any such speculations. Our experience, from which alone we can argue safely, is so limited in extent and duration as to afford us no probable conjecture concerning the whole of things.

If you agree that our limited experience is an unequal standard by which to judge of the unlimited extent of nature, a too narrow stretch upon which to erect hypotheses concerning so vast a matter, you entirely abandon your case, and must admit of the absolute incomprehensibility of the author of nature.

If one allows the principle of causal analogy to apply to the universe, and if one, selects design-designer as the analogy by which to understand the origin and nature of the universe, then one would have to show why the analogies of an animal or a vegetable are to be rejected. That would be an especially difficult task in view of the fact that the case made for the design-designer analogy (like the animal and vegetable analogies) lacks adequate evidential support and is the product of mere conjecture. Suppose, however, that we allow the proponents of the design argument to reject the other analogies and to use the design-designer analogy (even though its use is unwarranted), the next question Hume would ask is, "Why do proponents of the design argument select only certain qualities of human designers and ascribe those to the divine designer? Why not ascribe to the deity the plurality, mistakes, imperfections, and perversity of human designers?"

By this argument from analogy, how prove the unity of Deity? Many men join in building a house or ship or city or commonwealth. Why may not several deities have combined in framing a world? This is only so much greater similarity to human affairs, to the operation of human intelligence. By dividing thus the work among several, you would get rid of that extensive power and knowledge which must be supposed in one deity.

Were one deity, who possessed every attribute necessary to the production of the universe, and not many deities, proved by this argument from analogy, it would be needless to suppose any other deity. But while it is still an open question whether all these attributes are united in one deity or dispersed among several independent deities, by what phenomena in nature can you pretend to decide the controversy? On this kind of argument from nature, polytheism and monotheism are on a like footing. Neither has any advantage over the other.

By this method of reasoning from analogy you renounce all claim to perfection in any of the attributes of the Deity. Imperfections in human productions you ascribe to imperfections in human producers. There are many inexplicable difficulties in the work of nature. Are you to ascribe these to the imperfections of the author of nature?

By representing Deity as so intelligible and comprehensible, so similar to a human mind, you make ourselves the model. Is this reasonable? The sentiments of the human mind include gratitude and resentment, love and hate, friendship and enmity, blame and approval, pity and scorn, admiration and envy. Do you propose to transfer such sentiments to a Supreme Being? Or suppose Him actuated by them? Do you propose to ascribe to Him only knowledge and power but no virtues?

Hume has raised some tough-minded objections to the argument from design. The bottom line of his objections is that even if we allow the principle of causal analogy to apply to the universe (which is unwarranted), and even if we allow the design-designer analogy to stand (which is also unwarranted), even then the argument does not establish that the designer of the universe is the single, supreme, intelligent, perfect being that proponents of the argument want. Hume, however, is not finished with this design argument. He has yet another powerful objection to register. The design argument seeks to say something about God on the basis of a scrutiny of his handiwork—nature. What, however, does a scrutiny of nature really reveal about its maker? Do not the suffering and evil in nature call into question the purported omnipotence and/or benevolence of God? Can one seriously maintain that imperfect nature, replete with pain and misery, is the work of a perfect being?

Can any man, by a simple denial, hope to bear down the united testimony of mankind? The whole earth is cursed and polluted. A perpetual war is kindled among all living creatures. Necessity, hunger, want, stimulate the strong and courageous; fear, anxiety, terror, agitate the weak and the infirm. The first entrance into life gives anguish to the newborn infant and to parent. Weakness, impotence, distress, attend each stage of many lives which are finished at last in agony and horror.

Is it not thus in nature? Observe the curious artifices of nature to embitter the life of living beings. The stronger prey upon the weaker, and keep them in perpetual terror and misery. The weaker, too, often prey upon the stronger. Consider those species of insects which are bred on the body of animals, or flying about, infix their stings into them. These insects have others, still more minute, which torment them. On every hand animals are surrounded with enemies which cause their misery and seek their destruction.

Why should man pretend to be exempted from the lot which befalls an other animals? Man is the greatest enemy of man. Oppression, injustice, contempt, slander, violence, sedition, war—by these men torment each other. The external ills of humanity, from the elements, from other animals, from men themselves, form a frightful catalogue of woes; but they are nothing compared with those that arise from conditions within.

How many lie under the lingering torment of disease? How many suffer remorse, shame, anguish, rage, disappointment, fear, despair? How many suffer those deep disorders of mind, insanity, idiocy, madness? Who has passed through life without cruel inroads from these tormentors?

Were a stranger to drop into this world, I would show him, as a specimen of its ills, a hospital full of diseases, a prison crowded with malefactors, a battlefield strewn with carcasses, a fleet floundering in the ocean, a nation languishing under tyranny, famine, or pestilence. Labor and poverty are the certain lot of the far greater number, while the few who enjoy riches and ease never reach contentment or true felicity. All the good things of life taken together make a man very wretched indeed.

You ascribe an author to nature, and a purpose to the author of nature. What, I beseech you, is the object fulfilled by these matters to which attention has been drawn? Our sense of music, harmony, beauty, has some purpose. But what of gout, gravels, megrims, toothaches, rheumatisms? How does divine benevolence and purpose display itself here? Why argue for the power and knowledge of the Deity while His moral qualities are in doubt?

You say: But this world is only a point in comparison of the universe; this life is but a moment in comparison of eternity. Present evils are rectified in other regions and future times. And the eyes of men, being then opened to large views of things see the whole connection of general laws, and trace with adoration the benevolence and wisdom of the Deity through all the mazes and intricacies of his providence.

I answer: The only method of supporting divine benevolence is for you to say to me, "Your representations are exaggerated; your melancholy views are mostly fictitious; your inferences are contrary to fact and experience; health is more common than sickness; pleasure, than pain; happiness, than misery; for one vexation we meet, we attain a hundred enjoyments."

I add: Can such apologetics be admitted? Even allowing your claim that human happiness exceeds human misery, yet it proves nothing. For an excess of happiness over misery is not what we expect from infinite power coupled with infinite wisdom and infinite goodness.

The questions asked by Epicurus, of old, are yet unanswered. Is Deity willing to prevent evil, but not able? Then He is not omnipotent. Is He able, but not willing? Then He is malevolent. Is He both able and willing? Then whence cometh evil? Is He neither able nor willing? Then why call Him Deity?

Evil and unhappiness are the rocks upon which all arguments for Deity must finally come to wreck. Why is there any misery and wickedness at all in the world? Not by chance, surely. From some purpose or cause then? Is it from the intention of the Deity? But He is perfectly benevolent. Is it contrary to his intention? But He is almighty. Nothing can shake the solidity of this reasoning, so short, so clear, so decisive; unless we agree that these matters lie beyond human capacity, that our human reason is not applicable to them. This is the counsel of skepticism that I have all along insisted on.

The whole matter is summarized in the two following passages.

In a word, a man who follows this kind of argument from analogy, where one of the terms of the analogy lies beyond his experience, may perhaps be able to conjecture that the universe arose from something like design. But beyond that he cannot go, except by the utmost license of thought.

On this argument for all you know to the contrary, this world may be a very faulty and imperfect copy compared to a superior standard; only the first rude essay of some infant deity who afterwards abandoned it, ashamed of his lame performance; only the work of some dependent, inferior deity, the object of derision to his superiors; only the product of old age and dotage in some superannuated deity, and ever since his death running on at adventures from the first impulse it received from him.

Thus far, we have the argument from the miracles and the argument from design. If these arguments from miracles and from design presented so many difficulties, would one fare better with the argument from the first cause? By this argument could one prove the infinity, the unity, and the perfection, of the author of nature? Hume states this argument as follows:

The argument from first cause is this. Whatever exists must have a cause of its existence. Nothing can produce itself. In mounting up, therefore, from effects to causes, we must go on tracing an infinite regression without any ultimate cause, or must finally have recourse to an ultimate cause. Now, it is insisted, the conception of an infinite regression, or utterly no beginning cause to which all others can be traced, is absurd. We must, therefore, have recourse to a necessarily existent being, the first cause of all things, who carries the reason of His existence in Himself, and whom we cannot suppose not to exist without embracing an absurdity. Such a being is the Deity.

His criticism is brief and to the point:

Wherein do we find the absurdity of an infinite regression? It leads us beyond our powers of conceiving? So also does the conception of an infinite deity.
Let us admit its absurdity. Let us admit the necessity of a first cause. Shall we then ask for a cause of this cause? If not, then may we not argue a material first cause of this material universe? If not, may we ascribe to the spiritual first cause the origin of evil and misery and waste which we noted in our analysis of the argument from analogy? If not, to what cause then are they to be traced? If so, wherein do we fare better with the argument from the necessity of a first cause than from the probability of an intelligent designer?

His conclusion to the whole business is a plea for skepticism in natural theology:

All religious systems are subject to insuperable difficulties. Each disputant triumphs in his turn, exposing the absurdities, barbarities, and pernicious tenets of his antagonist. But all of them prepare a complete triumph for the skeptic who tells them no system ought ever to be embraced with regard to such questions. A total suspense of judgment is here our only reasonable recourse.

The upshot of Hume's critique of natural theology is skepticism. Its historical importance is along several lines. In the first place, it was a nemesis visited upon the Age of Reason; for what Hume showed was the helplessness of reason to cope with the problems of natural theology. In some minds this work has never been undone. For them, Hume administered a deathblow to the speculations at which he directed his attention. Rational theology in the grand manner has never been completely restored to its former intellectual respectability. In the second place, Hume's handling of these questions led to an interesting attempt, by John Stuart Mill in the following century, to introduce into theology the conception of a finite God, and in the twentieth century, to the pragmatic approach to these matters in the writings of the American, William James.

NOTE ON SOURCES.   The material in this section is quoted, abridged, or paraphrased from David Hume, "On Miracles," *An Enquiry Concerning Human Understanding* (Oxford: Clarendon Press, 1975) and *Dialogues Concerning Natural Religion* (Indianapolis: Bobbs-Merrill, 1970), Parts 2–10.

---

4   THOMAS HENRY HUXLEY
Agnosticism—The Only Legitimate Response

FROM MILL TO HUXLEY.   Two famous books, both published in 1859, enter into discussion of a key question of this chapter. The first is Charles Darwin's *Origin of Species;* the second, John Stuart Mill's *On Liberty.* Our question has been: Can you use what you know about nature to justify what you believe about God? Both books focus on that question.

Darwin's book caused many persons to revise their conception of nature, thus causing them to question their conception of God. The book pictured plants and animals engaged in a ruthless and life-long struggle for existence. In one way or another they must eat or be eaten, kill or be killed. Tennyson's phrase "Nature red in tooth and claw" expressed the point. Under the pressure of this struggle for existence some species were eliminated and some survived. This was "natural selection": nature "selected" the fit and eliminated the unfit. If nature is created and sustained by God, then this natural selection is Divine Selection: God, through the struggle for existence, selects the fit and eliminates the unfit; in so doing, He brings about an evolution from the lowest beginnings of life up to the present stage of the higher animals and humans. Suppose this is what we know about nature. Can we use this knowledge to justify what we believe about God? Can we, as one writer asked, proceed "through nature to God"?

Mill's book, especially in its famous second chapter, argued for the right of the individual to think for himself or herself. It provided the classic plea for "the right to pro and con," on all questions, no matter how important or sacred or long established. Darwin's "downgrading" of nature, particularly if you thought about God as the author of nature, produced a crisis in public discussion of these matters. Mill's chapter was a timely warning against obscurantism and intolerance.

That was in 1859. In 1877 William Kingdom Clifford published a paper, *The Ethics of Belief,* in which he argued that ethics as well as logic has something to say on the justification of belief: If you are not logically entitled to hold a particular belief, then you are not morally entitled to hold that belief. Clifford included religious beliefs in this winnowing demand. The result was something of a paradox for many of his readers: they were familiar with the claim that in these matters doubt or disbelief was a sin, and here was Clifford insisting that in the absence of logical justification belief was immoral and sinful.

Thomas Henry Huxley's *Agnosticism,* which repeated and extended Clifford's thesis, became a symbol for the state of mind in which many found themselves. Huxley commanded a wider hearing than Clifford, spoke with greater authority, and ranged over a wider field. The paper in which he stated and applied his agnosticism provided Victorian England with one of its liveliest controversies. Since Clifford's paper expressed so much of what Huxley meant by agnosticism, we begin by looking at what Clifford had to say:

A shipowner was about to send to sea an emigrant ship. He knew that she was old, not overwell built, and often had needed repairs. It had been suggested to him that possibly she was not seaworthy. He thought that perhaps he ought to have her overhauled and refitted, even though this should put him to great expense.

Before the ship sailed, however, he said to himself that she had gone safely through so many voyages and weathered so many storms, that it was idle to suppose that she would not come safely home from this trip also. He would put his trust in Providence, which could hardly fail to protect all these unhappy families that were leaving their fatherland to seek for better times elsewhere. He would dismiss ungenerous suspicions about the honesty of builders and contractors. In such ways he acquired a sincere and comfortable conviction that his vessel was safe and seaworthy; he watched her departure with a light heart, and benevolent wishes for the success of the exiles in their new home; and he got his insurance money when she went down in mid-ocean and told no tales.

What shall we say of him? Surely that he was guilty of the death of those men. He sincerely believed in the soundness of his ship; but the sincerity of his conviction can in nowise help him, because he had no *right* to believe on such evidence as was before him. He had acquired his belief not by honestly earning it in patient investigation, but by stifling his doubts.

Let us alter the case a little, and suppose that the ship was not unsound after all; that she made her voyage safely, and many others after it. Will that diminish the guilt of her owner? Not one jot. The man would not have been innocent; he would only have been not found out. The question of right or wrong has to do not with whether his belief turned out to be true or false, but whether he had a *right* to believe on such evidence as was before him.

Although he had sincerely and "conscientiously" believed, yet he had no *right* to believe on such evidence as was before him. His sincere convictions, instead of being honestly earned, were stolen. The question is not whether his belief was true or false, but whether he entertained it on wrong grounds.

If he chose to examine himself *in foro conscientiae,* he would know that he had acquired and nourished a belief, when he had no *right* to believe on such evidence as was before him; and therein he would know that he had done a wrong thing.

No real belief, however trifling and fragmentary it may seem, is ever truly insignificant; it prepares us to receive more of its like, confirms those which resembled it before, and weakens others; and so gradually lays a stealthy train in our inmost thoughts, which may some day explode into overt action, and leave its stamp upon our character forever.

It is wrong to believe on insufficient evidence, or to nourish belief by suppressing doubts and avoiding investigation. Since no belief, however seemingly trivial, and however obscure the believer, is ever actually insignificant or without its effect, we have no choice but to extend our judgment to all cases of belief whatever. Belief, that sacred faculty, which prompts the decisions of our will, and knits into harmonious working all the energies of our being, is ours not for ourselves but for humanity. It is *rightly* used on truths which have been established by long tradition and waiting too, and which have stood in the fierce light of free and fearless questioning. It is desecrated when given to unproved and unquestioned statements, for the solace and private pleasure of the believer; to add a tinsel splendor to the plain straight road of our life and display a bright mirage beyond it; or even to drown the common sorrows of our kind by a self-deception which allows them not only to cast down, but also to degrade us. Whoso would deserve well of his fellows in this matter will guard the purity of his belief with a very fanaticism of jealous care, lest at any time it should rest on an unworthy object, and catch a stain which can never be wiped away.

It is not only the leader of men, statesman, philosopher, or poet, that has this duty to mankind. Every rustic who delivers in the village alehouse his slow infrequent sentences, may help to kill or keep alive the fatal superstitions which clog his race. No simplicity of mind, no obscurity of station, can escape the universal duty of questioning all that we believe.

It is the sense of power attached to a sense of knowledge that makes men desirous of believing, and afraid of doubting. This sense of power is the highest and best of pleasures when the belief on which it is founded has been fairly earned. But if the belief has been accepted on insufficient evidence, the pleasure is a *stolen* one. Not only does it deceive ourselves by giving us a sense of power which we do not really possess, but it is *sinful,* because it is *stolen* in defiance of our duty. That *duty* is to guard ourselves from such beliefs as from a pestilence, which may shortly master our own body and then spread to the rest of the town. What would be thought of one who, for the sake of a sweet fruit, should deliberately run the risk of bringing a plague upon his family and his neighbors?

Every time we let ourselves believe for unworthy reasons, we weaken our powers of self-control, of doubting, of judicially and fairly weighing evidence. We all suffer severely enough from the maintenance of false beliefs and the fatally wrong actions which they lead to. The evil born when one such belief is entertained is great and wide. But a greater and wider evil arises when the credulous character is maintained, when a habit of believing for unworthy reasons is fostered and made permanent.

It is *wrong* always, everywhere, and for any one, to believe anything upon insufficient evidence. Habitual want of care about what I believe leads to habitual want of care in others about the truth of what is told to me. The credulous man is father to the liar and the cheat.

If a man, holding a belief which he was taught in childhood or persuaded of afterwards, keeps down doubts which arise about it in his mind, purposely avoids the reading of books and the company of men that call in question or discuss it, and regards as impious those questions which cannot easily be asked without disturbing it; the life of that man is one long sin against mankind.

If this judgment seems harsh when applied to those simple souls who have never known better, who have been brought up with a horror of doubt, and taught that their eternal welfare depends of what they believe; then it leads to the very serious question, *Who hath made Israel to sin?*

Inquiry into the evidence of a doctrine is not to be made once for all, and then taken as finally settled. It is never lawful to stifle a doubt; for either it can be honestly answered by means of the inquiry already made, or else it proves that the inquiry was not complete.

"But," says one, "I am a busy man; I have no time for the long course of study which would be necessary to make me in any degree a competent judge of certain questions, or even able to understand the nature of the arguments." Then he should have no time to believe.

The beliefs about right and wrong which guide our actions in dealing with men in society, and the beliefs about physical nature which guide our actions in dealing with animate and inanimate bodies, these never suffer from investigation; they can take care of themselves, without being propped up by "acts of faith," the clamor of paid advocates, or the suppression of contrary evidence.

Since it is not enough to say, "It is wrong to believe on unworthy evidence," without saying also what evidence is worthy, we shall now go on to inquire under what circumstances it is lawful to believe on the testimony of others; and more generally when and why we may believe that which goes beyond our own experience, or even beyond the experience of mankind.

BIOGRAPHICAL NOTE.   Thomas Henry Huxley was born near London, England, in 1825, and died in 1895 at the age of seventy. He was a renowned biologist, and one of the most versatile scientists in nineteenth-century England. As a youth he was basically self-educated until the time when he undertook a medical apprenticeship. In 1842 he pursued studies, work, and research at Charing Cross Hospital where he won prizes in chemistry, anatomy, and physiology. For several years, from 1846 to 1850, he served as an assistant surgeon on a British vessel engaged in a surveying operation in Australian waters. Huxley used these voyages to good advantage, gathering data and writing papers that won him respect as a competent biologist. In 1851 he was elected a fellow of the Royal Society. After leaving the navy, he held a number of governmental posts during which time he launched an extended study of paleontology. His erudition, eloquence, clarity of thought, and earnest skepticism soon singled him out as an intellectual leader in Victorian England. For forty years he championed various causes ranging from support of Darwin's theory of evolution to educational reform. Illustrative of his exceedingly diverse interests and writings are his nine volumes of *Collected Essays* and his five volumes of *Scientific Memoirs.*

THE ARGUMENT OF THE PASSAGES.   In reading Huxley on these matters it is well to keep Mill, Darwin, and Clifford in mind. In the following material there are two extended quotations from Huxley. In the *first* he tells how he arrived at the position that he calls agnosticism, and why he coined that word as a name for it. In the *second* he gives a statement of the essential ideas he wants held together by the term *agnosticism.* To put it briefly, agnosticism is the claim that if you cannot use what you know to justify what you believe, then it is immoral to go on believing. Suppose a man asks himself "Am I morally entitled to entertain a certain belief of mine?" Agnosticism asks him: "Are you *logically* entitled to entertain the belief to which you refer?" If the answer is no, then agnosticism says to him: "Then you are not morally entitled to entertain the belief. You have no moral right to a belief you cannot justify logically."

Looking back nearly fifty years, I see myself as a boy, whose education has been interrupted, and who intellectually, was left, for some years, altogether to his own devices. At that time, I was a voracious and omnivorous reader; a dreamer and speculator, endowed with that courage in attacking any and every subject, which is the blessed compensation of youth and inexperience. Among the books and essays, on all sorts of topics from metaphysics to heraldry, which I read at this time, two left indelible impressions on my mind. One was Guizot's "History of Civilization," the other was Sir William Hamilton's essay "On the Philosophy of the Unconditioned." The latter was strange reading for a boy, and I could not possibly have understood a great deal of it; nevertheless, I devoured it with avidity, and it stamped upon my mind the strong conviction that, on even the most solemn and important of questions, men are apt to take cunning phrases for answers; and that the limitation of our faculties, in a great number of cases, renders real answers to such questions, not merely actually impossible, but theoretically inconceivable.

When I reached intellectual maturity and began to ask myself whether I was an atheist, a theist, or a pantheist; a materialist or an idealist; a Christian or a freethinker; I found that the more I learned and reflected, the less ready was the answer; until, at last, I came to the conclusion that I had neither art nor part with any of these denominations, except the last. The one thing in which most of these good people were agreed was the one thing in which I differed from them. They were quite sure they had attained a certain "gnosis,"—had, more or less successfully, solved the problem of existence; while I was quite sure I had not, and had a pretty strong conviction that the problem was insoluble. And, with Hume and Kant on my side, I could not think myself presumptuous in holding fast by that opinion.

This was my situation when I had the good fortune to find a place among the members of that remarkable confraternity of antagonists, long since deceased, but of green and pious memory, the Metaphysical Society. Every variety of philosophical and theological opinion was represented there, and expressed itself with entire openness; most of my colleagues were -*ists* of one sort or another; and, however kind and friendly they might be, I, the man without a rag of label to cover himself with, could not fail to have some of the uneasy feelings which must have beset the historical fox when, after leaving the trap in which his tail remained, he presented himself to his normally elongated companions. So I took thought, and invented what I conceived to be the appropriate title of "agnostic." It came into my head as suggestively antithetic to the "gnostic" of Church history, who professed to know so much about the very things of which I was ignorant; and I took the earliest opportunity of parading it at our Society, to show that I, too, had a tail, like the other foxes. To my great satisfaction, the term took; and when the *Spectator* had stood godfather to it, any suspicion in the minds of respectable people, that a knowledge of its parentage might have awakened was, of course, completely lulled.

This is the history of the origin of the terms "agnostic" and "agnosticism."

Huxley now proceeds to summarize the major contentions of agnosticism:

Agnosticism is properly described as a creed in so far as it expresses absolute faith in the validity of a principle which is as much ethical as intellectual. This principle may be stated in various ways, but they all amount to this: that it is wrong for a man to say that he is certain of the objective truth of any proposition unless he can produce evidence which logically justifies that certainty. This is what agnosticism asserts; and, in my opinion, it is all that is essential to agnosticism.

That which agnostics deny and repudiate as immoral is that there are propositions which men ought to believe, without logically satisfactory evidence; and that reprobation ought to attach to the profession of disbelief in such inadequately supported propositions. The justification of the agnostic principle lies in the success which follows upon its application, in natural or in civil history; and in the fact that, so far as these topics are concerned, no sane man thinks of denying its validity.

Agnosticism is a creed, in so far as its general principle is concerned. The application of that principle results in the denial of, or the suspension of judgment concerning, a number of propositions respecting which contemporary "gnostics" profess entire certainty.

The extent of the region of the uncertain, the number of the problems the investigation of which ends in a verdict of not proven will vary according to the knowledge and the intellectual habits of the individual agnostic. What I am sure about is that there are many topics about which I know nothing, and which, so far as I can see, are out of reach of my faculties. Relatively to myself, I am quite sure that the region of uncertainty is far more extensive than I could wish. Materialism and idealism; theism and atheism; the doctrine of the soul and its mortality or immortality—appear in the history of philosophy like the shades of Scandinavian heroes, eternally slaying one another and eternally coming to life again. It is getting on for twenty-five centuries, at least, since mankind began seriously to give their minds to these topics. Generation after generation, philosophy has been doomed to roll the stone uphill; and, just as all the world swore it was at the top, down it has rolled to the bottom again. All this is written in innumerable books; and he who will toil through them will discover that the stone is just where it was when the work began. Hume saw this; Kant saw it; since their time, more and more eyes have been cleansed of the films which prevented them from seeing it; until now the weight and number has begun to tell in practical life.

Between agnosticism and clericalism, there can be neither peace nor truce. The cleric asserts that it is morally wrong not to believe certain propositions, whatever the results of a strict scientific investigation of the evidence of these propositions. He tells us that "religious error is, in itself, of an immoral nature." He declares that he has prejudged certain conclusions, and looks upon those who show cause for arrest of judgment as emissaries of Satan. It necessarily follows that, for him, the attainment of faith, not the ascertainment of truth, is the highest aim of mental life. And, on analysis, it will be found to be the "power of saying you believe things which are incredible." Now I, and many other agnostics, believe that faith in this sense is an abomination; and we feel that the disagreement between ourselves and those who hold this doctrine is even more moral than intellectual. It is desirable there should be an end of any mistakes on this topic.

Those who appreciate our position will see that when any one declares that we ought to believe this, that, and the other, and are wicked if we don't, it is impossible for us to give any answer but this: We have not the slightest objection to believe anything you like, if you will give us good grounds for belief; but, if you can not, we must respectfully refuse, even if that refusal should wreck morality and insure our own damnation several times over.

Is one able to provide evidence from nature such that belief in the existence of God is *required* by reason? *allowed* by reason? Philosophers like Aquinas say that such belief is required by reason. Others like Pascal claim that belief is not required, but is allowed by reason. Those like Hume argue that belief in a supreme, perfect being is neither required nor allowed by reason. Still others like Mill maintain that the evidence from nature certainly allows belief in a finite deity, and may even require such a belief. For Clifford and Huxley and their agnostic compatriots, belief in a supreme, perfect being is not warranted by the evidence; indeed, such unevidenced belief in the existence of God is to be regarded as immoral. Our next author, William James, continues the debate by arguing that the believer and the agnostic are virtually on the same footing and that if the believer is to be judged to be immoral for embracing a belief in the existence of God, even so the agnostic and atheist are to be considered immoral for holding their positions. If reason allows affirmation of agnosticism, then reason must also allow affirmation of theism.

NOTE ON SOURCES.   The material in this section is quoted or abridged from William K. Clifford, "The Ethics of Belief," and T. H. Huxley, "Agnosticism."

---

5   WILLIAM JAMES
Legitimate Belief in Spite of Agnosticism

FROM HUXLEY TO JAMES.   It will be recalled that Pascal, writing in the seventeenth century, repudiated the possibility of deriving belief in God from beliefs about nature, but he clung to orthodox convictions. John Stuart Mill, writing two centuries later, reversed the procedure. He clung to the idea of deriving belief in God from beliefs about nature, but repudiated the orthodox convictions. The most humans can rationally justify through natural theology, he argued, is the belief in a finite God. William James, writing in America toward the close of the nineteenth and in the opening years of the twentieth centuries, attempted to blend the insights of Pascal and Mill. James was convinced that the appeal to natural theology was bankrupt. No one had ever properly answered Hume on his own grounds. But James found himself believing wholeheartedly in the existence of God. That, he could not shake off. Accordingly, he sought to combine perspectives from Pascal and Mill, respectively: an appeal to what he called "the will to believe" in support of the belief in a finite God. Although he differed from Pascal on the nature of God, James's "will to believe" seems to echo Pascal's recommendation that lacking compelling evidence from natural theology for belief in the existence of God those seeking God should act as if they had already found God and eventually they would be assured of His existence.

On the face of it, James's "will to believe," later his pragmatism, is closely related, historically, to Huxley's agnosticism. This is apparent on reading James's essay. Huxley had said that if you couldn't logically justify what you believe, then it was immoral to believe. Such belief would be "stolen." It is this note of moral censure in Huxley's agnosticism that caught James's attention. His argument is that among Huxley's own beliefs are some that he (Huxley) could not justify "logically," "intellectually," but that he (Huxley) nevertheless will not abandon. Such beliefs embody "the will to believe." Beliefs that are *appropriate* objects of the will to believe are not open to the moral criticism proposed by Huxley's agnosticism.

BIOGRAPHICAL NOTE.   William James was born in 1842 and died in 1910 at the age of sixty-eight. He was educated at Harvard, receiving his medical degree in 1869. He was appointed to the teaching staff of Harvard in the department of physiology. From physiology he moved later to psychology, writing his brilliant and epoch-making *Principles of Psychology* and *Varieties of Religious Experience*. From psychology he moved on to philosophy. His best-known and most controversial books were written during his years as professor of philosophy. He gathered about him, at Harvard, what was perhaps the most brilliant group of teachers and writers in philosophy ever assembled at any one time in any university in this country. These philosophical colleagues included Josiah Royce, George Herbert Palmer, George Santayana, and (in psychology) Hugo Münsterberg.

Although James was trained as a physiologist, he had many of the interests of a moralist and theologian. His robust assurance that the good life, in the long run, provides the deepest and most lasting satisfaction; his passionately felt need for a "Friend" sustaining the universe and reaching out to humans in their struggle for righteousness and truth, are convictions that pervade many of his writings. His three books, *The Will to Believe and Other Essays, The Varieties of Religious Experience,* and *Pragmatism,* contain popular presentations of these views.

THE ARGUMENT OF THE PASSAGES.   The passages quoted or abridged hereunder are, for the most part, from James's essay "The Will to Believe." He states somewhere that it might better have been called "The Right to Believe." His aim is to point out that, in certain cases, where the evidence is insufficient to justify belief on "rational" grounds, there may nevertheless be other grounds. In a word, sufficient evidence is not the only thing that justifies belief, is not the only thing that gives us a "right to believe." Agnosticism may not be the last word here. In such cases, upon what does our right to believe rest? Where the evidence is insufficient, is it necessary to say, with agnosticism, that belief is everywhere and always immoral?

That is the central problem of the essay. James begins with a few remarks on hypotheses in general. The purpose of these remarks is to explain what he means by a "genuine option" between rival hypotheses. Where we are faced with a genuine option between rival hypotheses, neither of which is backed by sufficient evidence, upon what principle may we legitimately exercise our will to believe? James then formulates the principle that, he thinks, justifies belief under such circumstances. The question now is: Are there any beliefs that present themselves for acceptance on this principle? James notes that moral judgments are of this nature. If this is so, then the moral judgments proposed by agnosticism, or moral principles embodied in such judgments, would be important exceptions to the rule laid down by agnosticism. However, and more important, the "religious hypothesis" is of this nature. He then states the terms of this hypothesis. In what follows, he deals with two possible lines of criticism that, he knows, will be directed against his position. The first of these is the objection of the agnostic, namely, that where evidence is insufficient to justify belief, we have no right to believe. The second objection is to the effect that once you set up any principle designed to justify belief on insufficient grounds, you have (in principle) obliterated the distinction between intelligent belief and any but the wildest superstition. Finally, in a few passages, we note his acceptance of Mill's limited theism.

James begins:

> Let us give the name of *hypothesis* to anything that may be proposed of our belief. And, just as electricians speak of live and dead wires, let us speak of an hypothesis as either live or dead. A live hypothesis is one which appeals as a real possibility to him to whom it is proposed.

Next, let us call the decision between hypotheses an *option*. Options may be of several kinds. They may be living or dead, forced or avoidable, momentous or trivial.

A living option is one in which both hypotheses are live. If I say to you: "Be a theosophist or be a Mohammedan," it is probably a dead option, because for you neither hypothesis is likely to be live. But if I say: "Be an agnostic or be a Christian," it is otherwise. Trained as you are, each hypothesis makes some appeal, however small, to your belief.

A forced option is one which arises when there is no standing outside of the alternative hypothesis. If I say to you: "Choose between going out with your umbrella or without it," I do not offer you a forced option. You can easily avoid it by not going out at all. But if I say: "Either accept this truth or go without it," I put on you a forced option, for there is no third alternative and no standing outside of these two alternatives.

A momentous option is one that is presented when the opportunity is unique, when the stake is significant, or when the decision is irreversible if it later prove unwise. If I were Dr. Nansen and proposed to you to join my North Pole expedition, your option would be momentous; for this would probably be your only opportunity, and your choice now would either exclude you from the North Pole sort of immortality altogether, or put at least the chance of it into your hands. *Per contra,* the option is trivial when the opportunity is not unique, when the stake is insignificant, or when the decision is reversible if it later prove unwise.

An option is genuine when it is of the living, forced, momentous kind.

So much for hypotheses and options. Suppose, now, that a person is confronted by a genuine option, a pair of rival beliefs, neither of which can be said to rest on sufficient evidence to justify belief. What is she to do? Upon what principle can she justify herself in accepting the one or the other? It is the following:

The thesis I defend is this: Our passional (emotional) nature not only lawfully may, but must, decide an option between propositions, whenever it is a genuine option that cannot by its nature be decided on intellectual grounds.

The essence of the matter is contained in this principle. We are curious to know where, among our beliefs, we shall find some that call for acceptance on this principle. One example would be our moral beliefs: that it is better to do this than that, better to be this sort of person than that, and so on.

The question arises: Are there any such forced options in our speculative opinions? Are there some options between opinions in which this passional influence must be regarded both as an inevitable and as a lawful determinant of our choice?

Moral questions immediately present themselves. A moral question is a question not of what exists, but of what is good, or would be good if it did exist.

Science can tell us what exists; but to compare the worths, both of what exists and what does not exist, we must consult not science, but what Pascal calls our "heart," i.e., our passional nature. Science, herself, consults her heart when she lays it down that the infinite ascertainment of fact and correction of false belief are the supreme goods for man. Challenge the statement, and science can only repeat it oracularly, or else prove it by showing that such ascertainment and correction bring man all sorts of other goods which man's heart in turn declares desirable.

Moral beliefs. Is that all? What about religious beliefs? Are they appropriate objects of our sheer "will to believe"?

Let us pass to the question of religious faith. What do we mean by the religious hypothesis? Broadly it is this: Science says things are: morality says some things are better than other things: religion says that the best things are the more eternal things, the things in the universe that throw the last stone, so to speak, and say the final word: and that we are better off, even now, if we believe her first affirmation to be true.

Now let us consider what the logical elements of this situation are in case the religious hypothesis in both its branches be really true. We must admit that possibility at the outset.

We see, first, that religion offers itself as a momentous option. We are supposed to gain, even now, by our belief, and to lose by our nonbelief, a certain vital good.

We see, second, that religion is a forced option so far as that vital good is concerned. We cannot escape the issue by remaining skeptical, because although we do avoid error in that way if religion be untrue, we lose the good, if it be true. Skepticism, then, is not an avoidance of the option.

In these matters, the skeptic's position is this: Better risk the loss of truth than the chance of error. But in this he is actively playing his stake as much as the believer is. He is backing the field against the religious hypothesis, just as the believer is backing the religious hypothesis against the field.

Now, to most of us, religion comes in a still further way. What I mean is this. The more perfect and more eternal aspect of the universe is represented in our religions as having a personal form. The universe is no longer a mere It, but a Thou, if we are religious; and any relation that may be possible from person to person might be possible here. We feel, too, as if the appeal of religion were made to our own active good will, as if evidence for its truth might be forever withheld from us unless we met the hypothesis halfway.

This feeling, forced on us we know not whence, that by obstinately believing that there are gods we are doing the universe the deepest service we can, seems part of the living essence of the religious hypothesis.

God is the natural appellation, for us Christians at least, for the supreme reality, so I will call this higher part of the universe by the name of God. We and God have business with each other; and in opening ourselves to His influence our deepest destiny is fulfilled. The universe, at those parts of it which our personal being constitutes, takes a turn genuinely for the worse or for the better in proportion as each one of us fulfills or evades God's demands.

God's existence is the guarantee of an ideal order that shall be permanently preserved. This world may indeed some day burn up or freeze up; but if it is part of His order, the old ideals are sure to be brought elsewhere to fruition, so that where God is, tragedy is only provisional and partial, and shipwreck and dissolution are not the absolutely final things.

Only when this farther step of faith concerning God is taken, and remote objective consequences are predicted, does religion, as it seems to me, get wholly free from subjective experience, and bring a real hypothesis into play.

What is this but to say that religion, in her fullest exercise of function, is a postulator of new facts? The world interpreted religiously is not the materialistic world over again, with an altered expression. It must have, over and above the altered expression, a natural constitution different at some point from that which a materialistic world would have. It must be such that different events can be expected in it, different conduct must be required.

All this on the supposition that our passional nature may be prophetic and right: and that the religious hypothesis is a live hypothesis which may be true.

We are now in possession of the essentials of James's position. We know what he means by a genuine option between rival hypotheses. We know the principle by which he would justify belief in such circumstances. We know that he considers the religious hypothesis a case in point. We know, finally, what he means by this religious hypothesis. His defense of the whole position is still to be made. He deals first with the skeptic. The point here is this: It may be all very well to talk about the demands of our "passional nature," but, as a matter of fact, why is it not just as legitimate to refuse to believe either hypothesis when neither is backed by sufficient evidence? Why may an agnostic not take the stand, in all conscience, that under the circumstances stipulated by James, the proper attitude is one of suspended judgment? Let us hear, through James, the agnostic's statement of the case:

> It does seem preposterous on the very face of it, to talk of our opinions being modifiable at will. Can our will either help or hinder our intellect in its perceptions of truth? . . . Indeed, the talk of believing by our volition seems from one point of view, simply silly. From another point of view it is worse than silly, it is vile. When one turns to the magnificent edifice of the physical sciences, and sees how it was reared, what thousands of disinterested moral lives of men lie buried in its mere foundations; what patience and postponement, what choking down of preference, what submission to icy laws of outer fact are wrought into its very stones and mortar; how absolutely impersonal it stands in its vast augustness—then how besotted and contemptible seems every little sentimentalist who comes blowing his voluntary smoke wreaths! Can we wonder if those bred in the rugged and manly school of science should feel like spewing such subjectivism out of their mouths? The whole system of loyalties which grow up in the schools of science go dead against its toleration; so that it is only natural that those who have caught the scientific fever should pass over to the opposite extreme and write sometimes as if the incorruptibly truthful intellect ought positively to prefer bitterness and unacceptableness to the heart in its cup.
> Clough sings:

> > It fortifies my soul to know
> > That, though I perish, Truth is so

> while Huxley exclaims: "My only consolation lies in the reflection that, however bad our posterity may become, so far as they hold by the plain rule of not pretending to believe what they have no reason to believe, because it may be to their advantage so to pretend, they will not have reached the lowest depth of immorality."
> And that delicious *enfant terrible,* Clifford, writes: "Belief is desecrated when given to unproved and unquestioned statements for the solace and private pleasure of the believer. Whoso would deserve well of his fellows in this matter will guard the purity of his belief with a very fanaticism of jealous care, lest at any time it should rest on an unworthy object, and cast a stain which can never be wiped away. If a belief has been accepted on insufficient evidence, even though the belief be true, the pleasure is a stolen one. It is sinful because it is stolen in defiance of our duty to mankind. That duty is to guard ourselves from such beliefs as from a pestilence which may shortly master our body and

then spread to the rest of the town. It is wrong, always, everywhere, and for everyone, to believe anything upon insufficient evidence."

Now, all of this strikes one as healthy, even when expressed by Clifford with somewhat too much of robustious pathos in the voice. Willing and wishing do seem, in the matter of our beliefs, to be only fifth wheels to the coach.

How shall this indictment be answered? It will be noticed that James has been fair to the agnostic in admitting the genuine possibility here of a moral issue. The agnostic's claim is not, at its best, that we are merely foolish to believe on insufficient evidence. It is the more serious claim that we *ought* not to believe on insufficient evidence; that belief, in such cases, is immoral. That is the point agnosticism adds to skepticism. That is the charge with which James is faced. The first move in his defense is to note that in this unique case of the religious hypothesis doubt is the equivalent of denial; and, the point is, denial is not suspended judgment. (It may be necessary to reread James's wording of the religious hypothesis, especially its *second* part, to follow his argument here.)

To preach skepticism in these matters is tantamount to telling us, when in the presence of the religious hypothesis, that to yield to our fear of its being false is wiser and better than to yield to our hope that it may be true.

As James points out, this puts a slightly different face on the matter. Why is it "wiser and better" to refrain from belief on all occasions where the evidence is insufficient?

This is not the case of "intellect" against "passion." It is only intellect, with one passion—the dread or horror of believing what may be false—laying down its law—never to believe what may be false when there is no evidence that it may be true.

And by what, forsooth, is the supreme wisdom of this passion warranted? Dupery for dupery, what proof is there that dupery through hope is so much worse than dupery through fear? I, for one, can see no proof; and I simply refuse to imitate the skeptic's option in a case where my own stake is important enough to give me the right to choose my own form of risk.

And what it comes down to is this:

We may regard the case for truth as paramount, and the avoidance of error as secondary; or we may treat the avoidance of error as more imperative, and let truth take its chance. Clifford exhorts us to the latter course. Believe nothing, he tells us, keep your mind in suspense forever, rather than, by closing on insufficient evidence, incur the awful risk of believing lies. You, on the other hand, may think that the risk of being in error is a very small matter when compared with the blessings of real knowledge, and be ready to be duped many times rather than postpone indefinitely the chance of guessing true.

This being so, he knows where he stands:

For my own part, I have also a horror of being duped. But I can believe that worse things than being duped may happen to a man in this world. So Clifford's exhortation has to my ears a thoroughly fantastic sound. Our errors are surely not such awfully solemn things. In a world where we are to sure to incur them, a certain lightness of heart seems healthier than this excessive nervousness on their behalf.

If the religious hypothesis be true, and the evidence for it still insufficient, I do not wish, by putting a skeptical extinguisher upon my nature, to forfeit my sole chance of getting upon the winning side; that chance depending, of course, on my willingness to run the risk of acting as if my passional need of taking the world religiously might be prophetic and right.

When I look at the religious hypothesis, as it really puts itself to men, and when I think of all the possibilities which it involves, then the skeptical command to put a stopper on our heart and wait—acting meanwhile more or less as if religion were not true—wait till doomsday, or till such time as our intellect and senses may have raked in enough evidence—this command, I say, seems to me the queerest idol ever manufactured in the philosophic cave.

If the religious hypothesis were true, then pure intellectualism, with its veto on our willingness to make advances, would be an absurdity; and some participation of our sympathetic nature would be logically required. I, therefore, for one, cannot see my way to accepting the agnostic rules for truth-seeking (never to believe any hypothesis when there is no evidence or insufficient evidence) or to willfully agree to keep my willing nature out of the game.

I cannot do so for this plain reason: A rule of thinking which would prevent me from acknowledging certain kinds of truth if those kinds of truths were really there, would be an irrational rule. That, for me, is the long and short of the logic of the situation.

The great empiricists are only empiricists on reflection; left to their instincts, they dogmatize like infallible popes. When the Cliffords tell us how sinful it is to be Christians on such "insufficient evidence," insufficiency is really the last thing they have in mind. For them the evidence is absolutely sufficient, only it makes the other way. They believe so completely in an anti-Christian order of the universe that there is no living option: Christianity, for them, is a dead hypothesis from the start.

As a kind of Parthian shot, James throws a question at the skeptics themselves:

Our belief in truth itself, for instance, that there is a truth and that our minds and it are made for each other—what is it but a passionate affirmation of desire in which our social system backs us up? We want to have a truth; we want to believe that our experiments and studies and discussions must put us in a continually better and better position toward it; and on this line we agree to fight out our thinking lives.

But if a skeptic asks us how we know all this, can our logic find a reply? It cannot. It is just one volition against another; we are willing to go in for life upon a trust or assumption which he, for his part, does not care to make. As a rule we disbelieve all facts and theories for which we have no use. Clifford's cosmic emotions find no use for Christian feelings. Huxley belabors the bishops because there is no use for sacerdotalism in his scheme of life. But Newman goes over to Romanism, and finds all sorts of reasons good for staying there, because a priestly system is for him an organic need and delight.

So Clifford notwithstanding, our nonintellectual nature evidently does influence our convictions. The state of things is far from simple, and pure insight and pure logic, whatever they may do ideally, are not the only things that really do produce our creeds.

If we had an infallible intellect, with its objective certitudes, we might feel ourselves disloyal to such a perfect organ of knowledge in not trusting to it exclusively, in not waiting for its releasing word. But if we believe that no bell in us tolls to let us know for certain when truth is in our grasp, then it seems a piece of idle fantasticality to preach so solemnly of our duty of waiting for the bell.

James has still to deal with another sort of critic, no less hostile. The charge this time is not that where evidence is lacking it is wiser and better to suspend judgment. It is, rather, this: If you start justifying belief on this basis, where and how are you going to draw the line? The justification is not, by its nature, the peculiar property of the man who desires to believe in God. It would seem to be equally available, as a principle of justification, for other beliefs as well, some of which might be incompatible with those beliefs James used it to defend. A man who advances a principle that would justify incompatible beliefs has some explaining to do. James knew this. Although convinced that his argument was sound, he knew that others would not be. Thus:

I confess I do not see how this logic can be escaped. But sad experience makes me fear that some of you may still shrink from saying with me that we have the right to believe at our own risk any hypothesis that is live enough to tempt our will.

If this is so, however, I suspect it is because you have got away from the logical point of view altogether, and are thinking of some particular religious hypothesis which for you is dead. The freedom to "believe what you will" you apply to the case of some patent superstition; and the faith you think of is the faith defined by the schoolboy when he said: "Faith is when you believe something that you know ain't true."

I can only repeat that this is a misapprehension of my position. The freedom to "believe what we will," for which I have been arguing, can only cover living options which the intellect by itself cannot resolve; and living options never seem absurd or superstitious to him who has them to consider.

Where there is no such forced option, the dispassionately judicial intellect with no pet hypothesis, saving us, as it does, from dupery, at any rate, ought to be our ideal.

It would appear that James has only restated his difficulty. It is still open to anyone to point out: "Yes, what you have said, you have said. The point is, however, that what you have not said, you have not said. What about the man whose passional nature inclines him to embrace, as true, a proposition that is incompatible with one that your passional nature has inclined you to embrace? As between two passional natures having divergent inclinations, how do you decide?" A glance through the published letters of William James shows that he was bothered by this point. Writing to his brother Henry, the novelist, he protests:

When I *say* that, *other things being equal,* the view of things that seems more satisfactory morally will legitimately be treated by men as truer than the view that seems less so, *they quote me as saying* that anything morally satisfactory can be treated as true, no matter how unsatisfactory it may be from the point of view of its consistency with what we already know or believe to be true about physical or natural facts, which is rot!!

James has drawn a two-edged sword. To vary the metaphor, his principle may be used to reinforce either theism or atheism, or for the matter of that, some third alternative equally removed from either, say skepticism or polytheism. In the last analysis he merely reinforces the most deeply congenial belief; he does not state which belief is or ought to be the most congenial. However, he is not done protesting. Writing to an English philosopher, he has much the same thing to say:

> Would to God I had never thought of that unhappy title for my essay. What I meant by the title was the state of mind of the man who finds an impulse in him toward a believing attitude, and who resolves not to quench it simply because doubts of its truth are possible. Its opposite would be the maxim: Believe in nothing which you can possibly doubt.
>
> My essay hedged the license to indulge in private overbeliefs with so many restrictions and sign boards of danger that the outlet was narrow enough. It made of tolerance the essence of the situation. It defined the permissible cases. It treated the faith attitude as a necessity for individuals, because the total "evidence" which only the race can draw includes their experiments among its data. It tended to show only that faith cannot be absolutely *vetoed,* as certain champions of "science" had claimed it ought to be.
>
> I cry to heaven to tell me of what insane root my "leading contemporaries" have eaten, that they are so smitten with blindness as to the meaning of printed texts.
>
> In my essay the evil shape was a vision of "Science" in the form of abstraction, priggishness and sawdust, lording it over all. Take the sterilest scientific prig and cad you know, compare him with the richest religious intellect you know, and you would not, any more than I would, give the former the exclusive right of way.

There are two parts to a man's exposition of his ideas concerning God. In the first place, he should make clear why he believes that God exists. In the second, he should make clear what he conceives God's nature to be. So far as God's existence goes, we know where James stands in this essay. "Why do I believe in God? Is it because I have experienced his presence? No; rather because I need that it be true." Before quitting James, it is worth noting that he used his principle to justify his belief in God's finiteness. Like Mill, and other recent and contemporary theologians, James repudiated the celebrated "omni's" of traditional theology.

> I simply refuse to accept the idea of there being no purpose in the objective world. On the other hand, I cannot represent the existence of purpose except as based in a mind. The "not-me," therefore, so far as it contains purpose, must spring from a mind; but not necessarily a *One and Only* mind.
>
> In saying God exists, all I imply is that my purposes are cared for by a mind so powerful as on the whole to control the drift of the universe. That is . . . merely a practical emotional faith.
>
> The only difficulties of theism are the moral difficulties and meanness; and they have always seemed to me to flow from the gratuitous dogma of God being the all-inclusive reality. Once think possible a pluralism of which He may be one member, and piety forthwith ceases to be incompatible with manliness, and religious faith with intellectual rectitude.
>
> In short, the only theism I defend is that of simple unphilosophic mankind. God, in the religious life of ordinary men is the name, not of the whole of things, heaven forbid, but only of the ideal tendency in things. . . . He works in an external environment, has limits, and has enemies. . . . If there be a God, how the devil can we know what difficulties

he may have had to contend with? Possible difficulties! They save everything. But what are they if not limitations to the all-inclusiveness of any single being!

Having an environment, being in time, and working out a history just like ourselves, He escapes from the foreignness from all that is human, of the static, timeless, perfect absolute.

My God, being part of a pluralistic system, is responsible only for such things as He knows enough and has enough power to have accomplished. The "omniscient" and "omnipotent" God of theology I regard as a disease of the philosophy shop.

The line of least resistance, as it seems to me, both in theology and in philosophy, is to accept, along with the Superhuman Consciousness, the notion that It is not all embracing; the notion, in other words, that there is a God, but that He is finite, either in power or in knowledge, or in both at once.

NOTE ON SOURCES.   The material in this section is quoted or abridged from "The Will to Believe." The concluding passages are from the chapters entitled "Conclusion" and "Postscript" in James's book *Varieties of Religious Experience.*

THE QUESTION POSED

The question "When can I say I know?" is central to the branch of philosophy called *epistemology,* which is derived from the two Greek words meaning "knowledge" and "the rationale of." It means an inquiry into the nature of knowledge. If the intention were carried out, it would provide us with the knowledge of the nature of knowledge. In the conception of epistemology, knowledge turns in upon itself and seeks to formulate a "theory" of itself. Here knowledge is itself made the object of investigation. How did philosophers find themselves involved in such an inquiry?

From an acquaintance with the questions we have been examining—especially the last one: "What things shall I call art?"—one can see in a general way how epistemology came about. Responses to these questions have often been speculative, and there is a cautious turn of mind to which all such speculations seem to be of doubtful value. Such a mind is impressed finally with the futility of such matters and with the confusion that emerges when humans seek to clarify their beliefs about such things. Out of this attitude toward speculation, two widely different things have resulted. There have come, in the first place, the genial and undisciplined doubts of such persons as Montaigne and Anatole France. Here the procedure is largely one of banter and ridicule. But that has not been the doubter's only weapon against the speculator. For in the second place, there has come the demand that flights of speculation be put aside until a preliminary inquiry is made into the nature of knowledge itself and the question faced: Can it be shown, from an analysis of the nature of knowledge itself, whether such speculations are justified, whether they lie within the actual or possible grasp of the mind?

The sections that follow may, therefore, be considered as approaches to a single problem: the condition that needs to be met if speculation is justified at all.

The authors chosen for consideration are David Hume and Immanuel Kant from the eighteenth century, A. J. Ayer and R. G. Collingwood from the early part of the twentieth century, and Alvin Goldman and Keith Lehrer, both examples of contemporary epistemologists.

6   DAVID HUME
An Appeal to Experience

For most readers, during the closing years of the seventeenth and most of the eighteenth century, the problem of knowledge meant John Locke's *Essay Concerning Human Understanding*. His general commonsense tone, his homely appeal to experience, his determination not to be led into unverifiable speculations, all combined to secure for him a wide circle of readers and followers. It was only natural, therefore, that the next stage in the development of epistemological theory should take the form of an attempt to "begin where Locke left off." His position briefly was this: All knowledge may be analyzed into ideas. All ideas come to us from experience. All experience is by way of the senses. This *empiricism,* as it is called, was Locke's contribution to epistemological theory. His successor in these matters, David Hume, wrote for a generation that was familiar with the appeal to experience as Locke had formulated it. Hume set himself a simple task: to deduce more rigorously the implications of Locke's position.

THE ARGUMENT OF THE PASSAGES.   Hume is a critic of natural theology. His method there was to show what happens in natural theology if one sticks closely to the terms laid down by traditional speculation in these matters. He applies the same method in epistemology. It is proposed to make an appeal to experience, he writes; let the appeal be made, then, and not abandoned because it is found to lead to inconvenient consequences. The argument of his position is simple and direct. All knowledge may be analyzed into impressions and ideas. All ideas are derived from earlier impressions.

We use certain "metaphysical" terms, such as "matter," "mind," "causal connection," "free will," "the uniformity of nature." These terms play a large part in human thinking and speculating. In fact, they are the fundamental terms in the modern person's general reflections about the world. What are they worth? From what "impressions" are they derived? What corresponds to them in that actual experience to which Locke proposed to appeal? In each case Hume's answer is "they have no basis in experience." Accordingly, any speculation that incorporates them is a waste of ink and paper. He begins by explaining that an inquiry into the nature of knowledge is directed toward eliminating as mere speculation all abstruse terms that clutter human thinking:

> The only method of freeing learning from abstruse questions is to inquire seriously into the nature of human understanding and show, from an exact analysis of its powers and capacity, that it is by no means fitted for such subjects.

The premises of his theory of knowledge are to be the following:

> We may divide all perceptions into two classes: impressions and ideas. By impressions I mean all our perceptions when we hear, see, feel, love, hate, desire, etc. Ideas are those less lively perceptions of which we are conscious when we reflect on any of those sensations mentioned above.

All ideas are copies of impressions. . . . Even those ideas which seem most wide of this origin are found, upon a nearer scrutiny to be derived from it. . . . We shall always find that every idea is copied from a similar impression. . . . it is impossible for us to think of anything which we have not antecedently felt by our senses.

The test of all terms is to be "show me the impression":

When we entertain any suspicion of a philosophical term, we need but inquire from what impression is that supposed idea derived. If it be not possible to assign any, this will serve to confirm our suspicion that it is employed without meaning. . . . By this means we can throw light upon ideas and render them precise. Produce the impressions or originals from which the ideas are copied.

The first idea to be tested by the appeal to impressions is the now familiar idea of substance, the concept so important to Descartes in Chapter 2.

Some philosophers found much of their reasonings on the distinction of *substance* and *quality.* I would fain ask them whether the idea of substance be derived from impressions of sensations or impressions of reflection. Does it arise from an impression? Point it out to us, that we may know its nature and qualities. But if you cannot point out any such impression, you may be certain you are mistaken when you imagine you have any such idea.

If the impression from which we derive our idea of substance be conveyed to us by our senses, I ask, by which of them? If by the eyes, it must be a color. If by the ears, it must be a sound. If by the palate, it must be a taste. And so of the other senses. But I believe none will assert that substance is either a color, a sound, or a taste.

Is the idea of substance, then, derived from an impression of reflection [i.e., introspection]? But impressions of reflection resolve themselves into our feelings, passions, and emotions, none of which can possibly resemble a substance. We have, therefore, no idea of substance, apart from that of a collection of qualities.

The idea of substance is nothing but a collection of ideas of qualities, united by the imagination and given a particular name by which we are able to recall that collection. The particular qualities which form a substance are commonly referred to an unknown something in which they are supposed to "inhere." This is a fiction.

We may well ask what causes us to believe in the existence of material substance. 'Tis certain there is no question in philosophy more abstruse. By what argument can it be proved that perceptions must be caused by external objects entirely different from them? By an appeal to experience? But here experience is and must be entirely silent. The mind has never anything present to it but its perceptions and cannot possibly have any experience of their connection with objects. The supposition of such a connection is, therefore, without any foundation in reasoning.

Philosophers distinguish betwixt *perceptions* and *objects*. The perceptions are supposed to be caused by the object, and to be interrupted, perishing and different at different times and for different people. The objects are supposed to cause the perceptions, and to be uninterrupted, continuous, and identical. But, however, this view may be esteemed, I assert that there are no principles, either of the understanding or the fancy which lead us to embrace this opinion of the double existence of perceptions and objects.

This hypothesis of the double existence of perceptions and objects has no primary recommendation to reason. The only existences of which we are certain are perceptions. Being immediately present to us by consciousness, they commend our strongest assent, and must be the foundation of all our reasonings. But, as nothing is ever present to the mind but perceptions, it follows that we can never observe any "object," or any connection, causal or otherwise, between perceptions and objects.

The idea of substance as something underlying a set of qualities is unable to produce its credentials. Away with it, then. As Hume remarks of all such ideas, "Commit it to the flames." From material substance he turns to the idea of mental or spiritual substance:

There are some philosophers (e.g., Berkeley) who imagine we are every moment intimately conscious of what we call our *self;* that we feel its existence and its continuance in existence, and are certain of its identity and simplicity.

Unluckily all these positive assertions are contrary to that very experience which is pleaded for them. Have we any idea of a self? From what impression could it be derived? It must be some impression that gives rise to every idea. But self or person is not any one impression. If any impression gives rise to the idea of one's self, that impression must continue to be the same, since one's self is supposed to continue to be the same. But there is no such continuing, constant impression.

For my part, when I enter most intimately into what I call my *self,* I always stumble on some particular perception or other, of heat or cold, light or shade, love or hatred, pain or pleasure, color or sound, etc. I never catch my self, distinct from some such perception.

If anyone thinks he has a different notion of his self, I must confess I can no longer reason with him. He may perceive something simple and continued which he calls his *self;* though I am certain there is no such principle in me.

Setting aside metaphysicians of this kind, I may venture to affirm of the rest of mankind that they are nothing but a bundle or collection of different perceptions which succeed each other with an inconceivable rapidity and are in a perpetual flux and movement, Our eyes cannot turn in their sockets without varying their perceptions. Our thoughts are still more variable. And all our other senses and powers con-tribute to this change.

The mind (or self) is a kind of theater where perceptions make their appearance, pass, repass, glide away, and mingle in an infinite variety. But there is no simplicity, no one simple thing present or pervading this multiplicity; no identity pervading this change; whatever natural inclination we may have to imagine that there is. The comparison of the theater must not mislead us: it persists, while the actors come and go. Whereas, only the successive perceptions constitute the mind.

The idea of mind or self or Spirit fails to reveal any basis in immediate impressions. That seals its fate. But the question persists: "Why do we entertain such a notion?" It is one thing to show that an idea is a mere fiction. It is another thing to account for its widespread presence in human thinking.

Why do we ascribe an identity amid these successive perceptions, and suppose our selves possessed of an invariable and uninterrupted existence through the whole course of our life? The identity which we ascribe to minds and selves is only a fictitious one, but why do we ascribe it?

Suppose we could see clearly into the mind of another, and observe that succession of perceptions which constitutes his mind. Suppose, too, that he always preserves the memory of a considerable part of past perceptions. It is evident that nothing could more readily contribute to bestowing a relation between these successive perceptions. Would not the frequent placing of these remembered perceptions in the chain of thought convey our imagination more easily from one to another? And so make the whole seem like the continuance of one object?

As memory alone acquaints us with the continuance and extent of a succession of perceptions, it is to be considered, on that account chiefly, as the source of personal identity. Had we no memory, we should never have any notion of that succession of perceptions which constitutes our self or person. But having once acquired this notion from the operation of memory, we can extend the same beyond our memory and come to include times which we have entirely forgot. And so arises the fiction of person and personal identity.

Material substance is gone. Mental substance is gone. Hume turns to the notion of causal connection between events. He is here proposing to invade the citadel of eighteenth-century science, a structure that was believed to rest squarely on the notion of causal connection. Hume's handling of this idea should be observed closely. His first question is, "What do people mean by the idea of causal connection?" His answer is that by causal connection they mean necessary connection; they believe that there is a necessary connection between a cause and its effect. His next question is the inevitable one: "What evidence, open to our senses, have we for believing that there is any necessity in causal connection?" His answer is, "None whatever."

There is no idea in metaphysics more obscure or uncertain than *necessary connection* between cause and effect. We shall try to fix the precise meaning of this term by producing the impression from which it is copied.

When we look at external objects, and consider the operation of causes, we are never able, in a single instance, to discover a necessary connection; any quality which binds the effect to the cause, and renders the one a necessary consequence of the other. We find only that the effect does, in fact, follow the cause. The impact of one billiard ball upon another is followed by the motion of the second. There is here contiguity in space and time, but nothing to suggest necessary connection.

The scenes of the universe are continually shifting, and one object follows another in an uninterrupted succession. But any "force" or necessary connection pervading the whole machine never discovers itself in any of the sensible qualities of the body. We know that heat is a constant attendant of flame. But as to any necessary connection between them, we have no room so much as to conjecture or imagine.

In single instances of causal connection we never, by our utmost scrutiny, discover anything but one event following another. We detect no necessary connection between the cause and its effect. All events seem loose and separate. One event follows another. But we observe no tie between them, beyond contiguity in space and time. They are contiguous, thus; but never connected. As we can have no idea of anything of which we have had no correspondent impression, the conclusion seems to be that we have no idea of necessary connection, and that these words are absolutely without meaning.

We are apt to imagine that we could discover effects from their causes by the mere operation of our reason, without experience. We fancy that, were we brought on a sudden into this world, we could have inferred that one billiard ball would communicate motion to another upon impact; and that we need not have waited for the event, in order to pronounce with certainty concerning it. Knowledge of this relation arises entirely from experience. We find that particular objects are constantly conjoined with each other.

Knowledge of this relation is not, in any instance, attained by reasonings *a priori*. Causes and effects are discoverable by experience, not by reason. Every effect is a distinct event from its cause. It could not, therefore, be discovered in the cause (prior to experience of their conjunction). Without the assistance of observation and experience, we should in vain pretend to determine any single event or infer any cause or effect. A man must be very sagacious who could discover by reasoning that ice is the effect of cold, without being previously acquainted with the operation of these qualities.

Hence no philosopher who is rational and modest has even pretended to assign the ultimate cause of any natural operation. Ultimate springs and principles (causes) are totally shut off from human curiosity and enquiry.

As in the case of our idea of mind or self, Hume pauses to inquire why we ascribe to the connection between cause and effect something that is not revealed in experience.

Why do we imagine a necessary connection? From observing many constant conjunctions? But what is there in a number of instances which is absent from a single instance? Only this: After a repetition of similar instances the mind is carried by habit upon the appearance of the cause, to expect the effect. This connection, which we feel in the mind, this customary and habitual transition of the imagination from a cause to its effect, is the impression from which we form the idea of necessary connection. There is nothing further in the case.

When we say a cause is necessarily connected with its effect we mean, therefore, that they have acquired a connection in our thought; a conclusion which is somewhat extraordinary, but seems founded on sufficient evidence.

Every idea is copied from some impression. In all single instances of causal connection there is nothing that can suggest any idea of necessity. But when many instances have been experienced, we begin to entertain the idea. We then feel a new impression, to wit, a customary transition in our thoughts or imagination between the cause and its effect. This impression is the original of that idea which we seek for. For, as this idea arises from a number of similar instances, it must arise from the circumstance in which the number of instances differ from each single instance. This customary transition is the only circumstance in which they differ.

Hume's rejection of the idea of cause as necessary connection suggests at once that he may be in a position to say something about the long-standing controversy over free will and determinism. That dispute arises when we hold (a) that human acts are caused, and (b) that causes are necessary connections. Hume's claim here is not that he can solve the problem but that he can dissolve it.

The question of man's free will has been long disputed among philosophers. Does man have freedom of will? Or are his acts determined? If motives determine acts, are motives themselves determined? This dispute has been much canvassed on all hands, and has led into such labyrinths of obscure sophistry that a sensible reader inclines to turn a deaf ear to the question, expecting neither instruction nor entertainment. I hope to make it appear that the whole controversy has hitherto turned merely upon words.

We ascribe necessity to matter. The degree and direction of every motion are prescribed with exactness. Do we similarly ascribe necessity to persons? Are the degree and direction of every action prescribed with exactness?

Two circumstances form the whole of the necessity we ascribe to matter: a constant conjunction between cause-events and effect-events, and a consequent inference in our minds from the one to the other. Beyond these two circumstances we have no notion of any necessity in the motion of matter.

Do not these two circumstances take place in the voluntary actions of men? Are not similar motives followed by similar actions? Are there not detectable uniformities in human action? Is it impossible to collect any general observations concerning mankind? Has experience of human affairs, however, accurately digested by reflection, no purpose?

The most irregular and unexpected resolutions of men may be accounted for by those who know every particular circumstance of their character and situation. A genial person, contrary to expectation, may give a peevish answer, but he has a toothache or has not dined. Even when, as sometimes happens, an action cannot be accounted for, do we not put it down to our ignorance of relevant details?

Thus it appears that the conjunction between motive and action is as regular and uniform as between cause and effect in any part of nature. In both cases, constant conjunction and inference from one to the other.

Though constant conjunction and customary transition be all that is discoverable between a cause and an effect in nature, men believe they perceive something like a necessary connection. Then, when they consider the operations of their own wills and feel no such necessary connection between motive and action, they suppose there is a difference between the cause-effect relation and the motive-action relation. And are hence to say that man's will, unlike matter, is free.

But our knowledge of causation, like our knowledge of motivation, is merely of a constant conjunction and a consequent inference in our minds from one to the other. It is the same in both cases. It is different only if it be pretended that the mind can perceive, in the operation of matter, some other connection between cause and effect than has place in the voluntary actions of intelligent beings. It is incumbent on those who pretend thus to make good their assertion. So long as we rashly suppose that we have an idea of some necessity in the operations of external nature, beyond constant conjunction and an habitual inference in our minds; and, at the same time, admit we can find nothing such in the voluntary actions of the mind, we shall continue confusion.

Thus far Hume has examined the ideas of material substance, of mental substance, of causal connection, of free will. Of each in turn he has asked one question: "Upon what impression, received by the senses, does it rest?" From each in turn he has received only silence for an answer. One more idea remains, namely, the idea of a uniformity of nature, the unquestioned premise of all our inductions and generalizations from nature. Why do we believe, so unquestioningly, that the "future will resemble the past"? Why do we argue, for instance, that fire will always melt ice, when our only ground for this belief is the fact that it has done so in the past?

All our conclusions from experience proceed on the supposition that the future will resemble the past. To prove that the future will resemble the past, by arguing from experience, is evidently going in a circle, and taking that for granted which is the very point in question.

As to past experience, it can be allowed to give direct and certain information of those precise objects only, and that precise period of time only, which fell under its cognizance. But why this experience should be extended to future times and other objects, is the question on which I would insist. So to extend it is a process of mind or thought of which I would willingly know the foundation.

Not by an argument from experience can we prove this resemblance of the past to the future, for all such arguments are founded on the supposition of that resemblance. Let the course of things be allowed hitherto ever so regular. That alone, without some new inference, does not prove that for the future it will continue so.

My practice, you say, refutes my doubts. But you mistake the purport of my question. In practice I am satisfied. As a philosopher, who has some share of curiosity, I will not say skepticism, I want to learn the foundation of this inference. No reading, no inquiry, has yet been able to remove my difficulty. Upon what grounds can we argue that the future will resemble the past? Upon what grounds expect similar effects from causes which are similar?

Geometry (or any mathematics), when taken into the assistance of science, is unable to remedy this defect. Every part of applied mathematics proceeds on the supposition that certain laws are established by nature in her operations. Mathematical reasonings are employed to assist experiences in the discovery of these laws, or to determine their influence in particular instances. But the discovery of the law itself is owing merely to experience, and all the mathematical reasoning in the world could never lead one step toward the knowledge of it.

In all reasonings from experience, then, there is a step taken by the mind (that the future resembles the past) which is not supported by any argument. Nevertheless, we take this step. There must therefore be some other principle (than rational or demonstrative argument).

Though none but a fool or madman will ever pretend to dispute the authority of experience, it may surely be allowed a philosopher to have so much curiosity as to examine the principle of human nature which gives authority to experience.

This principle is custom, or habit. Wherever repetition produces a propensity to renew the same act, without being impelled by any reasoning, we say this propensity is the effect of custom or habit. That habit or custom is the ultimate principle of all our conclusions from experiences, seems to be the only hypothesis which explains why we draw from many instances an inference which we are not able to draw from one instance that is in no respect different from them.

All inferences from experience are, therefore, effects of habit or custom, not of reasoning. The conclusions which we draw, based on reasoning, from considering one circle, are the same which we would draw from surveying all circles. But no man, having seen only one body impelled by another, could infer that every other similar body would move after a like impulse.

Custom, then, not reason, is the great guide of human life. It is that principle alone which renders our experience useful to us, and makes us expect, for the future, a similar train of events with those which have appeared in the past. Without the influence of custom, we should be entirely ignorant of every matter of fact beyond what is immediately present to the memory or the senses.

What, then, is the conclusion of the whole matter? A simple one, though, it must be confessed, pretty remote from the common theories of philosophy. All belief concerning matters of fact or real existence, is derived merely from some object present to the memory or the senses, and a customary conjunction between that and some other object. Having found, in many instances, that two kinds of objects have been conjoined (say, flame and heat), the mind is carried by custom to expect the same in the future, This is the whole operation of the mind in all our conclusions concerning matters of fact and existence.

Here, then, is a kind of pre-established harmony between the course of nature and formation of our beliefs. Custom or habit is the principle of human nature by which this correspondence, so necessary to the subsistence of our species and the regulation of our conduct, has been effected. Did not the presence of an object excite in us the ideas of other objects commonly conjoined with it, all human knowledge would be limited to the narrow sphere of our memory and senses. Those who delight in the discovery of purposes in nature have here ample subject to employ their wonder and admiration.

As this operation of the mind, whereby we infer like effects from like causes, is so essential to human life, it is not probable that it could be trusted to the fallacious deductions of our reason, which is slow in its operation and extremely liable to error and mistake. It is more comfortable to the ordinary wisdom of nature to secure so necessary an act of the mind by some instinct or mechanical tendency which may be infallible in its operations and independent of all the labored deductions of understanding.

Hume is now at the end of his review:

By way of conclusion to these reflections on diverse questions: When we run over libraries, persuaded of the principles here expounded, what havoc must we make? If we take in hand any volume, of divinity or metaphysics, for instance, let us ask: Does it contain any reasoning concerning quantity or number? No. Does it contain any experimental (probable) reasoning concerning matter of fact? No. Commit it then to the flames: for it can contain nothing but sophistry and illusion.

I am at first affrighted and confounded with that forlorn solitude in which I am placed by my philosophy, and fancy myself some strange uncouth monster, utterly abandoned and disconsolate. Fain would I run into the crowd for shelter and warmth. I call upon others to join me. But no one will hearken to me. Everyone keeps at a distance, and dreads that storm which beats upon me from every side. I have exposed myself to the enmity of all metaphysicians, logicians, mathematicians, and theologians. Can I wonder at the insults I must suffer? I have declared my disapprobation of their systems. Can I be surprised if they should express a hatred of my ideas and my person? When I look about me, I foresee on every hand, dispute, contradiction, anger, calumny, detraction. When I turn my eye inward, I find only doubt and ignorance. Every step I take is with hesitation; every new reflection makes me dread an error and absurdity in my reasoning.

NOTE ON SOURCES.   The material in this section is quoted, abridged, or paraphrased from David Hume, *An Enquiry Concerning Human Understanding* (Oxford: Clarendon Press, 1975), Sections 1, 2, 4, 5, 7, 8, and 12. However, since Hume had already, in an earlier book, *A Treatise of Human Nature,* worked over much of the materials in those sections of the *Enquiry,* we have sometimes drawn on corresponding sections of the *Treatise* to replace or supplement passages in the *Enquiry.*

4

What Shall I Say About Ultimate Reality?

THE QUESTION POSED

One of the best-known remarks in the history of philosophy is ascribed to the Greek thinker, Thales. He is said to have held that "all things are made of water." On the face of it, this seems both unimportant and false. Why then its historical importance? Why has Thales been bracketed, along with Copernicus and Darwin, as having initiated a line of thought that marked an epoch in human speculation?

The reason is this. It required, in the first instance, a bold mind to conceive any proposition having the general form "All things are made of . . . "; because if there is one proposition that would appear to be justified by the facts of our everyday experience, it is that all things are not made of any one thing. Multiplicity and variety are the obvious facts about the everyday world. The effort of thought required to break down testimony of the everyday world must have been considerable, as it certainly was subsequently fruitful.

Thales probably had his reasons. Such apparently diverse things as ice, snow, mist, vapor, steam are all "made of" water, if we use the term loosely. Why not other things, too? Whatever his reasons may have been, his remark, once made, continued to re-echo in the minds of generations that came after him. "All things are made of . . . "

In fact, the problem is with us to this day. What are all things made of? What do we intend by the phrase *made of?* If we brush aside Thales's answer, what do we propose in place of it? Speculations on this question constitute part of the philosophical discipline called metaphysics. That is, metaphysics is, in part, an inquiry into the question of what all things are "made of."

Suppose we consider a miscellaneous collection of things, a clay pipe, a bird's egg, a rainbow, a copy of *Hamlet*, an uprising in central China, an act of mercy, a cry in the night, a new planet. What are all these things made of? Varying the words, to what common substance are these all reducible? Of what "underlying reality" are they all manifestations? Is this underlying reality itself further reducible?

The notion that the observed multiplicity and variety of the everyday world are reducible to something common and uniform and *not* given as part of the everyday world is not an unreasonable notion. Few persons would care to deny it in principle, much as they might argue over what that something is to which all things are reducible. Granted the propriety of the notion of an ultimate reality, a "real" world in contrast to the "everyday" world, it is necessary to go one step further. In some sense or other, the everyday world is an appearance or a manifestation of the real world. There is the real world, the world as it really is, and there are its appearances, how it appears.

It is then possible to restate our central problem: What is the nature of that ultimate reality, that real world, of which the everyday world is the appearance? Answers to this question vary. If it is held that there is *an* ultimate reality, we have what is called *monism* in metaphysics, the belief that ultimate reality is one in kind. If it is held that there are at least two ultimate realities, we have what is called *dualism* in metaphysics, the belief that ultimate reality is two in kind. If it is held that there are three or more ultimate realities, we have what is called *pluralism* in metaphysics, the belief that ultimate reality is three or more inkind.

Within these classifications others will occur. You and I might agree that monism is a true belief. Our agreement might extend no further. When we came to the question of the nature of this ultimate reality, we might differ. I might claim that it was matter; you might claim that it was mind; a third person might claim that it was neither, but something more ultimate of which both matter and mind are manifestations.

In this topic we are to be concerned with such inquiries. A metaphysical claim is about the nature of ultimate reality. In considering any such claim, it will be helpful to ask, "Is it a form of monism, or dualism, or pluralism? What reasons are given, or may be given, in support of it? What reasons against it? What consequences follow from it? Do these agree with our experience of the everyday world? Or do they make nonsense of it?" Reflection upon the nature of ultimate reality is not the whole of metaphysics, but it is a large part of it. For a beginner in metaphysics, two things are of primary importance: to demand reasons for accepting any claim, and to note consequences that follow from accepting the hypothesis. If a materialist in metaphysics claims that all and only material things are real things ("If X is real, then X is matter"), we should ask the materialist *why* he or she thinks so; and what follows *from* this metaphysical claim.

The readings and comments that follow help in thinking about this question. These philosophers have been chosen because they are typical and because, among them, they provide good argument. Each is convinced of his views and eager to spread them among "all rational minds." Each realizes that he must be prepared to argue his case. There is among them no appeal to emotions; at least, not intentionally. They are all, in this respect, "hardheaded rationalists." Here, for the eye that can detect it, is one of humankind's supreme intellectual sports insofar as the human is a "rational" animal. Here are corrosive skepticism, caustic (if obscure) wit, resounding thwacks, closely built arguments, relentless determination to "begin at the beginning" and "think it through," and proud gestures directing attention to "positions established" and "positions overthrown." A taste for metaphysics and a flare for the practice of metaphysics are not widely diffused, but the genuine article, like a love for poetry or painting, is irrepressible once it has become aware of itself.

The readings are in chronological order, but the order exhibits development. Hobbes contributes the claim that all things are made of matter, that matter alone is real; "if X is real, then X is matter." This is monism and materialism, as full-blown as one could wish. The position taken up by Berkeley begins by a deliberate and reasoned-out rejection of Hobbes's materialism. All things, the claim here is, are either mind or objectifications of mind, spirit, *Geist*, and so on. Hobbes's materialism and Berkeley's idealism between them account for much traditional metaphysics. The term *voluntarism*, associated with Schopenhauer, who seems to have been familiar with the claims of both Hobbes and Berkeley, indicates a position somewhat closer to Berkeley than to Hobbes: it covers the claim that neither matter nor mind in the sense of intellect, but *will*, is the ultimate substance of all things. The ultimately real stuff, of which all things are manifestations, to which all things in the world of appearance are "reducible," is will, the power to act, to perform a deed. As Faust says, *Im Anfang war die Tat*, "in the beginning was the deed."

---

1   THOMAS HOBBES
The Claims of Materialism

BIOGRAPHICAL NOTE.   Thomas Hobbes was born in England in 1588, the year in which Elizabeth became queen of England, and died in 1679 at the age of ninety-one. The English had their major political revolution between 1641 and 1688. For them this was somewhat comparable to what the Americans had beginning in 1776, the French beginning in 1789, the Russians beginning in 1917, and the Chinese in the years that culminated in 1949. Hobbes was a close student of revolutionary politics and the then recent physical sciences. His life's work was to formulate a conceptual framework, given which a person could assimilate the outcomes of the political and scientific revolutions. He led a long and busy life, interesting in itself and also because of the years through which it was lived. He was educated at Oxford. Thereafter he became tutor and secretary to the Earl of Devonshire. In this capacity he made the acquaintance of Francis Bacon, Ben Johnson, and other literary figures. He published a translation of Thucydides. When his patron died, Hobbes took over the education of his son with whom he made the Grand Tour, making the acquaintance of Galileo, Gassendi, and other scientific luminaries in Europe. He returned to England to study politics. It was the time of England's civil war against Charles I. Hobbes as a Royalist, sided against Cromwell. Circulation of his book, *The Body Politic*, obliged him to leave England and reside in Paris. This time he met Descartes and engaged him in metaphysical controversy. The exiled Prince of Wales, afterward Charles II, was also in Paris. Hobbes became his tutor. He published again on the subject of politics, this time rousing the wrath of some of the Royalists. He returned to England and enjoyed such peace as obtained under Cromwell's regime, making friends with William Harvey, who discovered the circulation of the blood, with the poet Cowley, and others. Upon the restoration of Charles II to the English throne, Hobbes moved once more to a place in the sun and on the pension list. He was one of the most influential men of his day among persons who were open to ideas. He believed that matter is the ultimate reality; that our sense organs are transformers, not revealers; that humans do not have a free will; that all human action is motivated by complete selfishness; that an absolute sovereign is needed, whether in the form of a monarch or a parliament, to insure peace under law; and that religion is a "pill which it is better to swallow without chewing."

THE ARGUMENT OF THE PASSAGES.   The following passages give a simple formulation of metaphysical materialism. From a statement of the essential point, that all is matter moving according to laws, the passages follow Hobbes through the principal turns of his belief. They present a development and, in some cases, a defense of the implications of the fundamental belief. It should be remembered that Hobbes is writing here as a philosopher, not as a scientist. In the strict sense of the word, he was not a scientist, either by temperament or training. He is, where it is relevant, restating or referring to the labors of Copernicus, Kepler, Galileo, Harvey, and the rest. But the point of his writings, in effect, is this: If what such men are finding out, is once accepted without reservation, then over all we are committed to these more comprehensive beliefs.

> Think not, courteous reader, that the philosophy which I am going to set in order is that which makes philosophers' stones. It is the natural reason of man, busily flying up and down among the creatures, and bringing back a true report of their order, causes, and effects. Philosophy is therefore the child of the world and your own mind. Like the world, its father, as it was in the beginning, it is a thing confused. If you will be a philosopher in good earnest, let your reason move upon the deep of your own cogitations and experience; those things that lie in confusion must be set in order, distinguished, and stamped everyone with its own name.
>
> Philosophy excludes theology, I mean the doctrine of God. It excludes the doctrine of angels and also such things are neither bodies nor properties of bodies. It excludes history, natural as well as political, because such knowledge is but experience or authority and not reason. It excludes astrology and all such divinations. It excludes all such knowledge as is acquired by divine inspiration, or revelation, as not derived to us by reason but by some supernatural sense. Lastly it excludes the doctrine of God's worship as being not to be known by the light of natural reason but the authority of the church.
>
> I am not ignorant how hard a thing it is to weed out of men's minds inveterate opinions that have taken root there, and been confirmed by the authority of eloquent writers; especially since true philosophy rejects the paint and false colors, the ornaments and graces, of language. The first grounds of knowledge are not only beautiful; they are poor and arid, and, in appearance, deformed. Nevertheless, there being some men who are delighted with truth and strength of reason, I thought I might do well to take these pains for the sake of even those few. I proceed therefore and take my beginning from the definition of philosophy.

With these preliminary observations, Hobbes closes in on his theme:

> The subject of philosophy is every body [i.e., piece of matter] of which we can conceive any beginning, which we can compare with other bodies, or which is capable of composition and resolution; that is to say, every body of whose beginning or properties we can have any knowledge.
>
> The definition of body may be this: a body is that which, having no dependence upon our thought, is coincident or coextended with some part of space.

> The world—I mean the whole mass of things that are—is corporeal, that is to say, body; and that which is not body is no part of the universe. . . . The universe being the aggregate of all bodies, there is no real part thereof that is not also body.

The basic thesis once stated, Hobbes moves on to a series of implications, propositions that follow from the fundamental position. The first of these is that motion is the one thing that "really" takes place; all else is mere appearance, thrown off, so to speak, by matter in motion.

> There can be no cause of motion except in a body contiguous and moved.
> Mutation, that is, change, can be nothing but motion of the parts of that body which is changed. We say that that which appears to our senses is otherwise than it appeared formerly. Both appearances are effects produced in the sentient creature; and, if they be different, it is necessary that some part of the agent which was formerly at rest is now moved, and so the mutation consists in the motion; or some part which was formerly moved, is now otherwise moved, and so the mutation consists in this new motion; or which, being formerly moved, is now at rest, and so again mutation is motion.

A second corollary is rigid determinism, that is, the belief that everything happens of necessity, or inevitably.

> Whatever effect is produced at any time, the same is produced by a necessary cause. For whatsoever is produced had an entire cause, had all those things which, being supposed, it cannot be understood but that the effect follows; that is, it had a necessary cause. In the same manner, whatsoever effects are hereafter to be produced, shall have a necessary cause, so that all the effects that have been or shall be produced have their necessity in things antecedent.

From this determinism it would follow that, given enough knowledge of the past and present, one could predict all future events in the greatest detail. Hobbes is aware of this claim. It has been made off and on ever since his time. Better than a century later the French astronomer, LaPlace, wrote:

> We ought to regard the present state of the universe as the effect of its antecedent state and as the cause of the state that is to follow. An intelligence, who for a given instant should be acquainted with all the forces by which nature is animated, and with the several positions of the beings composing it, if his intellect were vast enough to submit these data to analysis, would include in one and the same formula the movement of the largest bodies in the universe and those of the lightest atom. Nothing would be uncertain for him, the future as well as the past would be present to his eyes.

Hobbes turns to noting further implications of his materialism. All living organisms, it would follow, are just so many complicated machines:

> Seeing that life is but a motion of limbs and organs, why may we not say that all automata (engines that move themselves by springs and wheels as doth a watch) have an artificial life? For what is the heart but a spring, and the nerves but so many strings, and the joints but so many wheels, giving motion to the whole body?

Materialism in metaphysics, he urges, implies sensationism in epistemology; implies, that is, that all knowledge originates in sensations.

> The original of men's thoughts is sense, for there is no conception in a man's mind which hath not, totally or by parts, been begotten upon the organs of sense. The rest are derived from that original.
>
> As I said before, whatsoever we conceive, hath been perceived first by sense, either all at once or by parts. A man can have no thought representing anything, not subject to sense.
>
> Imagination is nothing but decaying sense. From whence it followeth that the longer the time is after the sense, the weaker is the imagination.
>
> Imagination being only of those things which have been formerly perceived by sense, it followeth that imagination and memory are but one thing which for divers considerations have divers names.

Materialism. Determinism. Mechanism. Sensationism. And now the doctrine of representative perception, that is, the belief that sensations represent but do not reveal the real nature of the external world. Hobbes labors this point at great length.

> The cause of sense is the external object which presseth the organ proper to each sense either immediately or mediately. This pressure, by the mediation of the nerves and other strings and membranes, continueth inward and causeth there a reaction or counter-pressure; which endeavor because outward, seemeth to be some matter without. This seeming is that which men call sense; and consisteth as to the eye, in a light or colored figure; to the ear, in a sound; and so on. All which qualities, called sensible qualities, are, in the object that causeth them only so many several motions of the matter by which it presseth our organs diversely. Neither in us that are pressed, are they anything else but divers motions; for motion produceth nothing but motion. For if these sensible qualities (colors, sounds) were in the object which causeth them, they could not be severed from them as by mirrors and echoes they are.
>
> The cause of perception consisteth in this: When the uttermost part of the organ is pressed, it no sooner yields but the next part within it is pressed also. In this manner the pressure or motion is propagated through all the parts of the organ to the innermost. Also, the pressure of the uttermost part proceedeth from the pressure of some more remote body, and so continually till we come to the object. Sense therefore is some internal motion in the sentient organism, generated by some internal motion of the parts of the object, and propagated through all the media to the innermost part of the organ.
>
> I shall endeavor to make plain these points: that the object wherein color is inherent is not the object seen; that there is nothing without us, really, which we call image or color; that color is but the apparition unto us of the motion, agitation, or change which the object worketh in the brain or some internal substance of the head; that as in vision, so also in the other senses, the subject of their inherence is not the object but the sentient creature.
>
> As a color is not inherent in the object, but an effect thereof upon us, caused by motion in the object, so neither is sound in the thing we hear, but in ourselves. The clapper hath no sound in it, but action, and maketh motion in the internal parts of the bell; so the bell hath motion, and not sound, that imparteth motion to the air; and the air hath motion, but no sound, which it imparteth by the ear and nerve unto the brain; and the brain hath motion, but no sound.

> From hence it followeth that whatsoever qualities our senses make us think there be in the world, they be not there, but are seeming and apparitions only; the things that really are in the world without us are those motions by which these seemings are caused. And this is the great deception of sense.

Hobbes is stopped by a problem. If the sensation, say the red color of a cherry, is really so much motion of particles in the observer's head, how can we explain the fact that it appears out there in space, located where the cherry is? As Hobbes asks, "Why doth the sensation appear as something situated without the organ?" His answer is:

> Why doth the sensation appear as something situated without the organ? It is true: There is in the whole organ, by reason of its own internal natural action some reaction against the motion which is propagated from the object to the innermost part of the organ. In the organ there is an endeavor opposite to the endeavor which proceedeth from the object. That endeavor inwards is the last action in the act of sense. Then from the reaction, an idea hath its being, which by reason that the endeavor is now outward, doth always appear as something situated without the organ.
>
> But though all sense be made by reaction, as I have said, it is not necessary that everything that reacteth should have sense. I know there have been philosophers, and those learned men, who have maintained that all bodies are endued with sense. Nor do I see how they can be refuted if the nature of sense be placed in reaction only.

The argument turns from the subjectivity of sensations to the question of desires. These too must be admitted to be merely so much matter in motion.

> As that which is really within us, in sensation, is only motion caused by the action of external objects, so that which is really within us in appetite or desire is nothing but motion. But the appearance of that motion we call either pleasure or pain.
>
> When appetites and aversions arise alternately concerning the same thing, so that sometimes we have an appetite to it and sometimes an aversion from it, then the whole sum of desires and aversions is what we call *deliberation*.
>
> In deliberation, the last appetite or aversion, immediately adhering to the act or the omission thereof, is what we call *will*.

If this be the whole story of human preferences and desires, Hobbes is in a position to make short shrift of any lofty moral idealism. This he proceeds to do:

> Moral philosophy is nothing else but the science of what is good and evil in the conversation and society of mankind. Good and evil are names that signify our appetites and aversions; which in different tempers, customs, and doctrines of men, are different, and divers men differ not only in their judgment, on the sense of what is pleasant and unpleasant to the taste, smell, hearing, touch, and sight, but also what is comfortable or disagreeable to reason in the actions of common life. Nay the same man, in divers times differeth from himself and at one time praiseth, that is, calleth good what at another time he dispraiseth, that is, calleth evil.
>
> Every man calleth that which pleaseth him, *good*; and that which displeaseth him, *evil*. Since every man differeth from another in constitution, they differ also from one

another concerning the common distinction of good and evil. Nor is there any such thing as absolute goodness considered without relation.

Whatsoever is the object of any man's appetite or desire, that it is which he for his part calleth good; and the object of his hate and aversion, evil. For these words *good* and *evil* are ever used with relation to the person that useth them, there being nothing simply and absolutely so, nor any rule of good and evil to be taken from the nature of objects themselves; but from the man, where there is no commonwealth.

To the commitments thus far, Hobbes adds one more: a categorical denial of human free will:

I conceive that nothing taketh beginning from itself, but from the action of some other immediate agent without itself. Therefore, when a man hath an appetite or will to something, to which before he had no appetite or will, the cause of his will is not the will itself but something else not in his own disposing.

Neither is the freedom of willing or not willing greater in man than in other living creatures. For where there is appetite, the entire cause thereof hath preceded, and, consequently, the appetite could not choose but follow; that is, hath of necessity followed. Therefore such a liberty as is free from necessity is not to be found in the will.

If by *freedom* we understand the power, not of willing but of doing what we will, then certainly that freedom is to be allowed to both men and animals.

The ordinary definition of a *free agent* is that he is one that when all things are present which are needful to produce an effect, can nevertheless not produce it. This implies a contradiction that is nonsense, being as much as to say the cause of anything may be sufficient and yet the effect shall not follow. There is no such thing as an "agent," which when all things requisite to action are present, can nevertheless forbear to produce it. Or, which is all one, there is no such thing as freedom from necessity.

The essentials of Hobbes's materialism are now before us. The position evokes criticism. With unerring instinct Hobbes places his finger upon the one point which, more than any other perhaps, will be disputed: the denial of human free will. The following passages show Hobbes attempting to defend his determinism against anticipated objections:

To deny necessity is to destroy the power and foreknowledge of God Almighty. For whatsoever God hath purposed to bring to pass by man, or foreseeth shall come to pass, a man might frustrate and make not come to pass if he hath freedom from necessity. Then would God foreknow such things as never shall be, and decree such things as shall never come to pass.

Liberty and necessity are consistent: as in the water, that hath not only liberty but a necessity to descend by the channel. So likewise in the actions men voluntarily do; which because they proceed from their will are termed *voluntary*. And yet, because every act of man's will and every desire and inclination proceedeth from some cause, and that from some other cause, in a continual chain, it proceedeth from necessity. To him that could see the connection of those causes, the necessity of all men's voluntary actions would appear manifest.

The necessity of an action doth not make the laws that prohibit it unjust. Whatsoever necessary cause precede an action, yet if the action be forbidden, he that doth it willingly may justly be punished. For instance, suppose the law on pain of death prohibit stealing. Suppose there be a man who by the strength of temptation is necessitated to steal, and is thereupon put to death. Doth not this punishment deter others from theft? Is it not a cause that others steal not? Doth it not frame and make their wills to justice? To make the law is thereupon to make a cause of justice, and so to necessitate justice. The intention of the law is not to grieve the delinquent for that which is past and not to be undone; but to make him and others just who might otherwise not be so. It respecteth not the evil act past, but the good to come. But you will say, how is it just to kill one man to amend another, if what were done were necessary? To this I answer: men are justly killed, not because their actions are not necessitated, but because their actions are noxious. We destroy, without being unjust, all that is noxious, both beasts and men.

Repentance is nothing but a glad returning into the right way, after the grief of being out of the way. Even though the cause that made a man go astray were necessary, there is no reason why he should not grieve. So likewise, even though the cause that made a man return into the right way were necessary, there remaineth still the cause of joy. So that I say the necessity of actions taketh away neither of those parts of repentance, neither grief for the error nor joy for the returning.

As for praise and dispraise, they depend not at all on the necessity of the action praised or dispraised. For what is it to praise, but to say a thing is good? Good for me, good for someone else, or good for the commonwealth. What is it to say an act is good, but to say it is as I wish it, or as another wish it, or according to the law of the commonwealth? Can no action please me, or another, or the commonwealth, that should happen of necessity? Doth not praise and dispraise, reward and punishment, make and conform the will to good and evil by example?

Materialism is always with us. It is as old as the record of Western philosophy, having received an elaborate presentation in the fifth century B.C. in the writing—of which we now possess only as a few suggestive fragments—of the Greek materialist Democritus, and several centuries later, in the writings of the Roman materialist Lucretius. Our task is to grasp the meaning of materialism and its implications. To recapitulate: It is the belief that reality is moving particles of matter. Its adherents have usually felt committed to certain further claims, as, for example, all events are rigidly predictable; all organisms are only mechanisms; all knowledge, originating in sensations, is knowledge of appearances only, since sensations are entirely subjective; human conduct is strictly determined by antecedent and concomitant events; human motives are essentially egocentric; and the achievement of happiness, in the sense of the satisfaction of desire, is the only finally good thing. These assorted doctrines are not, of course, as logically interdependent as the materialist would have us believe. But they are temperamentally interdependent. They give expression to a mood or a temperament or a frame of mind which is sufficiently widespread to demand a courteous hearing.

NOTE ON SOURCES.   The material in this section is quoted, abridged, or paraphrased from Thomas Hobbes, *The Elements of Philosophy, Human Nature, Of Liberty and Necessity*, and *Leviathan*. From *The English Works of Thomas Hobbes*, Sir William Molesworth, ed. (London: J. Bohn, 1839).

2   GEORGE BERKELEY
The Claims of Idealism

FROM HOBBES TO BERKELEY.   It was to be expected that Hobbes's tough-minded materialism would provoke protest and criticism. Throughout the seventeenth and eighteenth centuries, it is not too much to say that materialism was the "specter" that haunted Western
metaphysics. Some resorted to the simple expedient of ignoring such views. Some reviled
the personal characters of those who held them. Some attacked the premises and disputed
the validity of the conclusions that comprised the materialist's position. Among these, in the
eighteenth century, was George Berkeley, the founder of modern idealism and one of the
shrewdest metaphysicians of modern times.

BIOGRAPHICAL NOTE.   George Berkeley was born in Ireland in 1685 and died in 1753 at the
age of sixty-eight. He was educated at the Trinity College, Dublin, where while yet an
undergraduate, he conceived the necessity of "refuting atheists and materialists." At the age of
twenty-five he published *A Treatise Concerning the Principles of Human Knowledge*, and
three years later his *Three Dialogues Between Hylas and Philonous*. These two small volumes, by one of the youngest and brightest philosophical mind of his generation, contain
the statement and defense of his case against materialism and his case for idealism. For a
while he was laughed at, as readers of Boswell's *Johnson* will remember. But the scattered
ranks of those who had been troubled by the fashionable materialism launched by Hobbes
and others in the preceding century soon closed in his support. Shortly after publication,
Berkeley visited England and was received into the circle of Addison, Pope, and Steele. He
traveled on the European continent in various capacities, and on his return was appointed
lecturer in divinity and Greek in Trinity College, Dublin. He received a D.D. and was made
an ecclesiastical dean. He was promised aid to found a college in Bermuda for training cler-
gymen for the colonies and missionaries for the Indians. He was made, finally, Bishop of
Cloyne. He died at Oxford, beloved and respected, if not clearly understood, by all who
knew him.

THE ARGUMENT OF THE PASSAGES.   Berkeley desires to establish the proposition that reality is spiritual, that a person's mind provides him or her with a better example of the
constituent "stuff" of things than is provided by a lump of matter. This is his idealism. The first
step is a critique of materialism. This Berkeley proceeds to construct. He starts from premises
the materialists themselves admit (any others would be irrelevant) and seeks to show that their
conclusions either (1) are incompatible with these premises, or (2) do not follow from these
premises. He then approaches materialism from another angle, seeking this time to explain
how materialists have come to hold their "misguided" conclusions. Methodologically this
procedure is usable. A Communist might apply it to capitalism as the first step in a general
statement of the case for communism. A free trader might apply it to protectionism as the
first step in a general statement of the case for free trade. A liberal might apply it to con-
servatism as the first step in a general statement of the case for liberalism. The same remarks
are applicable to capitalists, protectionists, and conservatives.

The case against materialism stated, Berkeley moves on to the case for idealism. He formulates a few premises that anyone, he thinks, will admit. From these he seeks to deduce his idealism. He turns then to consider possible objections that might be urged against it before they are made.

The case against materialism stated, the case for idealism stated, the possible objections anticipated, he closes in on what, after all, he considers to be the most important part of the whole business, namely, an elucidation of the implications of his metaphysical idealism, an enumeration of the propositions that are also true if his idealism is true.

The total argument begins as follows:

> It is plain that the notion of what is called *matter* or *corporeal substance* involves a contradiction,* so much so that I should not think it necessary to spend time exposing its absurdity. But belief in the existence of matter seems to have taken so deep a root in the minds of philosophers, and draws after it so many ill consequences, that I choose rather to be thought prolix and tedious than to omit anything that might conduce to the discovery and extirpation of that prejudice.

The following distinction between primary and secondary qualities and the claim that primary qualities are alone real, whereas secondary qualities are merely subjective, were familiar notions in Berkeley's day.

> Some there are who make a distinction between primary and secondary qualities. By *primary qualities* they mean extension, figure, motion, rest, solidity, and number. By *secondary qualities* they mean sensible qualities, as colors, sounds, tastes, and so forth.
>
> Our ideas of secondary qualities they acknowledge not to be the resemblances of anything existing without the mind or unperceived. But they will have our ideas of the primary qualities to be patterns or images of things which exist without the mind in an unthinking substance which they call *matter*. By *matter*, therefore, we are to understand an inert, senseless substance in which extension, figure, and motion do actually exist.
>
> Colors, sounds, heat, cold, and such like secondary qualities, they tell us, are sensations existing in the mind alone, depending on and occasioned by the different size, texture and motion of the minute particles of matter. This they take for an undoubted truth, which they can demonstrate beyond all exception.

By *materialism*, then, Berkeley proposes to mean the belief in an inert, senseless substance possessing primary qualities in its own right but not possessing secondary qualities in the same intimate fashion. His first criticism of this belief is as follows:

> But can anyone conceive the extension and motion of a body without any of its secondary qualities? It is not in my power to frame an idea of a body extended and moving but I must withal give it some color or other secondary quality which is acknowledged to

---

* The "contradiction" would seem to be in saying that all knowledge is from sense-data, and at the same time admitting that matter is not a sense-datum. How then do we know it?

exist only in the mind. In short, primary qualities abstracted from secondary qualities are inconceivable. Where therefore the secondary qualities are, to wit, in the mind and nowhere else, there must the primary qualities be also.

His second criticism is this:

Great and small, swift and slow, degrees of extension and motion, are allowed to exist only in the mind, being entirely relative, and changing as the frame or position of the sense organs varies. The extension therefore that exists independently of the mind is neither great nor small; the action, neither swift nor slow. That is, they are nothing at all.

His third criticism is this:

Number is entirely a creature of the mind. Even though the other primary qualities be allowed to exist without, it will be evident that the same thing bears a different denomination of number as the mind views it with different respects. Thus the same extension is one, or three, or thirty-six, according as the mind considers it with reference to a yard, a foot, or an inch. Number is so visibly relative and dependent on men's understanding that it is strange anyone should give it an absolute existence without the mind.

His fourth criticism is this:

One argument whereby modern philosophers would prove that secondary qualities do not exist in matter but in our minds may be turned likewise against primary qualities. Thus, it is said that heat and cold are affections only of the mind and not at all qualities of real things; for the same body which appears cold to one hand seems warm to another. Thus, too, it is proved that sweetness is not really in the sapid thing; because, the thing remaining unaltered, the sweetness is changed to bitterness, as in the case of a fever or otherwise vitiated palate.

Now, why may we not as well argue that figure and extension are not real qualities existing in matter? To the same eye at different stations, or to eyes of a different texture at the same station, they appear various. By parity of reasoning, therefore, they cannot be ideas of anything settled and determinate without the mind.

In short, those arguments which are thought to prove that secondary qualities (colors, tastes, etc.) exist only in the mind, may with equal force be brought to prove the same thing of primary qualities (extension, figure, motion, etc.).

His fifth criticism is this:

Suppose it were possible that material substances possessing only primary qualities do exist independent of the mind. Yet how is it possible for us to know this? Either we know it by our senses or by our reason. As for our senses, by them we have knowledge only of our sensations: but they do not inform us that things exist independent of the mind or unperceived by the mind, like to those which are perceived. This the materialists themselves acknowledge; nay, insist.

It remains, therefore, that, if we have any knowledge at all of material substances, it must be by our reason inferring their existence from what is immediately perceived by sense. But I do not see what reason can induce us to believe in the existence of bodies independent of the mind, from what we perceive, since the very patrons of matter themselves do not pretend there is any necessary connection betwixt them and our ideas.

His sixth criticism is this:

It may be thought easier to explain the production of our sensations by supporting external bodies, rather than otherwise; and so it might be at least probable that there are such things as bodies that excite ideas in our minds. But neither can this be said. For, though we give the materialists their "external bodies," they by their own confession are no nearer knowing how our ideas are produced, since they own themselves unable to comprehend in what manner body can act upon spirit (or mind) or how it could imprint any idea in the mind.

Hence it is evident that the production of ideas or sensations in our minds can be no reason why we should suppose matter or corporeal substances; since their production is acknowledged to remain equally inexplicable with or without this particular supposition. If therefore it were possible for bodies to exist without the mind, yet to hold that they do so must needs be a very precarious opinion. In short, if there were external bodies, it is impossible we should come to know it; and if there were not, we might have the very same reasons to think there were that we have now. Which consideration were enough to make any reasonable person suspect the strength of whatever arguments he may think himself to have, for the existence of external bodies independent of the mind.

His conclusion is this:

It is on this, therefore, that I insist, to wit, that the absolute existence of unthinking things are words without a meaning, or which include a contradiction. That is what I repeat and inculcate, and earnestly recommend to the attentive thoughts of the reader.

He turns now to an exploration of the reasons that may have led men "to suppose the existence of material substance":

It is worth while to reflect on the motives which induced men to suppose the existence of material substance; so that having observed the gradual ceasing and expiration of those motives, we may withdraw the assent that was grounded on them.

First it was thought that the sensible qualities did really exist without the mind. And for this reason it seemed needful to suppose that some unthinking substratum or substance wherein they did exist, since they could not be conceived to exist by themselves.

Then, in time, men being convinced that secondary qualities had no existence without the mind, they stripped this substratum or material substance of those qualities, leaving only the primary ones, which they still conceive to exist without the mind and consequently to stand in need of a material support.

But now, it having been shown that none even of these can possibly exist otherwise than in a spirit or mind which perceives them, it follows that we have no longer any reason to suppose the being of "matter," nay, that it is utterly impossible that there should be any such thing so long as that word is taken to mean an unthinking substratum or substance for qualities wherein they exist without mind. It is an extraordinary instance of the force of prejudice that the mind of man retains so great a fondness, against all the evidence of reason, for a stupid, thoughtless Somewhat as a support of the qualities we perceive.

Thus Berkeley on materialism. One is moved to ponder its effect upon Thomas Hobbes. A smile perhaps, a sharpening of his controversial quill as he prepared to do battle with this newcomer. For Berkeley, having "dethroned" matter, sets about to "enthrone" spirit. His first step is to secure one or two propositions that "any rational man" would admit.

It is evident to anyone who takes a survey of the objects of human knowledge, that they are either ideas imprinted on the senses; or such as are perceived by attending to the passions and operations of the mind; or lastly, ideas formed by help of memory and imagination—compounding, dividing, or merely representing those originally perceived in the aforesaid ways.

As several such ideas are observed to accompany each other, they come to be marked by one name, and so reputed as one thing. Thus a certain color, taste, smell, figure, and consistence having been observed to go together, are accounted one distinct thing, signified by the name *apple*. Other collections of ideas constitute a stone, a tree, a book, and the like.

Besides the ideas or objects of knowledge, there is something which knows or perceives them, and exercises divers operations as willing, imagining, remembering, about them. This perceiving active being I call "mind," "spirit," "soul," or "myself."

The existence of an idea consists in its being perceived. Its *esse* is *percipi*. The table I write on I say "exists"; that is, I see and feel it; and if I were out of my study, I should say it "existed"; meaning that if I was in my study, I might perceive it, or that some other spirit actually does perceive it. There was an odor, that is, it was smelt; there was a sound, that is, it was heard; there was a color or figure, that is, it was perceived by sight or touch. That is all I can understand by these and like expressions. Their *esse* is *percipi*. Nor is it possible they should have any existence out of the minds which perceive them.

All our ideas and sensations are visibly inactive. There is nothing of power or agency included in them. One idea or sensation cannot produce or alter another. The very being of an idea implies passiveness and inertness in it; insomuch that it is impossible for an idea to do anything, or be the cause of anything.

We perceive a continual succession of ideas. Some are excited anew, others are changed or totally disappear. There is therefore some cause of these ideas, whereupon they depend, and which produces and changes them.

Having premised the preceding facts, Berkeley proceeds to argue from them:

It is clear, from what hath been said, that this cause cannot itself be any idea or sensation since all such are passive and inert. It must therefore be a substance. But it has been shown that here is no corporeal or material substance. It remains therefore that the cause of our ideas and sensations is an incorporeal active substance, or spirit.

I find I can excite some of my ideas in my mind at pleasure, and vary and shift the scene as oft as I think fit. This making and unmaking of ideas doth very properly denominate the mind active. Thus much is certain and grounded on experience. But when we talk, as do materialists, of unthinking substances producing ideas, we only amuse ourselves with words.

But whatever power I have over some of my ideas, I find that others have not a like dependence on my will. When, for example, I open my eyes in broad daylight, it is not in my power to choose whether I shall see or no, nor to determine what I shall see. It is likewise as to hearing and the other senses. The ideas imprinted on them are not creatures of my will. There is, therefore, some other will or mind or spirit that produces them.

These ideas which I cannot control, these ideas of sense, are more strong, more lively, more distinct than those which I can control. They have, likewise, a steadiness, order, and coherence which belong not to those that are the effects of my will. They speak themselves the products of a mind more powerful and wise than human needs.

Some truths there are so near and obvious to the human mind that a man need only open his eyes to see them. Such I take this important one to be, namely, that all the choir of heaven and furniture of the earth, in a word, all those bodies which compose the mighty frame of the world, have not any subsistence, without a mind; that their being is to be perceived or known; that, consequently, so long as they are not actually perceived by me, or do not exist in my mind or the mind of any other created spirit, they must either have no existence at all or else subsist in the mind of some Eternal Spirit. For it is unintelligible to attribute to any single part of them an existence independent of (perception by a) Spirit.

Until his premises are effectively questioned, or his reasoning from these premises shown to be fallacious, Berkeley may now survey his work with satisfaction. Are there any loopholes? The passages that follow show Berkeley at work on this question.

Before we proceed any farther, it is necessary that we spend some time in answering objections which may probably be made against the principles we have hitherto laid down. In this, if I seem too prolix, I desire I may be excused, since all men do not equally apprehend things of this nature; and I am willing to be understood by every man.

It might be objected:

By the foregoing principles all that is real and substantial in nature is banished out of the world. All things that exist, it will be said, exist only in the mind, that is, are purely notional. What therefore becomes of the sun, moon, and stars? What must we think of houses, rivers, mountains, trees, stones, nay even of our own bodies? Are all these but so many chimeras and illusions?

To this objection he has an answer:

We are not deprived of any one thing in nature. Whatever we see, hear, feel, or any wise conceive or understand remains as secure as ever, and is as real as ever. I do not argue against the existence of any one thing that we can apprehend either by sense or reflection. That the things I see with my eyes and touch with my hands do really exist, I make not the least question. The only thing whose existence I deny is that which philosophers call *matter*. There are minds which will or excite ideas in themselves at pleasure. Other ideas, which they do not so excite, speak themselves the effects of a mind more powerful and wise than human spirits. These latter are said to be more real than the former. In this sense the sun I see is the real sun. In this sense, everything in the world is as much a real being by our principles as by any other. If the word *substance* be taken for a combination of sensible qualities, we cannot be accused of denying its existence.

It sounds harsh to say we eat and drink ideas, and are clothed with ideas. But, in common discourse, the word *idea* is not used to signify the several combinations of sensible qualities which are called *things*. But this concerns not the truth of the proposition, which says no more than that we are fed and clothed with those things which we perceive immediately by our senses. The sensory qualities which, combined, constitute the several sorts of victuals and apparel, have been shown to exist only in the mind that perceives them. This is all that is meant by calling them *ideas*. If you agree that we eat and drink and are clad with the immediate object of sense, which cannot exist unperceived, I shall readily grant that it is more conformable to custom that they should be called *things* rather than *ideas*.

"I will still believe my senses and will never suffer any argument, how plausible soever, to prevail over the certainty of them." Be it so. Assert the evidence of your senses. We are willing to do the same. That what I see, hear, feel, etc., doth exist, I no more doubt of than I do of my own being. But, *I do not see how the testimony of sense can be alleged as a proof for the existence of anything which is not perceived by the senses.* We are not for having any man turn skeptic and doubt his senses.

Again, it might be objected:

From these principles it follows that things are every moment annihilated and created anew. The objects of sense exist only when they are perceived. The trees are in the garden, the chairs in the parlor, only while there is someone there to perceive them. Upon shutting my eyes it is all reduced to nothing, and upon opening them it is again created.

His answer:

It is thought absurd that, upon closing my eyelids, all the visible objects around me should be reduced to nothing. Yet, is not this what my very critics and opponents commonly acknowledge when they agree on all hands that light and color, which are the immediate objects of sight, are mere sensations, mere "subjective states" which exist no longer than they are perceived?

Indeed we hold the objects of sense to be nothing else but ideas which cannot exist unperceived. Yet we may not hence conclude that they have no existence except only when they are perceived by us; there may be some other spirit that perceives them though we do not. It would not follow, hence, that bodies are annihilated and created every moment, or exist not at all during the intervals between our perception of them.

It might be objected:

If primary qualities exist only in the mind, it follows that mind is extended, since extension is a primary quality of things.

The answer:

It no more follows that the mind is extended because extension is in it alone, than that it is red or blue because those qualities exist in it alone and nowhere else. Yet my opponents admit that secondary qualities exist in the mind alone; i.e., are "subjective."

It might be objected:

There have been a great many things explained by matter and motion. Take these away and you destroy the whole atomic theory, and undermine those principles of mechanics which have been applied with so much success to account for things. In short, whatever advances have been made in the study of nature, do all proceed on the supposition that "matter" doth exist.

To which Berkeley replies:

To "explain" things is all one has to show why, upon such and such occasions, we are affected with such and such ideas. But, how "matter" operates on mind, or produces any idea in it, is what no philosopher will pretend to explain. Of what use it is, therefore? Besides, things are accounted for by figure, motion and other qualities; not by "matter." Such qualities are no more than ideas, and therefore cannot be the cause of anything, since ideas cannot be the cause of anything.

It might be objected:

Does it not seem absurd to take away "natural causes" and ascribe everything to the operation of spirit? To say, not that fire heats or water cools, but that a spirit heats or a spirit cools, etc. Would not a man be deservedly laughed at who should talk after this manner?

To which Berkeley rejoins:

In such things we ought to think with the learned and speak with the vulgar. Those who are convinced of the truth of Copernican astronomy do nevertheless say "the sun rises," and "the sun sets." Yet it doth not. But if such persons affected a contrary style in common talk, it would appear ridiculous. It is the same with our tenets.

It might be objected:

Is not the universal assent of mankind an invincible argument on behalf of matter? Must we suppose the whole world to be mistaken? If so, what cause can be assigned of so widespread and predominant an error?

To which Berkeley responds:

It will perhaps not be found that so many do really believe in the existence of "matter." Strictly, to believe that which involves a contradiction, or has no meaning, is impossible. I admit men act as if the cause of their sensations were some senseless, unthinking being. But, that they clearly apprehend any meaning thereby, that they have formed a settled speculative opinion, is what I am not able to conceive.

Adding, too:

Even though we should grant a notion to be universally and steadfastly held to, yet that is but a weak argument for its truth. A vast number of prejudices and false opinions are everywhere embraced by the unreflecting part of mankind. There was a time when the antipodes and the motion of the earth were looked upon as monstrous absurdities even by men of learning.

It is demanded that we assign a cause of this prejudice that matter exists and is the cause of our sensations. I answer: Men, knowing they perceived several ideas whereof they themselves were not the author, nor depending on their wills, first maintained that those ideas had an existence independent of and external to the mind. But, seeing that the immediate objects of perception do not exist except they are being perceived, they then argued that there are objects, distinct from the colors, etc. immediately perceived by the mind, of which those latter are images or resemblances or effects imprinted on us by those objects. So the notion of an imperceived and unthinking "matter" owes its origin to the consciousness that we are not the author is of our sensations, which must therefore have some cause distinct from our minds upon which they are imprinted.

It might be objected:

You say: Though the ideas themselves do not exist without the mind, yet there may be things like them whereof they are copies or resemblances, which exist without the mind in an unthinking substance.

To which Berkeley counters:

It is indeed an opinion strangely prevailing among men that houses, mountains, rivers, in a word, all sensible objects, have an existence distinct from their being perceived by the understanding. But this principle involves a manifest contradiction. For what are the aforementioned objects but the things we perceive by sense? And what do we perceive besides our own ideas or sensations? Could any of these exist unperceived? There was an odor, that is, it was smelt; there was a sound, that is, it was heard; there was a color or figure, that is, it was perceived by sight or touch. That is all I can understand by these and like expressions. Their *esse* is *percipi*. Nor is it possible they should have any existence out of the minds which perceive them.

An idea can be like nothing but an idea; a color can be like nothing but a color. It is impossible for us to conceive a likeness except only between our ideas.

I ask whether the supposed originals or external things, of which our ideas are pictures or representations, be themselves perceivable or no? If they are, then they are ideas, and we have gained our point. If they are not, I appeal to anyone whether it be sense to say a color is like something which is invisible; to say hard or soft is like something intangible and so of the rest.

It might be objected:

> Let us admit that the notion of "matter" as the cause or support of the perceived qualities of things, is not needed. Yet there may perhaps be some inert, unperceiving substance, as incomprehensible to us as colors to a man born blind; supporting, it may be, qualities of which we know nothing because we have no senses adapted to them, but which, if we had other senses we should know of.

To which Berkeley replies:

> If by *matter* you mean the unknown (and unknowable) cause or support of unknown (and unknowable) qualities, I see no point in affirming or denying its existence. I see no advantage in disputing about something we know not what and we know not why.

And adds:

> If we had those other senses, they could only furnish us with new ideas or sensations. In which case we should have the same reason against their existing in an unperceiving substance that has been already offered with relation to such qualities as we do perceive; they would exist only in a mind perceiving them. This is true not only of ideas we are acquainted with at present but likewise of all possible ideas whatsoever.

The case is by now almost completed. He has stated and refuted materialism. He has stated and established idealism. He has anticipated and parried every objection that he can imagine. He proceeds to indicate some implications of his position for a number of traditional issues.

> Having posed and met possible objections, we proceed to take a view of our principles with regard to their consequences. After what hath been premised, I think we may lay down the following conclusions.
> First: It is plain that men amuse themselves in vain when they inquire for any natural cause distinct from a mind or spirit.
> Second: Since the whole creation is the workmanship of a wise and good Agent, it should seem to be in order to employ our thoughts about the final causes, or purposes of things. This not only discovers to us the attributes of the Creator and Sustainer, but may also direct us to the proper uses and applications of things.
> Third: The natural immortality of the soul is a necessary consequence of these principles. To assert natural immortality is not to assert that it is incapable of annihilation by the Creator who first gave it being but only that it is not liable to be broken or dissolved by the laws of nature or motion. Bodies are ideas in the mind or soul. The latter is indivisible, incorporeal, unextended, and consequently indissoluble. Changes, decays, dissolutions, which we see in bodies cannot affect a spirit which hath none of their properties. Such a being, a mind or soul or active spirit, is therefore indissoluble by the forces of nature.
> Fourth: From what hath been said, it is plain that we cannot know the existence of other minds or spirits otherwise than by their operations or the ideas excited by them in us. I perceive combinations of ideas, and changes thereof, that inform me that there are

agents like myself which accompany them and concur in their production. But the knowledge I have of these other spirits or mind is hence indirect; not as is the knowledge of my ideas, but depending on the intervention of ideas by me referred to minds as spirits distinct from myself.

Fifth: Though there be some things (i.e., combinations of sensations) which convince us that human agents are concerned in producing them, yet it is evident that nature, that is, the far greater part of the ideas or sensations perceived by us, is not produced by or dependent on the wills of men. There is therefore some other Spirit that causeth them. But if we consider the regularity, order, and concatenation of natural things, the surprising magnificence, beauty, and perfection of the larger, and the exquisite contrivance of the smaller parts of creation, we shall clearly perceive that the attributes One, Eternal, Infinitely Wise, Good, and Perfect, belong all of them to the aforesaid Spirit, who "works in all" and "by whom all things consist."

Hence it is evident that God is known as certainly and immediately as any other mind or spirit, distinct from ourselves. We may even assert that the existence of God is more evident than the existence of men; because the effects of nature are more numerous and considerable than those ascribed to men. There is not any one mark which denotes a man, or effect produced by him, that does not more strongly evince the being of that Spirit which is the author of nature. A human spirit is not perceived by sense: when we perceive the color, size, etc. of a man, we perceive only sensations or ideas excited in our own minds. These being exhibited to our view in sundry distinct collections, serve to mark out unto us the existence of finite spirits like ourselves. And after the same manner we see God. All the difference is that whereas some one finite and narrow assemblage of ideas denotes a particular human mind, on the other hand wherever we direct our view we perceive manifest tokens of the Divinity, "in whom we live and move and have our being."

It will be objected here that monsters, untimely births, fruits blasted in the blossom, rains falling in desert places, waste, miseries incident to human life, and so on, are evidence that the whole frame of nature is not actuated and superintended by a Spirit of infinite wisdom and goodness. If, that is to say, God is the author of all things, is He not the author of evil and undesirable things? Is this coherent with His infinite wisdom and goodness?

I answer: The very blemishes and defects of nature are not without their use. They make an agreeable variety and augment the beauty of the rest of creation, as shadows in a picture serve to set off the brighter parts.

I add: We do well, before we tax the author of nature with wastefulness, to examine whether such accusation be not the effect of prejudice contracted by our familiarity with impotent and saving mortals. In man, thriftiness with what he cannot easily secure may be wisdom. But, an Omnipotent Spirit can produce everything by a mere fiat. Hence nature's splendid profusion should not be interpreted as wastefulness in the author of nature. Rather it is an evidence of the riches of His power.

I add: As for the pain which is in the world, pursuant to the general laws of nature and the actions of finite imperfect spirits, this is indispensably necessary to our well-being. We consider some one particular pain and account it an evil. But our view is too narrow. If we enlarge our view, so as to comprehend the various ends, connections, and dependencies of things, we shall be forced to acknowledge that those particular things which, considered in themselves, appear to be evil, have the nature of good when considered in connection with the whole system of beings.

From what hath been said, it will be manifest that it is merely for want of attention and comprehensiveness of mind that there are any atheists or Manichaeans. Little and unreflecting souls may indeed burlesque the works of Providence, the beauty and order whereof they have not the capacity or will not be at the pains to comprehend. But those who are masters of any justness and extent of thought can never sufficiently admire the tracks of wisdom and goodness that shine through the economy of nature.

Since it is downright impossible that a soul pierced and illumined with a thorough sense of the omnipresence, holiness, and justice of that Spirit, should persist in a remorseless violation of His laws, we ought therefore earnestly to mediate on those important matters, that so we may attain conviction without scruple.

For, after all, what deserves the first place in our studies, is the consideration of God and duty; which to promote, was the main drift and design of my labors.

What is to be said of this flight of the metaphysical imagination? A generation later it caught the attention of David Hume. He observed, somewhat tartly, "The speculations of the ingenious Dr. Berkeley—they admit of no refutation, but they produce no conviction," and proceeded to deal with idealism as Berkeley had dealt with materialism, rejecting spiritual substance as Berkeley had rejected material substance. Meanwhile, one does well to know the argument. It has long served as a kind of rallying point for the like-minded in each generation. He provided an apparently coherent case against the "specter" of materialism. He gave articulation to that perennial temperament that dreads and despises and mistrusts the "appeal to matter." For his premises, others have been substituted. To his conclusions, especially his repudiation of materialism, little of importance or variety has been added.

NOTE ON SOURCES.   The material in this section has been quoted, abridged, or paraphrased from George Berkeley, *A Treatise Concerning the Principles of Human Knowledge*, Part I in Mary Calkins, ed., *Berkeley Selections* (New York: Charles Scribner's Sons, 1957).

5

Am I Free or Determined?

THE QUESTION POSED

In the pursuit of self-understanding, people have often claimed that the human being is simply a part of nature. That claim, which is rather ancient has received substantial support from the emergence of modern science. Those who make the claim usually intend thereby to deny at least four things about the human being. They intend to say that humans do not have immaterial minds, that humans are not free, that humans are not creatures of God, and that humans do not survive the death of their bodies. We explored the first of those denials in the previous chapter. In the next chapter which deals with the existence of God, we will address the third denial. In the present chapter we will consider the second denial as we examine the question, "Am I free or determined?"

Suppose you have an examination tomorrow and a friend asks you to forgo studying and spend the evening at a party. Your friend does not urge or threaten or coerce you. You consider the alternatives, and after a moment's thought, decide to give up studying for that night, and go to the party. We would ordinarily say that you are responsible for your decision. We think of such cases as actions in which you are free to decide one way or the other. Contrast this to a situation in which a migraine headache just about forces you to lie down and fall asleep on your bed instead of continuing to study. Contrast this latter case with your knee reflex. The doctor hits your knee with the little rubber hammer in just the right place and your knee pops up. It is very difficult for a person with normal reflexes to keep that knee still.

In the case of the migraine headache, it would not make nearly as much sense as in the party case to say that you are free to decide one way or the other about studying. With the reflex, it is much easier to say that you are not free at all. Now consider a case where a robber points a revolver at you and says, "Your money or your life" and it is clear that she means it. Are you free to choose? The dispute between advocates of free will and advocates of determinism is basically a dispute whether incidents like those cited, which feel so different, are really radically and essentially different.

Someone might think that we are always free to act no matter what the circumstances. They might say that the knee reflex is not an action; it is a behavior. Actions are behaviors that spring from our desires and wills. If we have a desire and act on it, we are free. Still others might argue that we are never free to act, no matter what the circumstances and no matter how free the act feels. In effect, such a view denies the distinction between behavior and action. The claim that some acts are free and some are not free would be a middle ground.

Determinists fall into two general categories. First, there are hard determinists who hold that all actions are caused and so no acts are free. These determinists must tell us at the very least, what happens to our ideas of moral responsibility. Second, there are soft determinists who hold that all acts are caused but that some acts are free while others are not. Soft determinists at the very least, must tell a convincing story that universal causality does not exclude freedom. Compatibilists hold one of two views: (1) soft determinism as defined above; or, (2) determinism may co-exist with moral responsibility. Libertarians hold that some acts are free from the deterministic causal network. Libertarians must at the very least, make sense out of the notion of an "uncaused" act.

The hard determinist might argue that although it is quite reasonable for you to believe that your decision to stay home to study for the exam instead of to party was an expression of free choice, nevertheless closer scrutiny would reveal that your behavior was not really free after all. What you thought was a free choice was really a choice dictated by your desires, which in turn spring from your character, which in its turn is fashioned by the forces of heredity and environment, which are clearly beyond your control. Again, the central claim of determinism is that every event has a cause. By an analysis of the causes of any one of your actions, the determinist would show that so-called freedom vanished in a chain of causes that stretched back into the remote recesses of your heredity and environment. Nature and nurture, genes and society—those are the facts that made you what you are and cause you to act the way you do. The notion that you are free is really a misapprehension, an illusion.

The battle between determinists and advocates of free will is an old one. The first of the combatants we have selected for study is the eighteenth-century advocate of determinism, Baron d'Holbach. In a clear and uncompromising fashion, he presents the position of determinism. To cross swords with him we have Jean-Paul Sartre who will appeal to his version of existentialism and his idea of what a person is to argue for libertarianism. Walter Stace will argue for soft determinism by claiming that actions caused by internal desires should be considered free. Our next contributor, John Hospers, modifies and refines Stace by appealing to contemporary psychology, and ends up affirming hard determinism. Then John Bender leads us through a thought experiment meant to support the compatibilist position that freedom and determinism can coexist. Finally, Karl Popper will offer an argument that a proper understanding of science will reveal that we are free.

Remember that this issue has important ramifications. If no one is truly free, if choice is an illusion, then how can anyone be held responsible for what they do? Ethics seems to presuppose at least compatibilism. Our criminal justice system certainly allows "I couldn't help it" as an excuse. Might it be that we can never help it?

1   BARON D'HOLBACH
I Am Determined

Descartes exploited the method of hyperbolic doubt in order to defeat doubt. The seventeenth century in which Descartes lived was a time when traditional ideas and institutions were challenged. The intellectual fires of the Renaissance and the Reformation had not died out. The skeptic Michel De Montaigne (1533–1592) had cast a cloud of doubt over the reliability of all human knowledge, and Descartes tried to dissipate that cloud. Descartes probably thought he was in step with the new science in that he had discovered by careful scrutiny an indubitable truth rooted in the concrete, empirical data of the thinking self, and in that he had used geometrical-style reasoning to construct his system of truth about reality. Yet, the harmony that Descartes and his followers (the Cartesians) thought they had with the new science was only partial. They seem to have missed the point that the mathematical reasoning of the new science was used to predict the behavior of phenomena, and was accordingly subjected to verification or falsification on the basis of observed data. Without prediction and testing, mathematical reasoning can generate systems of gratuitous fictions. That is precisely the charge that the eighteenth-century French intellectuals of the Enlightenment leveled at the Cartesians. These intellectuals had learned about the new science through the writings of John Locke (1632–1714) and Isaac Newton (1642–1727), for whom empirical data, prediction, and testing were essential. So impressed with the empirical bent of the new science were these French thinkers that they abandoned the dualistic perspective of Cartesian thought and went over to a purely materialistic world view. Perhaps the most radical of this group of French intellectuals was Baron d'Holbach, who affirmed that one's fate is fixed by external causes.

BIOGRAPHICAL NOTE.   Holbach was born in 1723 and died in 1789, aged sixty-six. His name was originally Paul Heinrich Dietrich. He was born in Germany, educated in the natural sciences at the University of Leiden, and came to Paris in 1749. He became a French subject and in 1753 inherited from his uncle the title of Baron d'Holbach and properties that made him financially independent for the rest of his life. He established a circle that included such Frenchmen as Diderot, Helvetius, D'Alembert, Rousseau, Condillac, Turgot, and Condorcet, and such foreigners as Hume, Gibbon, Adam Smith, Priestly, Walpole, Garrick, Sterne, Beccaria, and Franklin. He contributed some four hundred articles to Diderot's *Encyclopedia*. He propagandized and translated on behalf of materialism, atheism, revolution, and republicanism. Perhaps his best-known book, *Le Système de la Nature (The System of Nature)*, appeared in 1770 under the pseudonym of a certain Mirabaud who had been dead for ten years. The book bore the imprint of London as its place of publication, when in truth it had been published in Amsterdam. These fictitious devices were used, no doubt, to protect the author and publisher from reprisals that could result from the radical content of the book. Contrary to the prevailing opinions of the day, d'Holbach claimed that the human is a part of nature, and because there is no free will anywhere in the behavior of matter, there is none in nature and none in humans.

THE ARGUMENT OF THE PASSAGES.   Holbach's claim, called *determinism* or *necessitarianism,* is an answer to this question: "Is anyone ever responsible for *any* of his behavior? He being who *he* is, the circumstances being what *they* are, can he ever do anything other than he does do?" Holbach's answer is a categorical, unqualified no. Your thoughts and actions are the effects of causes over which you have no control. If you think you could have done otherwise, you are mistaken. We might add that even if you feel that you could have done otherwise, this is irrelevant, since the question is not how you feel but rather what is true about the world.

The following paragraphs are quoted from Holbach's historically important book *The System of Nature.* Nature, the title says, is a vast interlocked system in which every event is caused, necessitated, determined by all the other events that make up the total system. Many would grant this claim without argument when it is made of physical nature, nature taken as the subject matter of physics; but some demur when this claim is extended to include human nature and human behavior. They hold out for the possibility that some human behavior expresses a will that acts autonomously, is constrained neither by nature nor by events in nature. Holbach wrote these passages to deny any such claim.

He begins by reiterating his central claim. Note how the images he selects to depict the human being—"line," "bowl," "machine," "chains"—reinforce his claim that "No human behavior expresses free will." For emphasis, in these paragraphs we have printed the various wordings of that claim in italics.

> *In whatever manner man is considered, he is connected to universal nature, and submitted to the necessary and immutable laws that she imposes on all the beings she contains,* according to their peculiar essences or to the respective properties with which, without consulting them, she endows each particular species. Man's life is a line that nature commands him to describe upon the surface of the earth, without his ever being able to swerve from it, even for an instant. He is born without his own consent; his organization does in nowise depend upon himself; his ideas come to him involuntarily; his habits are in the power of those who cause him to contract them; he is unceasingly modified by causes, whether visible or concealed, over which he has no control, which necessarily regulate his mode of existence, give the hue to his way of thinking, and determine his manner of acting. He is good or bad, happy or miserable, wise or foolish, reasonable or irrational, without his will being for anything in these various states. . . .
>
> The will, as we have elsewhere said, is a modification of the brain, by which it is disposed to action, or prepared to give play to the organs. This will is necessarily determined by the qualities, good or bad, agreeable or painful, of the object or the motive that acts upon his senses, or of which the idea remains with him, and is resuscitated by his memory. In consequence, he acts necessarily, his action is the result of the impulse he receives either from the motive, from the object, or from the idea which has modified his brain, or disposed his will. When he does not act according to this impulse, it is because there comes some new cause, some new motive, some new idea, which modifies his brain in a different manner, gives him a new impulse, determines his will in another way, by which the action of the former impulse is suspended; thus, the sight of an agreeable object, or its idea, determines his will to set him in action to procure it; but if a new object or a new idea more powerfully attracts him, it gives a new direction to his will, annihilates the effect of the former, and prevents the action by which it was to be procured. This is the mode in which reflection, experience, reason, necessarily arrests or suspends the

action of man's will; without this he would of necessity have followed the anterior impulse which carried him towards a then-desirable object. In all this *he always acts according to necessary laws from which he has no means of emancipating himself. . . .*

This will, or rather the brain, finds itself in the same situation as a bowl, which, although it has received an impulse that drives it forward in a straight line, is deranged in its course whenever a force superior to the first obliges it to change its direction. The man who drinks the poisoned water appears a madman; but the actions of fools are as necessary as those of the most prudent individuals. The motives that determine the voluptuary and the debauchee to risk their health, are as powerful, and their actions are as necessary, as those which decide the wise man to manage his. But, it will be insisted, the debauchee may be prevailed on to change his conduct; this does not imply that he is a free agent; but that motives may be found sufficiently powerful to annihilate the effect of those that previously acted upon him; *then these new motives determine his will to the new mode of conduct he may adopt as necessarily as the former did to the old mode. . . .*

Man, then, is not a free agent in anyone instant of his life; he is necessarily guided in each step by those advantages, whether real or fictitious, that he attaches to the objects by which his passions are roused; these passions themselves are necessary in a being who unceasingly tends toward his own happiness; their energy is necessary, since that depends on his temperament; his temperament is necessary, because it depends on the physical elements which enter into composition; the modification of his temperament is necessary, as it is the infallible and inevitable consequence of the impulse he receives from the incessant action of moral and physical beings. . . .

There is, in point of fact, no difference between the man that is cast out of the window by another, and the man who throws himself out of it, except that the impulse in the first instance comes immediately from without whilst that which determines the fall in the second case, springs from within his own peculiar machine, having its more remote cause also exterior. . . .

He may be compared to a heavy body that finds itself arrested in its descent by an obstacle whatever; take away this obstacle, it will gravitate or continue to fall; but who shall say this dense body is free to fall or not? Is not its descent the necessary effect of its own specific gravity? The virtuous Socrates submitted to the laws of his country, although they were unjust; and though the doors of his jail were left open to him, he would not save himself; but *in this he did not act as a free agent;* the *invisible chains* of opinion, the secret love of decorum, the inward respect for the laws, even when they were iniquitous, the fear of tarnishing his glory, *kept him in his prison;* they were motives sufficiently powerful with this enthusiast for virtue, to induce him to wait death with tranquility.

We are no more than just parts of nature. Like all the parts of nature, everything we do is governed by laws. These laws are deterministic in nature. Deterministic laws rule out free will. So, there is no free will. Not everyone, however, is so convinced as Holbach. Some people believe they are free; they have the "feeling," the "experience" of acting freely. But such "experience," says Holbach, is illusory, based upon *ignorance* of the many and complex causes operating in human life.

Man believes he acts as a free agent, every time he does not see any thing that places obstacles to his actions; he does not perceive that the motive which causes him to will, is always necessary and independent of himself.

From whence it may be seen, that the same necessity which regulates the physical, also regulates the moral world, in which every thing is in consequence submitted to fatality. Man, in running over, frequently without his own knowledge, often in spite of himself, the route which nature has marked out for him, resembles a swimmer who is obliged to follow the current that carries him along; he believes himself a free agent, because he sometimes consents, sometimes does not consent, to glide with the stream, which, not withstanding, always hurries him forward; he believes himself the master of his condition, because he is obliged to use his arms under the fear of sinking.

It is, then, for want of recurring to the causes that move him, for want of being able to analyze, from not being competent to decompose the complicated motion of his machine, that man believes himself a free agent; it is only upon his own ignorance that he founds the profound yet deceitful notion he has of his free agency; that he builds those opinions which he brings forward as a striking proof of his pretended freedom of action. If, for a short time, each man was willing to examine his own peculiar actions, search out their true motives to discover their concatenation, he would remain convinced that the sentiment he has of his natural free agency, is a chimera that must speedily be destroyed by experience.

It is the great complication of motion in man, it is the variety of his action, it is the multiplicity of causes that move him, whether simultaneously or in continual succession, that persuades him he is a free agent; if all his motions were simple, if the causes that move him did not confound themselves with each other, if they were distinct, if his machine were less complicated, he would perceive that all his actions were necessary, because he would be enabled to recur instantly to the cause that made him act.

The errors of philosophers on the free agency of man, have arisen from their regarding his will as the *primum mobile,* the original motive of his actions; for want of recurring back, they have not perceived the multiplied, the complicated causes which, independently of him, give motion to the will itself; or which dispose and modify his brain, whilst he himself is purely passive in the motion he receives. . . .

To be undeceived on the system of his free agency, man has simply to recur to the motive by which his will is determined; he will always find this motive is out of his own control. It is said: that in consequence of an idea to which the mind gives birth, man acts freely if he encounters no obstacle. But the question is, what gives birth to this idea in his brain? Was he the master either to prevent it from presenting itself, or from renewing itself in his brain? Does not this idea depend either upon objects that strike him exteriorly and in despite of himself, or upon causes, that without his knowledge, act within himself and modify his brain?

Nevertheless it must be acknowledged that the multiplicity and diversity of the causes which continually act upon man, frequently without even his knowledge, render it impossible, or at least extremely difficult for him to recur to the true principles of his own peculiar actions, much less the action of others; they frequently depend upon causes so fugitive, so remote from their effects, and which, superficially examined, appear to have so little analogy, so slender a relation with them, that it requires singular sagacity to bring them into light.

Other people insist that humans are free in order to preserve the meaningfulness of praising or blaming various people for their actions. If people are not free agents how can they possibly merit reward or deserve punishment from either God or society for their actions? Holbach dismisses this argument for freedom as a piece of rationalizing rooted in human vanity that tries to present the human as in some sense "special" when compared with other physical beings in nature.

Nevertheless, in spite of the shackles by which he is bound, it is pretended he is a free agent, or that independent of the causes by which he is moved, he determines his own will, and regulates his own condition.

However slender the foundation of this opinion, of which everything ought to point out to him the error, it is current at this day and passes for an incontestable truth with a great number of people, otherwise extremely enlightened; it is the basis of religion, which, supposing relations between man and the unknown being she has placed above nature, has been incapable of imagining how man could merit reward or deserve punishment from this being, if he was not a free agent. Society has been believed interested in this system; because an idea has gone abroad, that if all actions of man were to be contemplated as necessary, the right of punishing those who injure their associates would no longer exist. At length human vanity accommodated itself to a hypothesis which, unquestionably, appears to distinguish man from all other physical beings, by assigning him the special privilege of a total independence of all other causes, but of which a very little reflection would have shown him the impossibility.

By way of concluding these selections from Holbach's *System of Nature*, let us examine half a dozen paragraphs in which he moves from abstract formulation of his determinism to some concrete applications of it. The passage is clear-cut and vivid. He imagines himself summoning an ambitious man, a miserly man, a voluptuary man, a choleric or bad-tempered man, and a zealous man, and letting each in turn testify to the truth of Holbach's claim:

The *ambitious man* cries out: you will have me resist my passion; but have they not unceasingly repeated to me that rank, honors, power, are the most desirable advantages in life? Have I not seen my fellow citizens envy them, the nobles of my country sacrifice every thing to obtain them? In the society in which I live, am I not obliged to feel, that if I am deprived of these advantages, I must expect to languish in contempt, to cringe under the rod of oppression?

The *miser* says: you forbid me to love money, to seek after the means of acquiring it: alas! does not every thing tell me that, in this world, money is the greatest blessing; that it is amply sufficient to render me happy? In the country I inhabit, do I not see all my fellow citizens covetous of riches? but do I not also witness that they are little scrupulous in the means of obtaining wealth? As soon as they are enriched by the means which you censure, are they not cherished, considered and respected? By what authority, then, do you defend me from amassing treasure? What right have you to prevent my using means, which, although you call them sordid and criminal, I see approved by the sovereign? Will you have me renounce my happiness?

The *voluptuary* argues: you pretend that I should resist my desires; but was I the maker of my own temperament, which unceasingly invites me to pleasure? You call my pleasures disgraceful; but in the country in which I live, do I not witness the most dissipated men enjoying the most distinguished rank? Do I not behold that no one is ashamed of adultery but the husband it has outraged? Do not I see men making trophies of their debaucheries, boasting of their libertinism, rewarded with applause?

The *choleric man* vociferates: you advise me to put a curb on my passions, and to resist the desire of avenging myself; but can I conquer my nature? Can I alter the received opinions of the world? Shall I not be forever disgraced, infallibly dishonored in society, if I do not wash out in the blood of my fellow creatures the injuries I have received?

The *zealous enthusiast* exclaims: you recommend me mildness; you advise me to be tolerant; to be indulgent to the opinions of my fellow men; but is not my temperament violent? Do I not ardently love my God? Do they not assure me, that zeal is pleasing to him; that sanguinary inhuman persecutors have been his friends? As I wish to render myself acceptable in his sight, I therefore adopt the same means.

In short, the actions of man are never free; they are always the necessary consequence of his temperament, of the received ideas, and of the notions, either true or false, which he has formed to himself of happiness; of his opinions strengthened by example, by education, and by daily experience.

If he understood the play of his organs, if he were able to recall to himself all the impulsions they have received, all the modifications they have undergone, all the effects they have produced, he would perceive that all his actions are submitted to that fatality, which regulates his own particular system, as it does the entire system of the universe; no one effect in him, any more than in nature, produces itself by chance; this, as has been before proved, is word void of sense. All that passes in him; all that is done by him, as well as all that happens in nature, or that is attributed to her, is derived from necessary causes, which act according to necessary laws, and which produce necessary effects from whence necessarily flow others.

Fatality, is the eternal, the immutable, the necessary order, established in nature; or the indispensable connexion of causes that act with the effects they operate.

Jean-Paul Sartre, our next author, refuses to surrender human freedom and dignity.

NOTE ON SOURCES.   The material in this section is quoted from Baron d'Holbach, *The System of Nature*, trans. by H. D. Robinson (Boston: J. P. Mendum, 1899), Chapter 11.

---

2   JEAN-PAUL SARTRE
I am Free

FROM HOLBACH TO SARTRE.   As determinism marched from the eighteenth century of Holbach through the nineteenth century of Buckle to the twentieth century of Sartre, it assaulted the freedom and dignity that humans had ascribed to themselves for centuries. That assault received monumental support from the brilliant achievements of the physical sciences which operated with a deterministic model of the universe. The impressive work of Darwin and advances in the biological sciences made the assault seem invincible. Must we not view the human as an organism devoid of freedom and driven by forces beyond its control? Voices of protest against this assault were raised in the nineteenth century by several intellectual giants. The Danish philosopher, Sören Kierkegaard (1813–1855), for example, ridiculed philosophers like Hegel (1770–1831) who generated grandiose systems to answer all questions—except one: What does it mean to be an existing individual person? The Russian writer, Fyodor Dostoevsky (1821–1881), poured out his anxieties in mighty novels like *Brothers Karamazov* and *Crime and Punishment* as he declared his belief in human freedom and dignity. The German philosopher and cultural historian, Friedrich Nietzsche (1844–1900), celebrated the freedom of the self-surmounting person who rose above the mediocrity and conformity of the masses in order to create meaning and values to live dangerously and joyfully. The Germany social analyst, Karl Marx (1818–1883), protested vigorously against the reification or "thingification" of persons in bourgeois capitalist society—a society which was stifling the free, conscious activity that distinguishes the human being from the rest of nature.

In the twentieth century the voices of protest have grown in numbers and eloquence. Atheistic philosophers like Martin Heidegger, Christian philosophers like Nicholas Berdyaev, Protestant theologians like Paul Tillich, Roman Catholic thinkers like Gabriel Marcel, Jewish philosophers like Martin Buber—despite their differences—have joined their voices in an affirmation of human freedom and dignity. Perhaps the most intense and famous of these twentieth-century voices of protest is Jean-Paul Sartre, the founder of French existentialism. His published lecture *Existentialism is a Humanism*, from which the material of this section is taken, is an excellent introduction to his protest.

There is much in Sartre that is reminiscent of Descartes; e.g., Sartre's distinction between a *pour soi* and an *en soi* is some sort of descendant of Descartes' distinction between a *res cogitans* and a *res extensa*. Descartes' efforts to track down a not-doubtable as a starting point is detectable in the following passage paraphrased from Sartre's lecture:

> Our point of departure is the subjectivity of the individual (the individual regarded as a *subject* who thinks, not as an *object* thought about). It is because we seek to base our teaching upon the truth. Any doctrine of probabilities which is not attached to a truth will crumble. To define the probable one must possess the true. And there is such a truth. At the point of departure there cannot be any other truth than this: "I think, therefore I am." This theory does not begin by taking man as an object but as a subject. All kinds of materialism treat man as an object, a set of predetermined reactions, no different in this respect from a table or a chair or a stone.

Sartre's insistence on starting with the human as subject, as one who knows and wills and judges, not as some external object that is known and willed and judged, is fundamental to his existentialism. A subject, in contrast to an object, is come at through the activities that it performs, and in performing which it is conscious, aware, of itself as free. Unlike Holbach, Sartre sees no reason to write off this consciousness, this awareness, this experience of freedom as illusory. If freedom is an ineluctable fact about man apprehended as *subject*—as knower, willer, and judger—and if, as Sartre says, "man is condemned to be free," then man makes himself to be whatever he essentially becomes. He does this as he goes along, in the exercise of his freedom. He is the author of his own essential nature. In his case, then, his existence *precedes* his "essence." Whatever he now essentially is, he has made himself to be, and he *existed* before and while he was doing so. This is a step beyond Descartes.

BIOGRAPHICAL NOTE.   Jean-Paul Sartre was born in Paris in 1905. His academic training in philosophy was received in colleges and universities in France and Germany. He taught philosophy in French colleges before and for a few years after World War II. His war experiences included service in the French army, prisoner of war in Germany, and work with the French Resistance movement. He wrote many philosophical monographs, novels, plays, and literary essays. He was a founder and editor of the journal *Modern Times*. He refused the Nobel Prize for literature in 1964 because he believed that the award had become politicized and did not want to become a tool in the cultural struggle between East and West. Of his many publications, we should note *Nausea* (1938), an existentialist novel; *Being and Nothingness* (1943), the major philosophical statement of his existentialism; *No Exit* (1944), his most famous play; and *Existentialism Is a Humanism* (1946), a philosophical conference paper. Sartre died in 1980, unable to complete the huge biography of Gustave Flaubert he had been working on for about two decades.

THE ARGUMENT OF THE PASSAGES.   The passages in this section have been taken from Sartre's lecture *Existentialism Is a Humanism*. The design of his lecture is clear and straightforward: he announced his intention to defend his position against some typical reproaches; formulates his position as clearly as possible; and proceeds to fend off specific attacks on existentialism.

Sartre begins, then, with a brief review of some of the typical reproaches leveled at existentialism: it leads to the quietism of despair; it emphasizes all that is shameful in the human situation; it ignores the solidarity of humankind; and it denies the seriousness of human affairs.

My purpose here is to offer a defence of existentialism against several reproaches that have been laid against it.

First, it has been reproached as an invitation to people to dwell in quietism of despair. For if every way to a solution is barred, one would have to regard any action in this world entirely ineffective, and one would arrive finally at a contemplative philosophy. Moreover, since contemplation is a luxury, this would be only another bourgeois philosophy. This is, especially, the reproach made by the Communists.

From another quarter we are reproached for having underlined all that is ignominious in the human situation, for depicting what is mean, sordid, or base to the neglect of certain things that possess charm and beauty and belong to the brighter side of human nature: for example, according to the Catholic critic, Mlle. Mercier, we forget how an infant smiles. Both from this side and from the other we are also reproached for leaving out of account the solidarity of mankind and considering man in isolation. And this, say the Communists, is because we base our doctrine upon pure subjectivity—upon the Cartesian "I think": which is the moment in which solitary man attains to himself; a position from which it is impossible to regain solidarity with other men who exist outside of the self. The *ego* cannot reach them through the *cogito*.

From the Christian side, we are reproached as people who deny the reality and seriousness of human affairs. For since we ignore the commandments of God and all values prescribed as eternal, nothing remains but what is strictly voluntary. Everyone can do what he likes, and will be incapable, from such a point of view, of condemning either the point of view or the action of anyone else.

It is to these various reproaches that I shall endeavor to reply today; that is why I have entitled this brief exposition "Existentialism Is a Humanism." Many may be surprised at the mention of humanism in this connection, but we shall try to see in what sense we understand it. In any case, we can begin by saying that existentialism, in our sense of the word, is a doctrine that does render human life possible; a doctrine, also, which affirms that every truth and every action imply both an environment and a human subjectivity. The essential charge laid against us is, of course, that of overemphasis upon the evil side of human life. I have lately been told of a lady who, whenever she lets slip a vulgar expression in a moment of nervousness, excuses herself by exclaiming "I believe I am becoming an existentialist." So it appears that ugliness is being identified with existentialism. That is why some people say we are "naturalistic," and if we are, it is strange to see how much we scandalize and horrify them, for no one seems to be much frightened or humiliated nowadays by what is properly called naturalism. Those who can quite well keep down a novel by Zola such as *La Terre* are sickened as soon as they read an existentialist novel. Those who appeal to the wisdom of the people—which is a sad wisdom—find ours sadder still. And yet, what could be more disillusioned than such sayings as "Charity begins at home" or "Promote a rogue and he'll sue you for damage, knock him down and he'll do you homage"? We all know how many common sayings can be quoted to this effect, and they all mean much the same—that you must not oppose the powers-that-be; that you must not fight against superior force, must not meddle in matters that are above your station. Or that any action not in accordance with some tradition is mere romanticism; or that any undertaking which has not the support of proven experience is foredoomed to frustration; and that since experience has shown men to be invariably inclined to evil, there must be firm rules to restrain them, otherwise we shall have anarchy. It is, however, the people who are forever mouthing these dismal proverbs and, whenever they are told of some more or less repulsive action, say "How like human nature!"—it is these very people, always harping upon realism, who complain that existentialism is too gloomy a view of things. Indeed their excessive protests make me suspect that what is annoying them is not so much our pessimism, but, much more likely, our optimism. For at bottom, what is alarming in the doctrine that I am about to try to explain to you is—is it not?—that it confronts man with a possibility of choice. To verify this, let us review the whole question upon the strictly philosophical level. What, then, is this that we call existentialism?

Because many of these reproaches arise from a misunderstanding of what existentialism really is, Sartre proceeds to provide for his audience an authentic picture of existentialism. He acknowledges that his task is complicated at the outset by a division within the ranks of existentialists: some existentialists believe in God and some do not. Furthermore, the atheistic existentialists insist that existentialism's central claim is incompatible with all or most traditional forms of theism. Allowing for this source of ambiguity, Sartre identifies a central claim common to all existentialists: "*existence precedes essence.*" With this slogan existentialists intend to affirm human freedom in a radical way. They claim that the human being first of all exists and that through subsequent thinking, willing, choosing, and acting, the human defines himself or herself. Each human creates his or her own essence, his or her own self. Accordingly, the human is *responsible* for what he or she becomes. Furthermore, in choosing to be a certain kind of self, the human is really making a statement of what a self in that situation should be like. Therefore, the human is choosing not simply for himself or herself, but for all humankind. As Sartre observes, "In fashioning myself I fashion man." Consequently, one is responsible not simply for oneself but for all humankind. We can understand now why Sartre titles his lecture "Existentialism Is a Humanism."

. . . there are two kinds of existentialists. There are, on the one hand, the Christians, amongst whom I shall name Jaspers and Gabriel Marcel, both professed Catholics; and on the other the existential atheists, amongst whom we must place Heidegger as well as the French existentialists and myself. What they have in common is simply the fact that they believe that *existence* comes before *essence*—or, if you will, that we must begin from the subjective. What exactly do we mean by that?

If one considers an article of manufacture—as for example, a book or a paper-knife—one sees that it has been made by an artisan who had a conception of it; and he has paid attention, equally, to the conception of a paper-knife and to the pre-existent technique of production which is a part of that conception and is, at bottom, a formula. Thus the paper-knife is at the same time an article producible in a certain manner and one which, on the other hand, serves a definite purpose, for one cannot suppose that a man would produce a paper-knife without knowing what it was for. Let us say, then, of the paper-knife that its essence—that it to say the sum of the formulae and the qualities which made its production and its definition possible—precedes its existence. The presence of such-and-such a paper-knife or book is thus determined before my eyes. Here, then, we are viewing the world from a technical standpoint, and we can say that production precedes existence.

When we think of God as the creator, we are thinking of him, most of the time, as a supernal artisan. Whatever doctrine we may be considering, whether it be a doctrine like that of Descartes, or of Leibniz himself, we always imply that the will follows, more or less, from the understanding or at least accompanies it, so that when God creates he knows precisely what he is creating. Thus, the conception of man in the mind of God is comparable to that of the paper-knife in the mind of the artisan: God makes man according to a procedure and a conception, exactly as the artisan manufactures a paper-knife, following a definition and a formula. Thus each individual man is the realization of a certain conception which dwells in the divine understanding. In the philosophic atheism of the eighteenth century, the notion of God is suppressed, but not, for all that, the idea that essence is prior to existence; something of that idea we still find everywhere, in Diderot, in Voltaire and even in Kant. Man possesses a human nature; that "human nature," which is the conception of human being, is found in every man; which means that each man is a particular example of a universal conception, the conception of man. In Kant, this universality goes so far that the wild man of the woods, man in the state of nature and the bourgeois are all contained in the same definition and have the same fundamental qualities. Here again, the essence of man precedes that historic existence which we confront in experience.

Atheistic existentialism, of which I am a representative, declares with greater consistency that if God does not exist there is at least one being whose existence comes before its essence, a being which exists before it can be defined by any conception of it. That being is man or, as Heidegger has it, the human reality. What do we mean by saying that existence precedes essence? We mean that man first of all exists, encounters himself, surges up in the world—and defines himself afterwards. If man as the existentialist sees him is not definable, it is because to begin with he is nothing. He will not be anything until later, and then he will be what he makes of himself. Thus, there is no human nature, because there is no God to have a conception of it. Man simply is. Not that he is simply what he conceives himself to be, but he is what he wills, and as he conceives himself after already existing—as he wills to be after that leap toward existence. Man is nothing else but that which he makes of himself. That is the first principle of existentialism. And this is what people call its "subjectivity," using the word as a reproach against us. But what do we mean to say by this, but that man is of a greater dignity than a stone or a table? For we mean to say that man primarily exists—that man is, before all else, something which propels itself towards a future and is aware that it is doing so. Man is, indeed, a project which possesses a subjective life, instead of being a kind of moss, or a fungus or a cauliflower. Before that projection of the self nothing exists; not even in the heaven of intelligence; man will only attain existence when he is what he purposes to be. Not, however, what he may wish to be. For what we usually understand by wishing or willing is a conscious decision taken—much more often than not—after we have made ourselves what we are. I may wish to join a party, to write a book or to marry—but in such a case what is usually called my will is probably a manifestation of a prior and more spontaneous decision. If, however, it is true that existence is prior to essence, man is responsible for what he is. Thus, the first effect of existentialism is that it puts every man in possession of himself as he is, and places the entire responsibility for his existence squarely upon his own shoulders. And when we say that man is responsible for himself, we do not mean that he is responsible only for his own individuality, but that he is responsible for all men. The word "subjectivism" is to be understood in two senses, and our adversaries play upon only one of them. Subjectivism means, on the one hand, the freedom of the individual subject and, on the other, that man cannot pass beyond human subjectivity. It is the latter which is the deeper meaning of existentialism. When we say that man chooses himself, we do mean that every one of us must choose for all men. For in effect, of all the actions a man may take in order to create himself as he wills to be, there is not one which is not creative, at the same time, of an image of man such as he believes he ought to be. To choose between this or that is at the same time to affirm the value of that which is chosen; for we are unable ever to choose the worse. What we choose is always the better; and nothing can be better for us unless it is better for all. If, moreover, existence precedes essence and we will to exist at the same time as we fashion our image, that image is valid for all and for the entire epoch in which we find ourselves. Our responsibility is thus much greater than we had supposed, for it concerns mankind as a whole. If I am a worker, for instance, I may choose to join a Christian rather than a Communist trade union. And if, by that membership, I choose to signify that resignation is, after all, the attitude that best becomes a man, that a man's kingdom is not upon this earth. I do not commit myself alone to that view. Resignation is my will for everyone, and my action is, in consequence, a commitment on behalf of all mankind. Or if, to take a more personal case, I decide to marry and to have children, even though this decision proceeds simply from my situation, from my passion or my desire, I am thereby committing not only myself, but humanity as a whole, to the practice of monogamy. I am thus responsible for myself and for all men, and I am creating a certain image of man as I would have him to be. In fashioning myself I fashion man.

Suppose you have given a concise exposition of the typical and central claims of some doctrine. You might then go on to single out three or four particular notions consequent upon, diagnostic of, the doctrine you had expounded. Sartre is now at that point. He has provided a concise account of his existentialism. He now selects three notions familiar and important to any Sartrean existentialist, namely, anguish, abandonment, and despair. There are others he might have chosen—bad faith, nausea, absurdity, for example. Given the doctrine that there are two modes of being in the world, *être en soi* and *être pour soi*, being which is not conscious or aware of itself and being which is conscious or aware of itself; call the mode of being that is conscious or aware of itself *existence pour soi*. Sartre's doctrine, existentialism, is about beings whose mode of existence is *pour soi*. You and I are such beings. We are conscious or aware that we exist. Our mode of existence is *pour soi*. A rock or a tree is not such a being. They are not conscious or aware that they exist. Their mode of existence is merely *en soi*. The present question is this: If you are a *pour soi*, why will anguish, abandonment, and despair be important, diagnostic, terms for you?

This may enable us to understand what is meant by such terms—perhaps a little grandiloquent—as anguish, abandonment and despair. As you will soon see, it is very simple. *First*, what do we mean by *anguish*? The existentialist frankly states that man is in anguish. His meaning is as follows—When a man commits himself to anything, fully realizing that he is not only choosing what he will be, but is thereby at the same time a legislator deciding for the whole of mankind—in such a moment a man cannot escape from the sense of complete and profound responsibility. There are many, indeed, who show no such anxiety. But we affirm that they are merely disguising their anguish or are in flight from it. Certainly, many people think that in what they are doing they commit no one but themselves to anything; and if you ask them, "What would happen if everyone did so?" they shrug their shoulders and reply, "Everyone does not do so." But in truth, one ought always to ask oneself what would happen if everyone did as one is doing; nor can one escape from that disturbing thought except by a kind of self-deception. The man who lies in self-excuse, by saying, "Everyone will not do it" must be ill at ease in his conscience, for the act of lying implies the universal value which it denies. By its very disguise his anguish reveals itself. This is the anguish that Kierkegaard called "the anguish of Abraham." You know the story: An angel commanded Abraham to sacrifice his son; and obedience was obligatory, if it really was an angel who had appeared and said, "Thou, Abraham, shalt sacrifice thy son." But anyone in such a case would wonder, first, whether it was indeed an angel and secondly, whether I am really Abraham. Where are the proofs? A certain mad woman who suffered from hallucinations said that people were telephoning her, and giving her orders. The doctor asked "But who is it that speaks to you?" She replied: "He says it is God." And what, indeed, could prove to her that it was God? If an angel appears to me, what is the proof that it is an angel; or, if I hear voices, who can prove that they proceed from heaven and not from hell, or from my own subconsciousness or some pathological condition? Who can prove that they are really addressed to me?

Who, then, can prove that I am the proper person to impose, by my own choice, my conception of man upon mankind? I shall never find any proof whatever; there will be no sign to convince me of it. If a voice speaks to me, it is still myself who must decide whether the voice is or is not that of an angel. If I regard a certain course of action as good, it is only I who choose to say that it is good and not bad. There is nothing to show that I am Abraham; nevertheless I am also obliged at every instant to perform actions which are examples. Everything happens to every man as though the whole human race had its eyes fixed upon what he is doing and regulated its conduct accordingly. So every man ought to say, "Am I a man who has the right to act in such a manner that humanity regulates itself by what I do." If a man does not say that, he is dissembling his anguish.

Clearly, the anguish with which we are concerned here is not one that could lead to quietism or inaction. It is anguish pure and simple, of the kind well known to all those who
have borne responsibilities. When, for instance, a military leader takes upon himself the
responsibility for an attack and sends a number of men to their death, he chooses to do
it and at bottom he alone chooses. No doubt he acts under a higher command, but its
orders, which are more general, require interpretation by him and upon that interpretation depends the life of ten, fourteen or twenty men. In making the decision, he cannot
but feel a certain anguish. All leaders know that anguish. It does not prevent their acting;
on the contrary it is the very condition of their action, for the action presupposes that
there is a plurality of possibilities, and in choosing one of these, they realize that it has value
only because it is chosen. Now it is anguish of that kind which existentialism describes,
and moreover, as we shall see, makes explicit through direct responsibility towards other
men who are concerned. Far from being a screen which could separate us from action,
it is a condition of action itself.

So much for existentialist anguish. Sartre's point has been this: if you are a *pour soi*,
conscious or aware of existence, especially of your own existence, in a world containing only
others who are also *pour soi*, and objects that are merely *en soi*, and that is all, you will
know anguish. Why so? Why is anguish one of the facts of life for a *pour soi*? He moves on
now to consider his second notion, *abandonment*. Thus:

And when we speak of "*abandonment*"—a favorite word of Heidegger—we only
mean to say that God does not exist, and that it is necessary to draw the consequences
of his absence right to the end. The existentialist is strongly opposed to a certain type of
secular moralism which seeks to suppress God at the least possible expense. Towards
1880, when the French professors endeavored to formulate a secular morality, they said
something like this:—God is a useless and costly hypothesis, so we will do without it. However, if we are to have morality, a society and a law-abiding world, it is essential that certain values should be taken seriously; they must have an *a priori* existence ascribed to
them. It must be considered obligatory *a priori* to be honest, not to lie, not to beat one's
wife, to bring up children and so forth; so we are going to do a little work on this subject,
which will enable us to show that these values exist all the same, inscribed in an intelligent heaven although, of course, there is no God. In other words—and this is, I believe,
the purport of all that we in France call radicalism—nothing will be changed if God does
not exist; we shall rediscover the same norms of honesty, progress and humanity, and we
shall have disposed of God as an out-of-date hypothesis which will die away quietly of
itself. The existentialist, on the contrary, finds it extremely embarrassing that God does
not exist, for there disappears with Him all possibility of finding values in an intelligible
heaven. There can no longer be any good *a priori*, since there is no infinite and perfect
consciousness to think it. It is nowhere written that "the good" exists, that one must be
honest or must not lie, since we are now upon the plane where there are only men. Dostoevsky once wrote "If God did not exist, everything would be permitted;" and that, for
existentialism, is the starting point. Everything is indeed permitted if God does not exist,
and man is in consequence forlorn, for he cannot find anything to depend upon either
within or outside himself. He discovers forthwith, that he is without excuse. For if indeed
existence precedes essence, one will never be able to explain one's action by reference
to a given and specific human nature; in other words, there is no determinism—man is

free, man *is* freedom. Nor, on the other hand, if God does not exist, are we provided with any values or commands that could legitimize our behavior. Thus we have neither behind us, nor before us in a luminous realm of values, any means of justification or excuse. We are left alone, without excuse. That is what I mean when I say that man is condemned to be free. Condemned, because he did not create himself, yet is nevertheless at liberty, and from the moment that he is thrown into this world he is responsible for everything he does. The existentialist does not believe in the power of passion. He will never regard a grand passion as a destructive torrent upon which a man is swept into certain actions as by fate, and which therefore, is an excuse for them. He thinks that man is responsible for his passion. Neither will an existentialist think that a man can find help through some sign being vouchsafed upon earth for his orientation; for he thinks that the man himself interprets the sign as he chooses. He thinks that every man, without any support or help whatever, is condemned at every instant to invent man. As Ponge has written in a very fine article, "Man is the future of man." That is exactly true. Only, if one took this to mean that the future is laid up in Heaven, that God knows what it is, it would be false, for then it would no longer even be a future. If, however, it means that, whatever man may now appear to be, there is a future to be fashioned, a virgin future that awaits him—then it is a true saying. But in the present one is forsaken.

Thus far, Sartre has claimed that if you are an existentialist you will hold that there are in the world only two modes of existence: existence that is conscious or aware of itself, *être pour soi*, and existence that is not conscious or aware of itself, *être en soi*. He went on to claim that if you are a *pour soi* among others who are *pour soi*, anguish will be one of the facts of life for you. There will be no avoiding that encounter. He has now added the further claim that if you are an atheist *pour soi*, then abandonment, lostness, cosmic aloneness, forlornness will be one of the ineluctable facts of life for you and your kind. There will be no avoiding encounter with the vast "emptiness" of the world. You will realize that you, and all others who are *pour soi*, are abandoned, lost, forlorn, alone. You are not an object of concern to any *en soi*; that would be impossible. And because for Sartre you are also an atheist *pour soi*, an atheist aware that he exists but committed to claiming that there is no super *pour soi*—no God, no Deity, no Creator and Sustainer—you are not an object of concern of any superhuman *pour soi*. There is, for the atheist existentialist, no God, but only other finite *pour soi* and *en soi*. Neither humanity nor nature is any substitute for God at this point. The knowledge that there are others, like yourself, who are *pour soi* will not rid you of this sense of being abandoned in and cast upon the world; *thrown*. The knowledge that every other being who is not a *pour soi* is merely an *en soi*, similar to a rock or a tree, will not rid you of this sense of abandonment, thrownness. He now turns to the existentialist concept of despair.

As for "*despair*," the meaning of this expression is extremely simple. It merely means that we limit ourselves to a reliance upon that which is within our wills, or within the sum of the probabilities, which render our action feasible. Whenever one wills anything, there are always these elements of probability. If I am counting upon a visit from a friend, who may be coming by train or tram, I presuppose that the train will arrive at the appointed time, or that the tram will not be derailed. I remain in the realm of possibilities; but one does not rely upon any possibilities beyond those that are strictly concerned in one's actions. Beyond the point at which the possibilities under consideration cease to affect my action, I ought to disinterest myself. For there is no God and no prevenient design which can adapt the world and all its possibilities to my will. When Descartes said, "Conquer yourself rather than the world," what he meant was, at the bottom, the same—that we should act without hope.

Marxists, to whom I have said this, have answered: "Your action is limited, obviously, by your death; but you can rely upon the help of others. That is, you can count both upon what the others are doing to help you elsewhere, as in China and in Russia, and upon what they will do later, after your death, to take up your action and carry it forward to its final accomplishment which will be the revolution. Moreover you must rely upon this; not to do so is immoral." To this I rejoin, first, that I shall always count upon my comrades-in-arms in the struggle, in so far as they are committed, as I am, to a definite, common cause; and in the unity of a party or a group which I can more or less control—that is, in which I am enrolled as a militant and whose movements are every moment are known to me. In that respect, to rely upon the unity and the will of the party is exactly like my reckoning that the train will run on time or that the tram will not be derailed. But I cannot count upon men whom I do not know, I cannot base my confidence upon human goodness or upon man's interest in the good of society, seeing that man is free and that there is no human nature which I can take as foundational.

Sartre has told us that he will defend his atheist existentialism against certain charges, certain reproaches. He has given us an account of his doctrine and some of its corollaries. He has explained that his doctrine is a form of humanism. In the second half of his lecture he will deal with some of the charges brought against this atheist or humanist existentialism. The first charge ("reproach") is that an existentialism such as his will lead to quietism and pessimism. Thus:

Quietism is the attitude of people who say, "let others do what I cannot do." The doctrine I am presenting before you is precisely the opposite of this, since it declares that there is no reality except in action. It goes further, indeed, and adds, "Man is nothing else but what he purposes, he exists only in so far as he realizes himself, he is therefore nothing else but the sum of his actions, nothing else but what his life is." Hence we can well understand why some people are horrified by our teaching. For many have but one resource to sustain them in their misery, and that is to think, "Circumstances have been against me, I was worthy to be something much better than I have been. I admit I have never had a great love or a great friendship; but that is because I never met a man or a woman who were worthy of it; if I have not written any very good books, it is because I had not the leisure to do so; or, if I have had no children to whom I could devote myself it is because I did not find the man I could have lived with. So there remains within me a wide range of abilities, inclinations and potentialities, unused but perfectly viable, which endow me with a worthiness that could never be inferred from the mere history of my actions." But in reality and for the existentialist, there is no love apart from the deeds of love; no potentiality of love other than that which is manifested in loving; there is no genius other than that which is expressed in works of art. The genius of Proust is the totality of the works of Proust; the genius of Racine is the series of his tragedies, outside of which there is nothing. Why should we attribute to Racine the capacity to write yet another tragedy when that is precisely what he did not write? In life, a man commits himself, draws his own portrait and there is nothing but that portrait. No doubt this thought may seem comfortless to one who has not made a success of his life. On the other hand, it puts everyone in a position to understand that reality alone is reliable; that dreams, expectations and hopes serve to define a man only as deceptive dreams, abortive hopes, expectations unfulfilled; that is to say, they define him negatively, not positively. Nevertheless, when one says: "You are nothing else but what you live," it does not imply that an artist is to be judged solely by his works of art, for a thousand other things contribute no less to his definition as a man. What we mean to say is that a man is no other than a series of undertakings, that he is the sum, the organization, the set of relations that constitute these undertakings.

Sartre's point is this: If, as existentialist, you tell a person that he is a *pour soi*, one who exists and is conscious of, aware of, existing, he may begin by agreeing with you. Why not? Your doctrine rates him above the world of the *en soi*. That is a gratifying, indeed a flattering, perception. However, if you go on to explain to him that his status as a *pour soi* endows him with free will, with perception of alternatives, with power to choose, hence with responsibility, with power to make of himself what he, not external events and forces, decides—if you go on to make this application of your existentialism to his handling of his life and affairs, he will take a dim view of your doctrine. He does not want to think of himself as essentially the architect of his own wrongdoings and of his character as a person. And he does not want your doctrine to constrain him into thinking that way about himself. He prefers to cop out, and your existentialism forbids him to do so. It tells him that he is the author of whatever he is. He has not "become" what he is. That is the way of the *en soi*. He has made of himself what he is, by his own wrong-headed and bad-willed thinking and acting. Hence, your doctrine denies or distorts the image he wants of himself. So what does he do? He contrives to misunderstand, to misinterpret, your doctrine. He will claim that your doctrine ends by inducing those who accept it to become quietists and pessimists. But as Sartre hastens to point out, such a person is only rationalizing his rejection of existentialism by refusing to understand that doctrine correctly. This refusal is an example of what Sartre means by *mauvaise foi*, bad faith. If the person will only snap out of his protective obtuseness, he will see that he is not "refuting" existentialism, not even proposing a relevant criticism, but merely setting up a straw man, and then clobbering it, only spitefully misunderstanding it.

In summary, Sartre has displayed his view of the human being in terms of radical freedom. According to Sartre, I first of all exist, and then by my own activity define my essence. I am free to create myself without having to obey guidelines or requirements established in advance by God or others. I am free to become the kind of person I choose to be. Accordingly, I am responsible for myself, and, Sartre adds, I am also responsible for all humankind. In creating myself, I experience the consequences of this radical freedom: anguish, abandonment, and despair. If instead of acknowledging responsibility for myself and pursuing the task of creating myself in radical freedom, I attempt to shift the responsibility from myself to some other entity (for example, God, others, or the environment), then I am treating myself as if I were an *en soi*, a thing that is manipulated by forces beyond its control. To shift responsibility in this fashion to entities beyond myself would mean that I would be attempting to be what I am not; I would be portraying myself as an *en soi* rather than a *pour soi*. I would be deceiving myself. I would be living a lie. I would be inauthentic. I would be expressing *mauvaise foi*, "bad faith." That is precisely what a determinist such as Holbach would be doing in the eyes of an existentialist like Sartre.

NOTE ON SOURCES.   The material in this section is quoted from Jean-Paul Sartre, translated by P. Mairet in Walter Kaufmann, ed., *Existentialism from Dostoevsky to Sartre* (New York: Meridian Books, 1956), pp. 287–311.

Glossary*

Absolutism: In the theory of value (ethics and aesthetics), the view that standards of value are objective rather than relative. In theory of knowledge, the view that objective, absolute (not merely relative) truth is possible. (Compare with **Objectivism** and contrast with **Subjectivism**.)

Ad hoc: From the Latin, "to this." The defense of a thesis against an objection by a claim that serves only to answer that particular objection. *Ad hoc* defenses are considered weak.

Aesthetics: The branch of philosophy that analyzes the human experience of beauty. Questions such as—What features make objects beautiful? Are there standards of beauty? What is the relation of works of art to nature?—are explored. The philosophy of art has a narrower focus than aesthetics because the former examines the experience of works of art and usually excludes the experience of beauty in nature.

After image: After having stared at a light for a few seconds, a person with normal vision will still see a faint glow after the light source is removed. That faint glow is called an after image.

Agnosticism: A term coined by T. H. Huxley (1825–1895) to describe his philosophical position: "It is morally wrong for a person to affirm that a proposition is true without evidence which logically justifies that affirmation." Following Huxley, people have called themselves "agnostics" to indicate that they believe that certain kinds of knowledge—especially knowledge of God—lack sufficient supporting evidence, and these are highly suspect.

Alienation: A term Marx borrowed from Hegel to describe the condition of the human producer who creates all the artifacts and institutions of culture and then becomes separated or divorced from those products which, in turn, are perceived as something foreign and alien to the human creator rather than as expressions of the human being's own creative energies. Such alien products appear to dominate and rule the human producer. Such is the human condition, according to Marx, in capitalistic society.

Anarchism: The doctrine which claims that all forms of government are evil and should be abolished.

Animism: A primitive belief that objects are infused by spirits or souls.

Antinomianism: The view which advocates freedom from law and the external regulation of human life.

A posteriori: A term used by Kant and others to characterize knowledge derived from sense experience.

Apparition: A ghost.

A priori: A term used by Kant and others to characterize knowledge derived by reason independent of sense experience. Such knowledge, says Kant, is true universally and necessarily; that is, true for everyone, and true in and of itself without reference to who believes or does not believe it, without reference to the consequences that follow from its being true or from its being believed.

Arguing in a circle: A fallacious form of argument in which one begins with some assertion, argues

---

* Taken from *Introduction to Modern Philosophy: Examining the Human Condition*, Seventh Edition by Alburey Castell, Donald M. Borchert, and Arthur Zucker.

using that assertion, and then concludes with that very same assertion—as if the original claim had been proved.

Atheism: The assertion that, given what most people *mean* by the term *God*, there is no God.

Autonomous inner man: B. F. Skinner's term for the mind or soul which has autonomy or independence from the body and its physical processes to the extent that human freedom is a reality. Skinner entirely rejects this notion of the inner man and freedom, and instead embraces a form of determinism.

Axiology: Theory of value.

Ayurvedic: An ancient Tibetan form of medicine. It stresses close attention to the pulse for diagnosis and the use of heavy metals such as gold in treatment. It is now also practiced widely in India.

Begging the question: A fallacious form of argument in which what is supposed to be proved is assumed. It differs from arguing in a circle in that, when begging the question, it is often not clear that the assertion meant to be proved has actually been assumed.

Behaviorism: The contemporary school of psychology associated with J. B. Watson and B. F. Skinner, which abandons the concepts of mind and consciousness, and restricts its analysis to the study of human and animal behavior. This approach usually denies the existence of human freedom and generally advocates a form of materialism.

Bona fides: A Latin phrase meaning "good faith." Also, one's credentials.

Bourgeoisie: In Marx's theory, the capitalist class, which controls the means of production and whose interests are expressed in and guaranteed by the social superstructure.

Cartesianism: The philosophy of René Descartes.

Casuistry: A method of determining right or wrong in matters of conscience and conduct by fastidiously applying general principles to particular concrete cases.

Catastrophists: Those who assume that differences in species are best explained by catastrophes, such as great floods. Catastrophists are opposed to Darwin's theory of evolution. This view conflicts with Uniformitarianism.

Categorical imperative: According to Kant, the supreme, absolute moral law which is understood by any rational creature to be one's duty without any qualifications or exceptions. Such duty involves acting on those principles which one could universalize (that is, make a universal law).

Categories of understanding: According to Kant, the forms of knowledge as distinguished from the content of knowledge. The mind brings to any knowing situation certain categories or forms through which it grasps the objects of knowledge. These categories such as unity and plurality, cause and effect, are not things known but are ways of knowing.

Category-mistake: According to Ryle, the error made when one assumes incorrectly that two different things exist in the same sort of way. To affirm that minds and bodies exist in the same sort of way is, says Ryle, to commit this mistake.

Cause: Something that is responsible for change, motion, or action in another thing. Hume questions the necessary connection that is often assumed to be present between two causally related events. According to Hume, the evidence of our senses may indicate that when event A happens, event B follows; but the evidence of our senses does not indicate that event A is responsible for event B.

Central state identity theory: Also called identity theory. The name calls attention to the fact that the mental is identical to states of the central nervous system and not to states of the entire nervous system.

Cerebral cortex of the brain: The grey matter on the outside of the mammalian brain.

Ceteris paribus: A Latin phrase meaning literally "with other things equal," or more smoothly "with other factors being the same."

Christian Science: A religion based on an interpretation of the Bible first given by Mary Baker Eddy in the mid-nineteenth century. In her view, disease is purely subjective, i.e., a defect of spirit, and can be overcome by prayer and improvement in character. There are Christian Science practitioners who help with the appropriate prayers.

Cogito, ergo sum: "I think, therefore I am." This statement is Descartes' *indubitandum,* the not doubtable and self-evident principle on which he attempts to construct a body of knowledge that is beyond the power of skeptics to destroy.

Cognition: From the Latin *cognoscere,* "to know," cognition refers, in the broadest sense, to knowledge or the act of knowing.

Cognitive symbol: A symbol, such as a word or group of words, used to indicate what you know or could know. Such symbols are usually assessed as true or false. Contrast with **Emotive symbol**.

Communism: The society of the future to which Marx and Engels believed historical process was irresistibly moving. In that society, exploitation of the masses by the ruling elite would no longer exist because the economic productive process would be owned and controlled by humankind at large for the benefit of all persons.

Contingency: A state of affairs or a being is said to be contingent when it may or also may not be. A contingent being depends on other beings and states of affairs for its existence: when those conditions are removed, the contingent being ceases to exist. (See **Empirical possibility**.)

Copernican Revolution: Sixteenth-century astronomer Nicolaus Copernicus reversed the traditional account of the solar system by substituting a heliocentric view for the prevailing geocentric view derived from second-century Greek astronomer Ptolemy. In epistemology, Kant considered his views to be something of a Copernican revolution in that he reversed the prevailing view by emphasizing the active role played by the mind in generating knowledge as opposed to the passive role of the mind emphasized by empiricists such as Locke and Hume. In the speculative philosophy of history, Spengler considered his position also to be a Copernican revolution in that he reversed the prevailing view which subdivided history into an ancient-medieval-modern scheme. In its place, Spengler presented the model of a process in which cultures mature and decline into civilizations.

Cybernetics: The comparative study of the human nervous system and complex electronic systems.

Cynicism: (1) The personal attitude which scorns and mocks the motives and virtues of others. (2) The doctrines of the Cynics, a school of Greek Philosophy founded by Antisthenes, a friend of Socrates. The Cynics claimed that a person's true happiness is to be achieved through a virtuous life which involves independence from events and facts external to the self. To achieve such independence, the Cynics attempted to master their desires and wants. In extreme cases, Cynics reduced their desires to a bare minimum and attempted to live an unencumbered, natural life in the midst of civilized society. No doubt, they appeared to be scorning civilization and perhaps

thereby facilitated the development of the broader meaning of cynicism when it refers to an attitude rather than to a school of philosophy.

Darwinian: Any of a number of theories of evolution stressing natural selection as opposed to miracles or goal-oriented evolution. Darwinian evolution conflicts with a teleological approach to evolution. (See **Teleology**.)

Deconstructionism: A twentieth-century movement with roots in Marxism and certain strands of contemporary European philosophy (especially French philosopher Jacques Derrida) that seeks to expose (deconstruct) the cultural influences that inescapably condition every language and the interpretation of any text and thereby relativize or disprivilege any particular interpretation. This perspective can lead to radical relativism and subjectivism. (See **Postmodernism, Relativism,** and **Subjectivism**.)

Deduction: A method of reasoning in which a conclusion is claimed to follow necessarily from one or more premises. (Compare with **Induction**.)

Deism: The view that after God created the world, he allowed it to function on its own without divine intervention. Deists depreciate supernatural revelation and confine religion to the realm of that which is accessible to human reason.

Democritean atomist: Democritus (460–370 B.C.) was a Greek philosopher who stressed the idea that everything is made of indivisible, small units which he called atoms.

Determinism: The doctrine that every event has a cause. Such a doctrine seems to preclude human freedom by explaining all human behavior in terms of chains of causes that stretch back into the dim recesses of one's heredity and environment.

Dialectic: The critical thinking process in which an idea is set forth, criticized, reformulated, and in its revised form set forth to be criticized and reformulated again. The process continues almost without end. Such dialectical thinking is as ancient as Socrates' question-and-answer method of philosophizing. In the dialectical process Hegel perceived what he considered to be the pattern of historical development: thesis, antithesis and synthesis (which becomes a new thesis, etc.).

Dialectical materialism: The view developed by some of Marx's disciples that reality is material and that matter develops according to the Hegelian pattern of thesis, antithesis, synthesis. In the realm of human history the dialectical movement of matter appears as the class struggle which is driving to its final synthesis in a Communist society.

Digital computer: A computer in which data is represented by discrete units—usually either the flow or lack of flow of an electric current.

Dilemma: An argument in which a choice between two or more alternatives (each being unsatisfactory if not fatal) is presented to an opponent.

Dualism: A theory which holds that in any given domain there are two independent and irreducible substances. For example, Descartes' view that the human being consists of *res cogitans* (a thinking thing or mind) and *res extensa* (an extended thing or body) is a metaphysical dualism. Other forms of dualism affirm pairs of substances such as the intelligible world of ideas and the material world of things, the forces of good and the forces of evil, the realm of light and the realm of darkness.

Economic substructure: Marx's term for the economic dimension of society which consists of all the raw materials, technology and interpersonal relations involved in producing and distributing the goods and services of a society. The key factor in the substructure is the relations of production which in all pre-Communist societies have been characterized by the struggle between the exploiting elite and the exploited masses.

Egoism: As a moral doctrine, ethical egoism declares that one ought to pursue his or her own interests exclusively. As a theory of motivation, psychological egoism declares that each person always acts in the pursuit of self-interest and can do no other.

Electron: A small negatively charged particle that orbits the nucleus of an atom. Electrons are not really particles and they do not really orbit the nuclei in the way that planets orbit the sun. (See **Quantum mechanics**.)

Elephant Man Syndrome: Also known as Von Recklinghausen's Syndrome. A genetic condition whose symptoms are many fibrous tumors on the body, often, but not always, on the face.

Emergent properties: The usual example is self-consciousness. From the physiology of the human brain, it could not have been predicted that humans would have self-consciousness. The properties of the chemicals that make up the brain do not themselves have self-consciousness. It is as if something is added when all the properties come together in a certain way. Emergent properties are more than just the sum of their parts. (See **Holism**.) Emergent properties are not reducible to their parts. (See **Reductionism**.)

Emotive symbol: A symbol used to express what you feel or could feel. Such symbols are usually assessed as fitting or unfitting, authentic or inauthentic, rather than as true or false. Contrast with **Cognitive Symbol**.

Emotivism: In ethics, emotivism claims that ethical sentences *express* the feelings of the speaker and seek to *evoke* similar feelings in the hearers. As such, ethical sentences do not make claims about the world that are either true or false. Some radical emotivists claim that ethical sentences merely *evince* emotions, which means that certain emotions are put on display by the speaker, without the claim being made that the speaker possesses those emotions. In aesthetics, emotivism maintains that a work of art is an emotive symbol with which the artist expresses his or her feelings. In contrast, a cognitive symbol expresses what one knows or believes rather than what one feels.

Empirical possibility: Factually possible; even if highly unlikely. (See **Contingent**.)

Empiricism: The theory that claims that all human knowledge is derived from the senses, which implies that humans neither possess inborn knowledge nor are able to generate knowledge by the use of reason alone.

En soi: Sartre's term for existence that is not conscious of itself. Such existence is "in itself." It does not project itself into the future and attempt to achieve that future self for itself.

Epiphenomenalism: The theory of the mind-body relation which holds that consciousness or mind is simply a by-product of the bodily neurological processes that underlie it, and that while mental events are caused by brain events, mental events never cause brain events.

Epistemology: An inquiry into the nature, origin, and validity of knowledge.

Eschatological verification: A term used by John Hick to refer to a future possible post-death situation in which the claims of Christian theism (such as "God exists" and "God is good") could be verified.

Esse est percipi: "To be is to be perceived." A slogan adopted by George Berkeley to convey one of his fundamental tenets that reality depends upon mind and is, accordingly, basically "spiritual." Berkeley developed this idealist position over-against the materialism of Thomas Hobbes.

Essence: The basic characteristic or function of a thing by virtue of which it is a distinct or unique entity.

Essence precedes existence: Sartre's term for describing the technological and theological viewpoints in which the idea of a thing appears first of all in the mind of a creator who then manipulates matter to make the thing appear in existence. Although Sartre accepts the technological view concerning things humans fashion, he rejects the claim that essence precedes existence in the case of the creation of humans. Each human creates himself or herself unencumbered by a prior essence which must be actualized. A prior essence would violate the fullness of human freedom which Sartre affirms.

Ethics: An investigation of the principles by which we distinguish goodness from badness and assess actions as right or wrong.

Existence precedes essence: Sartre's slogan with which he declares that the human being first exists and then defines himself or herself through his or her actions. The human creates his or her own existence rather than attempting to achieve a pre-established essence fixed by God. A pre-established essence would be incompatible with human freedom.

Existentialism: A philosophical movement rooted in nineteenth century philosophers such as Kierkegaard and Nietzsche who emphasized the importance of exploring meaning for the concrete existing individual as opposed to grandiose philosophical systems, such as Hegel's, which provide extensive explanations of reality without raising the question of what it means to be an existing, struggling, choosing individual. The movement flourished especially after the Second World War through the writings of such thinkers as Jean-Paul Sartre, Gabriel Marcel, Jacques Maritain, Nikolai Berdyayev, and Martin Heidegger.

Expressionism: The theory of art which holds that the distinctive function of the artist is to express emotions. A form of emotivism.

Fallibilism: The view that any knowledge claim may turn out to be false.

Fatalism: Occasionally used as a synonym for determinism. (See also **Determinism**.)

"Fido"—fido theory of meaning: The playful name given to the view that statements mean what they refer to just as the name "Fido" refers to Fido, the dog.

Folk psychology: Any common sense account of human behavior. Folk psychology is opposed to "scientific" psychologies such as Freudian, Jungian, physiological, behaviorist, etc.

Formalism: The theory of art which holds that only intrinsic features in a work of art are relevant to the interpretation and criticism of the art.

Foucault: Michel Foucault (1926–1984), a contemporary French philosopher who championed the postmodernist cause.

Galileo: Galileo Galilei (1564–1642) was a physicist and astronomer. He studied the motion of objects to discover the laws of motion and showed that Copernicus was correct in asserting that the sun, and not the Earth, is the center of the solar system. For this, Galileo was condemned for heresy by the Church. Most important, according to many scholars, was Galileo's insistence that science deal with those properties that could be expressed mathematically.

Gedankenexperiment: A thought experiment. A conceptual experiment. The tool of philosophers and theoretical scientists, such as Einstein and Hawking. Einstein once asked himself, "What would a light wave look like if I could run alongside it?" This is a thought experiment.

Genuine option: According to William James, an option that is living (both hypotheses are live or realistic alternatives), forced (one cannot walk away from the option without choosing one of the alternatives), momentous (the opportunity is unique, the stake significant, and the decision irreversible).

Gestalt shift: A total shift in the way one views something, first by focusing on foreground and then by focusing on background. The shift need not be intentional. Sometimes, one just sees differently. For example, the duck-rabbit:

Gnosticism: The name given by historians of religion to a cluster of religious movements widespread in the Graeco-Roman world, in which it was held that salvation involved release of the spirit from bondage to the flesh by means of secret knowledge (gnosis).

God: A being that transcends nature, is *more* than nature, and is often regarded as the creator, producer, and sustainer of nature.

Hedonistic paradox: The notion that "happiness to be gotten, must be forgotten." That is to say, one achieves happiness not as the goal of one's actions, but as the unintentional by-product of other intended goals.

Herbal medicine: Medicine based on the use of herbs as treatment for disease.

Heuristic: Helpful in teaching or learning.

Holistic: Systems are said to be holistic if their parts are so interrelated that the system cannot be understood except by appeal to the interconnectedness. Holistic systems are said to be more than the sums of their parts. Holistic systems cannot be properly understood by means of reductionism. (See **Reductionism.**)

Homeopathy: A medical theory based on the idea that disease should be treated with minute amounts of whatever caused the disease.

Homunculus: A scale model of a person. Originally it was thought that in the tip of sperm was an exact—but tiny—replica of a person.

Humanism: Any view in which concern for human beings, their achievements and welfare, is central.

Hydra: A small, tentacled coelenterate (jellyfish-like creature).

Hypothesis: Any statement proposed for one's belief. (William James)

Idealism: The view that mind (or soul, or spirit) is the ultimate reality and that matter is dependent upon mind, in contrast to materialism which regards reality as fundamentally material.

Imitation: The theory of art which suggests that the goal of the artist is to create the illusion that the copy is not a copy at all, but the original.

Incommensurability: Unable to be measured together against the same standard.

Indeterminism: The view that human decisions are in some sense independent of prior causes; the affirmation of free will.

Indubitandum: That which is not doubtable. (see also **Cogito, ergo sum.**)

Induction: A method of reasoning whereby one proceeds from a number of observed particular facts to a generalization about all such facts. Such generalizations can be supported by the particular facts, but the truth of those generalizations cannot be completely demonstrated by those facts. (Contrast with **Deduction.**)

Inductive inference: Usually contrasted to deductive inference. A statement is said to be inferred inductively when it might be false even if the beliefs (or statements, or facts) on which it is based are true. For example, "the water must be boiling because the water has been heating for 20 minutes" is an inductive inference; an inference inductively made. A statement is said to be made deductively when there is no way the statement inferred can be false if the supporting beliefs (statements, purported facts) are true.

Inferotemporal lobe of the brain: The lobe of the brain below (inferior to) the temporal lobe of primates, which is the lobe at the "side" of the brain; at the temples. Or, the lower part of the temporal lobe. The precise function of the temporal lobe is unknown. The term *inferotemporal* is unknown to contemporary American neuroanatomists. It is probably a British anatomical term that has long since ceased to be used.

Innate ideas: Ideas with which, according to Descartes and others, one is born. Such ideas are considered to be *a priori* and possessed by all rational humans.

Intentionality: Mental states such as beliefs have a content. Beliefs are always beliefs about something. Mental states that have content in this fashion are said to be intentional. Pain is a mental state that is not intentional.

Intrinsic good: That which is desirable for its own sake as distinct from an instrumental good which is desirable for the sake of something else.

Introspection: The act of turning one's attention inward so that it is focused on one's inner mental life. In doing this, one might notice slight aches previously gone unnoticed. One might also be able to concentrate on one's thoughts and feelings.

Intuition: The direct and immediate apprehension by the self of certain knowledge about the self and the world without the need for deductive or inductive reasoning as the basis for affirming the truth of certain propositions.

Jung: Carl Jung (1875–1961) was an early member of the Vienna Psychoanalytic Circle, a group studying psychological theories of, and with, Freud. He later broke with Freud and Freudian approaches. Jung is best known for his theory of archetypes, an attempt to explain personality characters by appeal to general patterns. Because Jung felt that these patterns were not culturally specific, he came to believe in the idea of a collective (human) consciousness.

Lakatos: Hungarian historian and philosopher of science and mathematics (1922–1974). Known for his critique of Karl Popper's views of falsification and Kuhn's ideas on paradigms.

Lamarckian: A follower of Lamarck; a view similar to Lamarck's. Lamarck held that evolution was a fact of nature and that its mechanism was a combination of inner desire on the part of organisms and the inheritance of acquired characteristics.

Lavoisier/Priestley/Phlogiston: In the late seventeenth century, phlogiston was the name for the principle that allowed for combustion. It is a substance since shown not to exist, although at the time there was good reason to believe that it might exist. Antoine Lavoisier (1743–1794) often gets credit for having discovered oxygen. Joseph Priestley (1733–1804) also isolated oxygen, but he thought it was dephlogisticated air, i.e., air which totally lacked phlogiston. The chemical reactions we explain by oxygen being taken up were explained by Priestley in terms of phlogiston being given off.

Law of parsimony: The widely accepted view that scientific explanation ought to use the fewest possible assumptions to generate an adequate account of natural phenomena.

Laws of science: Universal generalizations such as the ideal gas law, $PV = nRT$, or Newton's law of gravitational attraction, $\bar{F} = Gm_1m_2/r^2$. Finding such laws is sometimes said to be the goal of science.

Lesch-Nyhan Syndrome: First described in 1964 by Lesch and Nyhan, this is a condition characterized by severe mental retardation and a compulsion to gnaw the lips and fingers. The condition is controlled by a gene on the X chromosome; sometimes referred to as the self-immolator gene.

Libertarianism: The view which affirms freedom of the will.

Lingua mentis: Latin for "language of the mind."

Linguistics: The scientific study of language.

Logically follow: When an inference is deductive, it is said to follow logically from its premises. See the discussion of "deductive inference" in the entry for **Inductive inference**.

Logical positivism: A movement originating in Vienna in the early twentieth century, which tried to propagate "the scientific outlook" in all fields of human knowledge. A fundamental tenet of the movement was that statements are meaningful only if they can be verified or falsified either directly or indirectly through the data of experience. Applied to philosophy, this view eliminated as nonsense much of traditional philosophy which pursued knowledge in the non-empirical realms of theology, metaphysics, and ethics. (Note A. J. Ayer.)

Materialism: The doctrine which claims that matter is the primary feature of reality and relegates mind (or spirit) either to a secondary, dependent status or to no status at all.

Master morality: Nietzsche's term for the type of morality which originated in the ruling class and which values the exalted, proud noble who decides and decrees what is to be regarded as good and evil, right and wrong. (Contrast with **Slave morality**.)

Mauvaise foi: Sartre's term meaning "bad faith," a condition exhibited by the person who tries to avoid accepting responsibility for what he or she is, but instead tries to shift that responsibility to such factors as heredity and environment which are beyond the person's control. Such a person treats himself or herself as an *en soi* (or thing) instead of as a *pour soi* (a freedom, a person).

Metaphysics: The branch of philosophy which examines the nature of ultimate reality.

Micro/Macro: *Micro* refers to very small entities. *Macro* refers to large entities. Obviously, these are relative terms. Roughly, anything readily visible with the naked eye could be considered macro. Anything requiring a microscope should be considered micro.

Miracle: A violation of the laws of nature. (Hume) An interference with nature by a supernatural power. (Lewis)

Monism: The view which holds that in any given domain there is but one fundamental substance. For example, Smart attacks any mind-body dualism and affirms body (or matter) as the fundamental human substance.

More geometrico: Latin for "in the manner of geometry." That is, in the style of geometrical proofs.

Naturalism: The doctrine that nature is the whole of reality, and that nature is a self-existent and self-operating interlocking system in which no part can claim the slightest independence from the total event. As such, naturalism precludes free will. (Contrast with **Supernaturalism**.)

Natural theology: Knowledge, or beliefs, about God based on knowledge, or beliefs, about nature. Contrast with *revealed* theology in which knowledge about God is derived from divine revelation.

Necessary condition: A condition, C, is said to be necessary for an event, E, when (and only when) E cannot occur without the presence of the condition, C. For example, the presence of oxygen is a necessary condition for combustion. But notice that the presence of oxygen is not enough to insure combustion. Thus the presence of oxygen is a necessary, but not sufficient, condition for combustion.

Neuron(e): A nerve cell.

Neurophysiology: The study of the physiology of the nervous system.

Neurosis: A functional disorder of the mind or emotions without obvious organic injury or change that results in anxiety, phobia, or other abnormal behavioral symptoms. Frankl refers to this kind of neurosis as psychogenic neurosis (arising from conflicts between drives and instincts) in order to distinguish it from what he calls noögenic neurosis

which emerges from moral conflicts or spiritual problems.

Newtonian mechanics: The branch of physics that studies the motion of objects on the macro scale. The laws governing the motion of such objects originally discovered by Newton. For example, $F = ma$.

Nihilism: Based on the Latin word for "nothing" (*nihil*), this term has been used to describe people who say that there are no rationally justified moral norms or standards, and perhaps more frequently on the current scene to characterize people who claim that life has no meaning.

Nomic: Law-like, from the Greek word for "law" (*nomos*).

No-saying: Nietzsche's term for describing those moralities which advocate selflessness in one form or another. Selflessness is a no-saying to life, a negation of the self and of life which is, at its core, the will to survive.

Noumena: According to Kant, things-in-themselves or reality as it is. Knowledge is a joint product of the mind and the external world. The external world "appears" through the forms and categories of the mind. Accordingly, we only know "phenomena" or "appearances." We never really know noumena or things-in-themselves apart from the forms and categories our minds impose on them in the knowing situation.

Objectivism: In ethics, the view that moral values and principles exist objectively, that is to say, independent of a particular person's views and tastes. Such objective values and principles provide norms by which ethical statements can be judged as true or false. (Contrast with **Subjectivism**.)

Official doctrine: Gilbert Ryle's term for mind-body dualism which is derived chiefly from Descartes. (See also **Dualism**.)

Optimism: The personal attitude of hopefulness about human destiny and a positive evaluation of the world.

Option: The decision between two hypotheses. (William James)

Pantheism: The doctrine which identifies God (*theos*) with all things (*pan*). All things are appearances or manifestations of God.

Paranormal: Beyond the range of normal experience.

Pessimism: The personal attitude of despondency, hopelessness, and gloom toward the self and the world. The most famous philosophical justification of this attitude is that presented by Schopenhauer.

Phenomena: Derived from the Greek word meaning "that which appears," *phenomena* refers to reality as it appears to us, as contrasted with *noumena* which is reality without the structures of knowledge we impose on things in order to know them. Kant made much of this distinction.

Phenomenalism: The doctrine that percepts and concepts in the mind (that is, phenomena) are the sole object of knowledge or the only form of reality.

Phlogiston: See **Lavoisier/Priestley/Phlogiston**.

Phylogenetic scale: A continuum of organisms or species based on closeness of evolutionary relationships.

Platonic Forms: Abstract entities postulated to exist by Plato. They were perfectly real and, therefore, unchanging. Earthly objects were just copies—mere shadows—of the Forms.

Pluralism: The doctrine that there are many ultimate substances, as opposed to monism (which affirms only one) and dualism (which affirms two).

Positivism: A term first associated with Auguste Comte's doctrine that the highest form of knowledge is the scientific or positive. (Note his law of the three stages.)

Postmodernism: A point of view that has become prominent during the second half of the twentieth century which insists that it is impossible to achieve any sort of cognitive reliability. Humans can achieve only various interpretations, none of which can claim to the *the* truth. No point of view is privileged. All points of view are "decentered." (see also **Deconstructionism**.)

Postulates of morality: Three fundamental features of reality—freedom, immortality, and God—which one is justified in postulating or assuming if one is to be able to take seriously and interpret meaningfully the moral experience of humankind. (Kant)

Pour soi: Sartre's term for existence that is conscious of itself. Such existence is "for itself." It selects various possible future selves and tries to actualize those possibilities for itself. The "for itself" is the locus of freedom.

Pragmatism: A philosophical position, associated with such thinkers as C. S. Peirce and William James, which interprets the meaning of a statement or ideas generally in terms of its practical consequences. Also, pragmatists often assess propositions as true or false on the basis of their practical consequences.

Predestination: The theological doctrine which is often taken to hold that before the creation of the world, God foreordained all that would come to pass. More accurately, the doctrine refers to the notion that before creation (or perhaps shortly after the Fall) God decreed the eternal destiny of every individual intelligent creature.

Presupposition: A postulate or assumption which must be taken for granted if a desired result is to be achieved. R. G. Collingwood argues that scientific thinking rests upon "absolute" presuppositions which are themselves not pieces of scientific thinking, and which are incapable of proof or disproof.

Priestley: See **Lavoisier/Priestley/Phlogiston**.

Primary qualities: The qualities or characteristics believed to be inherent in bodies, such as extension, figure, motion, rest, solidity, and number. Such qualities are seen as constant within objects and inseparable from them, in contrast to secondary qualities, such as color, which are variable and thought not to exist in objects in the same way. (John Locke)

Pro tanto: Latin for "to that extent" or "so far."

Procrustean: A method whereby something is made to fit a decided-upon scheme, whether it really fits or not. From the mythological giant, Procrustes, who had a bed which he would make his victims fit either by cutting off their legs or stretching their legs.

Proletarians: In Marx's theory, the working class, the wage-laborers, who are exploited by the capitalist class, and who are destined to revolt and to abolish forever the exploitation of the masses by a ruling elite.

Providence: The theological doctrine that embraces the idea that God preserves and guides his creation to ensure that his purposes will be accomplished.

Pushpin: A game, something like tic-tac-toe, played with pins and a pin-cushion.

Quantum mechanics: The branch of physics that deals with the properties of entities that are so small (subatomic) that they do not have the properties of the objects dealt with in Newtonian mechanics. In Newtonian mechanics, entities are either waves or particles but never both. In quantum mechanics, this clear duality does not seem to hold.

Quietism: A view which advocates passive contemplation and restraint of the passions.

Rationalism: The philosophical view which appeals to reason rather than to sense impressions as the source of knowledge. Descartes's philosophy, built on his *cogito, ergo sum,* is a fine example of rationalism.

Realism: In medieval thought, realism stood for the doctrine that universals (ideas or essences of things) have a real, objective existence. In modern times, realism stands for the view that material objects exist externally and independently of our sense experience. Often realism is now used to refer to views that emphasize literalism and pragmatism. (See **Pragmatism**.)

Reductio ad absurdum: Literally, from the Latin, a reduction to absurdity. A style of argument. The idea is to take a statement and show that from it follows a conclusion that is absurd; suggesting that the original statement itself must be absurd.

Reductionism: A method which assumes that entities with parts are best studied by studying their component parts. A variation insists that the only proper way to learn about anything is to use the reductionistic method. Thus to study why people enjoy sweet food one would study the physiology of the taste buds along with the neurophysiology of certain parts of the brain. The comment, "It just tastes good" would not be an acceptable reductionistic answer. This view conflicts with a teleological approach and with a holistic approach.

Reincarnation: The belief that when the body dies the soul returns to earth, reborn or reincarnated in another body or physical form.

Relations of production: Marx's term for the way people relate to each other in order to produce the goods and services of society. In all pre-Communist societies (with the possible exception of an early primitive Communism) the relations of production have been conflictual: exploiting elite versus the exploited masses. In the future Communist society, Marx maintained that exploitation would be replaced by cooperation and mutual good will.

Relativism: The view that there is no absolute truth because what is regarded as true varies from person to person and from age to age. Truth, accordingly, is seen as relative to a person's time, place, and circumstances.

Representation: The theory of art which holds that art neither imitates nor copies an object outside the work of art, but rather is a symbol which stands for or represents the object.

Res cogitans: A thinking thing; the mind. (Descartes)

Res extensa: An extended thing; the body. (Descartes)

Revolution: In Marx's thought, the transformation of a society that occurs when the prevailing relations of production are supplanted by a new set and the social superstructure is reconstituted to reflect the interests of the new ruling class. In a communist revolution, non-exploitative socialistic relations of production replace the exploitative capitalistic relations and the social superstructure is altered to reflect the interests of all humankind.

Scholastics: Disciplines or adherents of scholasticism, the dominant system of theological and philosophical teachings in the Middle Ages, based on the authority of the Latin church fathers and Aristotle and his commentators. A term sometimes applied to persons who are dogmatic or pedantic.

Secondary qualities: Those sensible qualities, such as colors, sounds, tastes, smells, which do not exist *in objects* but are generated *in us* through the impact of the primary qualities (which do exist in objects) on our sense organs. (John Locke)

Semantic: Referring to the truth or meaning of statements. Contrasted to syntax, which refers to the form of a statement. Thus, "The girl hit the ball" and "The ball was hit by the girl" are identical in semantics (they mean the same and if one is true/false, then so must be the other) but they differ in syntax, or form (one is in the active voice and the other is in the passive voice).

Skepticism: Proponents of this view doubt that the knowledge we have achieved thus far is absolute and advocate a continued search for more carefully refined truth. Some skeptics doubt whether perfect certainty about some or all forms of knowledge is ever attainable.

Slave morality: Nietzsche's term for the type of morality which originated among the slaves in their need for comfort and mutual support, and which highly valued benevolence, submissiveness, selflessness, patience, etc. (Contrast with **Master morality**.)

Social contract: The original agreement by which individual persons united to form a state and consented to be governed. Although the idea of a social contract is ancient, it is likely that no such ancient agreement ever existed. The idea has, however, served as a criterion against which to judge whether governmental acts actually possessed the consent of the governed.

Social superstructure: Marx's term for all the prevailing social constructs other than the economic ones, ranging from the educational system to religion, state, and law. All these constructs, says Marx, are generated by the economic exploiting class to express and guarantee its interests.

Soft determinism: The view which seeks to affirm both determinism and human free will by regarding free will as one of the causes in the causal network responsible for human behavior.

Solipsism: The view that only I exist. Not you—me!

Sophists: Itinerant Greek scholars of the fifth century B.C. who popularized knowledge and offered lessons in rhetoric, especially to the politically ambitious youth.

Spiritualism: The belief that spirits or souls can survive bodily death and can and do communicate with the living, especially through people called mediums who, in a trance, temporarily become the mouthpieces for those departed spirits.

State of nature: The hypothetical condition of humankind prior to the social contract and the birth of the state. Some thinkers emphasize the individual rights and liberty which existed in the state of nature, and which have been curtailed through the social contract. Others emphasize the chaotic struggle of each against all in the state of nature, and celebrate the social contract which has brought a measure of peace, security, and progress to humankind.

Stoicism: A school of Greek philosophy founded by Zeno (about 308 B.C.), which holds up the model of the virtuous person who achieves happiness through knowledge. The virtuous person has mastered self and passions so that the self's happiness is internal and independent of the changing conditions of the external world.

Subjectivism: A view which emphasizes the individual self or subject as the creator of meaning, truth, or values. In ethics, subjectivism involves the claim that moral values and principles represent the individual's subjective feelings and reactions which, in the absence of objective moral norms, cannot be assessed as true or false. (Contrast with **Objectivism**.)

Substance: (1) The essence of a thing; that which makes a thing what it is rather than something else. (2) Also, that which underlies the things of the experienced world; matter. Substance in this second sense is severely criticized by Hume.

Sufficient condition: See **Necessary condition**.

Summum bonum: The highest or supreme good. The ultimate intrinsically worthy goal of human conduct. (See also **Intrinsic good**.)

Supernaturalism: The doctrine that nature is not the whole of reality and that part of reality transcends, or is beyond, nature. That part which transcends nature possesses an independence from nature that allows for the existence of such things as free will and rational thought. (Contrast with **Naturalism**.)

Syllogism: A form of deductive reasoning consisting of a major premise, a minor premise, and a conclusion. For example, "All men are mortal." (major premise); "Socrates is a man." (minor premise); "Therefore, Socrates is mortal." (conclusion).

Synchronicity: A view put forward by psychologist Carl Jung. He claimed that there are instances of coincidences that are so meaningful and appropriate that they cannot be true coincidences; somehow they are caused not by the usual causal chain, but by what he termed an "acausal connecting principle." A standard example is thinking of a friend you haven't heard from in a long time, then the phone rings and it is your friend calling. She says, "I don't know, I just felt like calling you." (See **Jung**.)

Syntactic: See **Semantic**.

Teleological: A term derived from two Greek words: *telos* meaning "purpose or goal" and *logos* meaning "principle or reason." Hence, teleological is "reasoning related to goals." The teleological argument for God's existence proceeds from alleged purposes in nature to a Divine Designer. A teleological ethic assesses an act as right or wrong on the basis of the goals or consequences it produces.

Teleology: The view that everything has a design or purpose and that this is the best way to understand anything. This view conflicts with a reductionistic approach.

Theism: A religion or philosophy that involves belief in the existence of a god or gods.

Theodicy: The attempt to reconcile God's attributes (divine goodness, omnipotence, justice) with the existence of evil and suffering in the world.

Theoretical entity: An entity postulated in order to fill out an explanation. The entity itself is not observed. In Freud's depth psychology, the *id* is a theoretical entity. When Newton first put forward his three laws, gravity was a theoretical entity.

Transvaluation of values: Nietzsche's term for the inversion of good and evil affected by the aristocracy when it declared aggressive egoism to be evil (when initially it had been regarded as good) and selfless altruism to be good (when initially it had been regarded as evil). Nietzsche calls for a new transvaluation of values which will celebrate aggressive egoism as good and regard selflessness as evil.

Übermensch: Nietzsche's term for the superman (the overman or self-transcending person) who discerns the current deterioration of civilization, stands apart from the mediocrity of the masses, legislates for himself what is right and wrong, and thereby sets himself beyond the prevailing good and evil.

Uniformitarianism: In geology, the view that the laws acting now have always acted. Thus, there is uniformity in the earth's history.

Utilitarianism: The ethical theory which recommends that we ought to do that act which, more than any other act open to us on a particular occasion, is likely to maximize the happiness (or pleasure) or humankind; that is, is likely to generate the greatest happiness for the greatest number of people. (Jeremy Bentham and John Stuart Mill)

Verification: The procedure of checking up on a statement to determine if it is true or false.

Verification principle: A tenet of the logical positivists according to which a sentence that purports to be cognitive is, in fact, cognitive only if it is able to be confirmed in principle.

Voluntarism: In metaphysics, the doctrine that blindly striving universal will is the ultimate reality of which all things are manifestations. (Schopenhauer)

Whewell: William Whewell (1794–1866) was a British scientist. He studied geology, physics, and astronomy. Whewell is considered one of the first philosophers of science. His name is pronounced Hūăl.

Wicket: A term from the game cricket.

Will to believe: According to William James, when one confronts two opposing hypotheses in a genuine option (e.g. to believe in God vs. not to believe in God), and when the available evidence is insufficient to demonstrate the truth or falsify of either hypothesis, then one is justified in exercising one's will to believe—that is, assenting to the hypothesis which one hopes is true because its rejection as false would generate very undesirable practical consequences.

Wittgenstein: Ludwig Wittgenstein (1889–1951) was a philosopher best known for his thoughts on the workings of language and philosophy itself.

Yes-saying: Nietzsche's term for assessing those moralities which advocate aggressive egoism. Because life involves the will to survive, the will to power, aggressive egoism is an affirmation of, a yes-saying to, life.